THE MUSICAL LIFE

HEDWIG STEIN: ÉMIGRÉE PIANIST

THE
MUSICAL
LIFE

Hedwig Stein: Émigrée Pianist

Helen Marquard

Matador
9 Priory Business Park,
Wistow Road, Kibworth Beauchamp,
Leicestershire. LE8 0RX
Tel: 0116 279 2299
Email: books@troubador.co.uk
Web: www.troubador.co.uk/matador
Twitter: @matadorbooks

ISBN 978 183859 514 2

British Library Cataloguing in Publication Data.
A catalogue record for this book is available from the British Library.

Printed and bound by CPI Group (UK) Ltd, Croydon, CR0 4YY

Typeset in 12pt Book Antiqua by Troubador Publishing Ltd, Leicester, UK

Matador is an imprint of Troubador Publishing Ltd

To
Anna,
whose unstinting help, encouragement and friendship made this possible;

for
Brian,
who knows why;

and
with my profound thanks to the many people who have been so generous in sharing memories, places, information, and ideas with me along the way and who I hope will enjoy reading the composite story.

Hedwig Stein programme Wigmore Hall 1956

Contents

Illustrations

ONE
MY LETTER TO ANNA

Here is the past and all its inhabitants miraculously sealed as in a magic tank; all we have to do is to look and to listen and to listen and to look and soon the little figures – for they are rather under life-size – will begin to move and to speak, and as they move we shall arrange them in all sorts of patterns of which they were ignorant, for they thought when they were alive that they could go where they liked; and as they speak we shall read into their sayings all kinds of meanings which never struck them for they believed when they were alive that they said straight off whatever came into their heads. But once you are in a biography, all is different.

VIRGINIA WOOLF, THE ART OF BIOGRAPHY[1]

Dearest Anna

This letter, with its considerable appendix, is surely going to be the longest letter anyone has ever written to you. At its heart is one of the people most close to you: your mother, Hedwig. What more can I possibly tell you about your own mother, you must surely ask – especially when you know that the bulk of the material I have drawn on is what you have provided me with: diaries, letters, photographs, concert programmes, your recollections. But I couldn't countenance simply compiling and editing those, and leaving it at that. No, what I'd like to share with you, and others, are my impressions of Hedwig and her life, *my* story of how I came to write *her* story, and her account of the events that impinged or crashed on her, together with the characters who played various roles and were influential in her thinking or her actions. Music took centre stage in her life; what she read, the art she saw, and the countrysides she loved of course added to that. I wanted to explore, as far as I could, how this deeply colourful woman changed through her life, as a pianist, as a teacher, as a wife, and as a mother, and how she affected others.

Of the many people I have met in my life, Hedwig stands out. Her sparkle for life, her ideas and her passion for music, all of which she was so ready to share with others, were irresistible. Time spent with her was as exhilarating as being on the top of a mountain, the wind blowing through your hair, while you share your feelings with the good friend at your side. Add to that the currents that flowed through her life, the kindnesses of strangers in helping her as an émigrée, and people she or her family and friends associated with, a few of whom I had already heard of when I first met her: Albert Einstein, Brahms, Max Reger, Peter Maxwell Davies, Jacob Epstein, Albert Schweitzer, Margaret Mead, JB Priestley. The mix was as powerful as the strongest of cocktails.

Attempting to tell the story of anyone's life is daunting. Maybe the clue is in the word 'story' rather than 'biography'. It implies a fusion of the writer's imagination and experience with the facts about another's life, the aim being to portray that person and what it was about her that was distinctive. Even when there are resources to hand, the gaps are inevitably larger than the material available; interpretation of diaries, letters and accounts will at the very least be tinged with, or even drastically coloured by, the storyteller's own perceptions and experience.

Thinking back to my early teenage years, I remember finding out about the local library, and there making the discovery that there were books about people. The kind librarian told me they were 'biographies'. These were not the fairytales or made-up stories I'd read when I was smaller, but much thicker, 'proper' books, some about people I had come across, others about people completely unknown to me. Physically they were contained within the binding of the books. And yet, as I sampled some of those on offer, I started to form clear impressions of their subjects until at the end, I felt as though I had been a companion through their lives. The sense of knowing the people personally, almost of owning them, persisted, even today. The individuals became, in some strange way, part of my circle of associates. Some I liked, others I did not; some I even felt I could identify with, to a greater or lesser extent. Some led me to examine my own life and preoccupations and positions, opening new doors and maybe closing existing ones. Of those, a few triggered quite radical changes in me, or in my plans for and attitude to my life, in particular Virginia Woolf and the Bloomsbury Group, Yehudi Menuhin, Jean Paul Sartre and Simone de Beauvoir, and Bertrand Russell. It was almost as good as meeting the people first-hand. The power of people and their stories…

Hedwig Stein, or even the wife Hedwig Elinson, is not a name that trips off anyone's lips, other than those of her immediate family. Even within her profession, she is little known. She died in 1983, and were I not embarking on relating her story, her immediate fate would be as most peoples': talked about occasionally by her surviving daughter and grandchildren, and possibly by some of the people she taught, and then becoming lost from everyone's consciousness. Yet she is someone whose life is worth remembering and reflecting on – in part because of who she was and what she did, and in part because of what she lived through, experienced, and passed on. I wanted to find a place for her today, to rediscover the person who had played a role in many others' lives, who thought deeply about what she had experienced and shared it, and who was able to convey much colour and emotion through music.

As I got going, I thought about other biographies; of, say, philosophers. There one might work through the evolution of their thoughts through their writings. For painters and sculptors, one can trace changes in technique or approach. Novelists adapt their styles. And in each of these cases, their work would have been influenced by events that happened to them, not only by their internal reflections. Much the same is true for those outside the arts. Scientists work through ideas, experimentation, and postulates, and develop theories; politicians are necessarily shaped by events and are seen in the light of how they deal with them. All these can be captured in concrete ways; the impacts are often traceable. But musicians, especially performing musicians? Music is ephemeral. It exists only from one millisecond to another as individual notes are played. After that it is confined to memories, unless a performance is recorded – and in Hedwig's day, that was relatively uncommon. The broadcasts she made no longer exist. We have nothing other than what critics wrote at the time and the impressions of the very few people who are still alive, to the extent that they can remember and describe how she played. No wonder the name Hedwig Stein draws a complete blank today.

In seeking to counter that by putting Hedwig's story together, all those letters bundled up in plastic freezer bags, her diary, the journal she kept of your trip to the Dolomites, the 1976 Boots diary, the disorderly address book crammed with odd notes and comments, her jottings, the photographs, the memoirs of your grandfather and great-grandfather, the books about Reger, the press cuttings, and of course your memories, gave me an invaluable base. There was even the old 'Kochbuch', a recipe book transformed into a cornucopia of scribbles: the meanings and pronòunciation of numerous English words; Hedwig's loves of musical works and her opinions of composers and performers; musings on her family; and interspersed, recipes written out in German in the self-conscious hand of an adolescent. What a blessing that Hedwig wrote and kept so much. Indeed, what could I possibly have made of the story without it? It would have been no more than a crude attempt to piece together the various building blocks of Hedwig's life, to a very large extent through my imagination. Many events and much of the nuance would have been lost. At the same time, I found it almost daunting to have so much material. How would I now start on this adventure, what might I use, and what should I leave to one side? How much should I quote from the diary and would my choice of quotes radically change the portrait? And how different would it be to approach such a task after my lifelong 'other' writing – research papers about the molecular events during the early stages of cancer formation, policy papers on the use of chemicals in the environment, on how to regulate biotechnology, and on the needs of start-up social and environmental enterprises in developing countries? The answers appeared over time and as I went along.

To the information you gave me, I have added my own store of books, documents, articles and contacts, chasing mentions of people and events so as to be able to dig deeper. Inevitably, I have had choices to make about what to follow and what to note but leave to one side, maybe for someone else to pick up. The huge enjoyment of the research aspect was my unbridled freedom to pursue anything that grabbed my interest. In many instances, there were topics I had not expected to encounter or had not known about at all. It has been a wonderfully indulgent and pleasing experience, imagining different microcosms, circles and worlds; and rewarding, if uncomfortable at times, to push myself through the intellectual and emotional examination of how I might have reacted in certain circumstances, often with no clear answer. Taking the decision to leave Germany in 1933 is one example I continue to find especially challenging.

I have not been a true researcher, chasing after every single jot and tittle. I had to decide how wide to cast the net of characters who appear. I started, if you remember, by trying to put together a family tree – a complex matter when confronted with snippets and throwaway comments dispersed through Hedwig's diary, and a host of names and locations and relationships, all at that time completely unknown to me. What a relief it was when you said it looked right. And then I set to work to compile a dramatis personae, to help myself as much as any reader. It grew, and it grew, and still more it grew. Several times, as you well know, I came a cropper: Leslie Linder was the theatrical agent? Not at all, you said; rather, he had been an engineer and philanthropist. Then there was all the confusion about the various Kilby sisters, and the two Ollys (or one Olly and one Olli?) – Stutchbury and Adelmann. And as concerns places, the muddling references to events that happened in and around Platt Lane which were resolved only when you explained that you as a family had lived in Platts Lane in Hampstead, and by a strange coincidence Hedwig and Iso had later had a flat in Platt Lane in Manchester. Over time, I managed to sort things out. The dramatis personae proved almost as fascinating as the diary itself, so rich were the friendships and associations Hedwig struck up. I decided to include it here, with my basic family tree. From these, it will be easy to see where I drew the defining limits for my story.

As with all individuals' lives, Hedwig's story is about other lives too, lives that crossed hers and influenced her, some over many years, others for much shorter times. They were lives lived through the total disruption of norms, involving Germany, Russia and England, when no one could escape involvement. They all add to the colour and complexity of Hedwig's long life, and I could not resist following a few of their stories and retelling odd anecdotes as well.

I started by saying I wanted to write my story about Hedwig's story. I hope that thought will remain with you as you read, especially if you come to parts that feel odd to you. I hope too that readers not so conversant with the world of classical music will stick with me through the mentions of various musicians, composers, and works, and read beyond them. Music was indeed the cornerstone of Hedwig's life, but her art of inspiring goes way beyond that. It was about the ways in which she communicated the essence of feelings and thoughts evoked by the creative arts, all enriched by her direct experience of situations and encounters and friendships with some remarkable people. I have included some of my favourite stories of Hedwig as related by others. Overall though, what you read now is very much mine. I realise that to you, Anna, it may in some parts ring not quite true. Different perspectives are inevitable – yours intimate; mine rather more distant.

In giving me the green light, the treasures of words in letters and diaries, and the many stories from your past, you opened the door for me to dwell again in those heady times when, through Hedwig, my world suddenly exploded, bringing the far removed to where I might be able to grasp it. My good fortune in being able to write about Hedwig stems from you alone.

Here then is my story, my portrait of Hedwig, interwoven with Hedwig's own telling of her story, with my profound thanks and love.
Helen

Two
Genesis

The starting point, of course, is how I first came to know Hedwig.

It was the autumn of 1973. I was just starting a post-doc at Manchester University in the biochemistry department, and had asked around in the lab for any advice about piano teachers I might approach. Peter, a dentist venturing into the world of scientific research and a keen lover of art, said he himself didn't know of anyone, but he had come across someone who might just be able to help. He added, with an enigmatic emphasis, 'She's eccentric, and she's German.' It turned out that Peter had met her on some committee or other to do with the arts in the north-west. Then came the crunch information: 'She's a *concert* pianist. But still, maybe she could help you.' He looked in his address book and scribbled down her telephone number on a scrap of paper.

And now here I was, having waited for over half an hour in the queue for my nearest telephone box in south Manchester, trying not to notice its inevitable and distinctive stink of stale cigarette smoke, dankness and urine, dialling the seven digits of the number, not sure whether I didn't rather hope she wouldn't be at home. She was. In a thick German accent, she said, 'We should meet,' after my very brief introduction about how I had a passion for the piano and music but hadn't played for ten years and wondered whether she could advise me of a teacher who might consider taking me on. I hadn't expected for a second that we might meet. What could I say except 'that would be very nice'? She gave me her address and we arranged the following Saturday morning.

Platt Lane formed something of a boundary between what was generally viewed as the 'acceptable' part of Manchester and the 'unacceptable' part that morphs into Moss Side, with its countless identical brick terrace houses, for the most part run down, and with its reputation for danger. There the streets were dirty, peppered with small shops filled with tacky household items and groceries, or displaying trayfuls of colourful Indian sweets, and with the odd eating place and its envelope of spices that wafted out into the streets.

I found though that Rusholme Gardens – a posh-sounding name – turned its back on all that. It was a block of rather fine-looking flats, each of which had a view across the road into the park opposite with its magnificent old trees. That Saturday morning I walked along from the bus stop, turned into Rusholme Gardens, and looked at the array of doorbells. 'Elinson'. That was it! I pressed the bell and shortly heard a voice saying, 'Come up. First floor.' The front door sprung open. The stairs and passageways were rather well carpeted, though my ascent was to the accompaniment of variously pitched creaks. I found the door of the flat I was hunting, took a breath and rang the bell.

'Coming,' was the loud, sung response, and very quickly I faced Hedwig Elinson, a woman of considerable stature with what looked like fair, artificially wavy hair that matched her beige-ish clothes. The striking things about her, though, were her warm and somewhat impish smile and the direct way she looked at me from her rather deep-set blue-grey eyes.

We went in, and the first thing I noticed – inevitably, given their size and imposing nature – was not one grand piano, but two; both, as I soon learned, Steinways. Hedwig explained how she and her husband had played together (from which I took it that her husband was no longer alive), and how she had very often played an orchestral accompaniment on the second piano while he practised the solo part. I tried to imagine what this husband might have been like, what life must have been for them, playing so much of the time, and what magnificent sounds they must have created together. But I couldn't reflect for very long. Coffee – instant – had been offered, and a chair in the bay window that faced on to the park, at an angle to the other one where Hedwig sat. She asked me about myself and my love of music. I gave a potted history: I'd never had proper lessons, except for a brief period and then from an organist, but had fallen in love with the sound of the piano as soon as I had discovered it as a child, in a darkened back room at my grandfather's. I had taught myself, and played of the easier core classical works what I could manage until I left home for university. I hadn't played since. But now, having just finished my doctorate, I was keen to see whether I could go back to it. Hedwig looked intently at me as I was talking, and then asked me if I didn't have some central or eastern European relatives – I looked as though I must have. This was preposterous! As much as I knew about my family – admittedly not a great deal – our stock was Yorkshire through and through. Hedwig was not persuaded. 'There must be something, maybe far in the past,' she said. The next surprise came when she asked to look at my hands. I have always been rather sensitive about my hands, since they are rather stubby. I held them out and she took them in hers and examined them. 'Not too bad…'

We continued to talk for a while longer and then Hedwig said, 'Very good. I take you.' I was stunned. I had simply thought she might *know* of someone with enough patience to take on a beginning non-beginner. 'The only thing is,' she continued, 'that I must ask you for some money. I have to help to pay for my grandchildren's education. Shall we say £2?' She added, 'We might try the Brahms Op. 117 Intermezzo to start with.' By now I was completely lost for words. My expectation had been that I would have to devote months to simple exercises, scales and arpeggios, and only then move slowly to pieces. Brahms to start? One of my musical loves? I left still in a daze, having agreed a time for my first lesson. Me? Lessons from someone described as a concert pianist? Who I knew by now had herself played at the Wigmore Hall and lectured at the Royal Manchester College of Music? Whose husband, Iso Elinson, had played in the major concert venues in the UK and beyond? It seemed far too good to be true.

But it was true. And over the subsequent weeks, my lessons became entire evenings. Hedwig would cook supper for us both when I came after a day in the lab, and she would regale me with stories of her past and of the present. She would play to me on one of the Steinways and on her clavichord, and she would teach me on both instruments. She would talk about literature and philosophy – German, English, and French – and tell stories about her life in Germany and in the UK, about her husband Iso, her family, her daughters and their children, their marriages. As on that first occasion, my ring at her doorbell would always produce a loud, singing 'Coming'. The door would open in a rush and Hedwig would immediately tell me something like, 'I have just been reading Schopenhauer,' followed by a few reflections, and then, with a little laugh and a twinkle in her eyes, 'I have been playing Bartók on my clavichord. You see, most people would not think it would work. But it does!' And she would bustle along to the room where her clavichord stood open, and demonstrate. Her opening comment on the day when the Prime Minister, Edward Heath, lost his nephew in a yachting accident was, 'That poor man. I feel sure, you see, that he will now be playing Bach.' And she went across to one of the Steinways, and played *Jesu, Joy of Man's Desiring* – forever one of her favourites – followed by one of Bach's 48 Preludes and Fugues. Always, you felt her playing was straight from the heart, and her personality lit up the music. But she was by no means always serious. Almost ever-present was her sense of fun, and she delighted in the preposterous.

I had never ever encountered anyone like her. Edward (Teddy) Crankshaw, who had earlier become a good friend of both Hedwig and Iso, wrote in the introduction to Artur Schnabel's *My Life and Music:*[2] 'his whole life, his conversation, was unending discovery, and it applied to everything he touched or that interested him.' That, absolutely, was true of Hedwig also.

My life had suddenly been expanded almost beyond description. These were not events and people I was reading about, but ideas and tales told by a woman who was also sharing her love and understanding of music with me. Edward Crankshaw went on to say that with Schnabel, he had one of those friendships that come only to the exceptionally lucky, and then only once or twice in a lifetime. An encounter with someone that is coupled with some personal and emotional trigger, such as music, a painting, a sculpture, or a landscape, can take on enormous significance and sometimes provoke a profound change. So it was for me with Hedwig.

The friendship grew quickly. I became very attached to my Hedwig evenings. Everything about Hedwig added sparkle to life, and that has remained, even though I was able to study with her for only a year before I took up a position in cancer research in Germany. I never saw Hedwig again. We exchanged letters sporadically over a number of years, but then the Christmas cards stopped arriving. I waited a couple of years before approaching the College, by now called the Royal Northern College of Music. Someone there was very understanding and helpful, and put me in touch with one of Hedwig's daughters, Anna, who told me Hedwig had died.

The memory of Hedwig nonetheless stayed with me. How could it be otherwise? She was instrumental in opening doors and ideas of all sorts for me. She had shared some of the main happenings in her life with me and her constant curiosity about all sorts of things was infectious. Slowly, the idea of trying to write about Hedwig took hold. Anna was immediately enthusiastic and gave me access to much of her mother's memorabilia. I learned that, about six months after Iso's death, Anna had encouraged Hedwig to write about her life, which she did through a 'diary' – here called the Diary – pursuing that task until 1977. When I came to read it, I was almost overwhelmed by the detail, and the seeming honesty. She found it 'a difficult task':

'I, so little inclined to measure or remember by dates (silver wedding, exams passed etc) must let impressions make up for this fact – how things and people, colours and smells and events seemed to me – how I reacted to them! I can at best hope that out of the kaleidoscopic landscape some things stand out as I honestly saw and felt them at the time.'

This, then, is not a diary as often construed, a daily recording of events and impressions, but is assembled very much post hoc from Hedwig's and

Iso's appointment diaries (referred to always as 'Boots diaries' because of where many of them were purchased – the one week to two pages planning variety), from odd jottings and letters, and from her recollections. They extend over 60-ish years, which amounts to many Boots diaries, most of which I have not seen. But the one Anna did lend me showed this was a true working diary. Writing is in no way confined to the space foreseen for a single day and consists of a miscellany of scribbles at all sorts of angles and in various colours – red, black, blue. One day, which I chose at random, gives a good impression. It is for Friday 7ᵗʰ May 1976 and the main entries are:

> dearest Iso (the day of his death in 1964);
> earthquake in Italy;
> university students esp Rosemary and Hans;
> thunderstorms;
> Mme Aron came and 2 Dr Hickmans and Thompson;
> Mozart Fantas C moll vv;[a] Schubert 7 and 8 vv; Beethoven d moll
> 1-2 v good; 3 errors; Noct C# minor; 3 Études; E♭ polonaise;
> Debussy Soirée (little error), Puerta, Cathédrale vvv (little error)
> and Pour le Piano vvv; encores: f minor Chopin, Schubert f minor;
> warmest applause of my life – 2 gorgeous bouquets.

From such snippets, Hedwig's memories were triggered, bringing back in some form the composite pictures of people, situations, weather, and countryside that form the Diary entries. Reliability and 'truth' are not guaranteed, therefore. But the Diary certainly captures Hedwig's personal experiences and some wider events and her feelings about them. Even if these had become distorted by the time she wrote, that seemed to me not to matter; how Hedwig viewed and relived her life in later years still tells us much about her. It differs little from the telling of stories from the past in conversation.

The Diary is itself worth comment. I surmise that it is different from

---

a   I take 'v' to represent a tick and hence Hedwig's self-assessment of her performance at a concert the previous evening.

those of many of the well-known diarists of her time in that – at least as far as she expressed it – she really did not expect anyone other than her family to read it, and even there she had her doubts. Using blue ink and a fountain pen, Hedwig entirely filled two large, thick, lined, red-bound exercise books that after all these years are rather battered and have that unmistakeable slightly dry yet distinct musty smell of old paper. It looks almost as though the physical capacity of the books determined when she finished, with just a few free lines left after the last entry in the second book. As far as I knew from Anna, Hedwig went to the extraordinary trouble of writing two diaries. Not only that. Anna unearthed a *draft* of the first years – itself a full exercise book, though with many fewer pages. One diary was intended for Anna, and the other for her sister, Marga. Until later in my writing, I had no idea whether Marga's still existed, or whether the entries were identical, or whether there were differences – large or small – between them. Nor did I know whether Hedwig wrote them in parallel or in tandem. But why did she go to the trouble of writing two? Photocopying was fairly sophisticated by the time she was writing. Here was the first unanswered question. What exactly lies behind these two versions of her diary, how and why they came to be as they are, remains a conundrum.

Hedwig comments on the tidiness and legibility of diarists before her time and on the common and frequent use of letters. Thankfully for me, on the whole her handwriting is similarly easily readable, though inevitably I was stumped here and there by an indecipherable scrawl. The main variations are in the size of the writing. Throughout, hers was a strong hand – like her strong voice – with a forward lean. I could sense the weight of her arm (remember, she was a pianist) directing her pen. It is tempting to say her voice and writing reflect her strong personality. Whether she felt her written 'voice' was a true expression of her feelings, we cannot be sure, the written voice inevitably having been refracted as a consequence of the writing itself. What might emerge does not always reflect the inner self and its emotions and thoughts. Furthermore, she really had only the option of using her adopted language in the main, given her likely audience. Only rarely did she turn to a German word or phrase.

Handwriting such long texts can have been no mean feat: Anna's copy comes to around 600 pages of continuous script. Despite Hedwig's lifelong love of good literature, in her own diary there is no subdivision of the text into paragraphs or sections; a change of day or month or even year hardly warrants a new line. Nearly every fourth or fifth sentence or phrase (they are well mixed throughout – about fifty-fifty) includes some words or phrases that are underlined, in blue or red, in biro. Some of these underlines may have been added later, on re-reading her Diary, for she rarely went back to anything without adding some comment or other from her later perspective. But it is clear there were other words or phrases underlined at the time of writing.

Extracts from Hedwig's Diary

The main text, after an initial and rather self-conscious start in 1964, appears to have tumbled out at quite a pace, even though it was written over a period of 13 years. Often an opening bracket is inserted without any closure. Full stops appear and she uses dashes very liberally; inverted commas to signify something slightly off-centre are common. For an outsider, what this simple mechanism achieves is an unusually direct connection between the reader and Hedwig. You can hear the emphases.

As I was fortunate enough to have spent a good number of hours together with her, I can almost hear her voice in my ear, its strong upbeat and heavily German-accented middle-pitch, and the timbre of that voice; I can picture the mischievous look that accompanied her frequent outbursts of deep laughter, and the expressions of delight on her face when she encountered something unusual or quirky. For those who have no such memories to draw on, you will have to imagine those characteristics as best you can, superimposing them on the illustrations and your impressions from the stories.

Her story, my story… to let Hedwig speak for herself where I knew she alone must hold centre stage, I have only minimally edited the extracts from her Diary. Who better to make her leap off the page and become a person we can relate to? Some of her wording and phrases could no doubt be polished, but then I feared something of Hedwig's essence would be lost. When she spoke, she would jump from one topic to another, each one being introduced with gusto and often reaching *con fuoco* – in a fiery manner – and invariably with full-blown delight. There was no need always to finish sentences. The ideas cascaded out, not necessarily having an obvious connection to one another; that could take a bit of time to work out. So it is with her Diary.

Hedwig was conscious of the way in which previous generations had kept diaries and of the publications of her relatives, such as the poems of her mother, the musicological writings of her father, and the writings of her great-grandfather and grandfather, physicians Kussmaul and Czerny, a number of which record in particular their professional experiences. This, then, may well have spurred her on in those times when she expressly questioned the point of what she was doing, for she was far from sure that even her daughters would read her Diary. Maybe, deep down, she hoped posterity would pick it up.

The Diary is not the only source for this story. I have had access to a good number of letters, mainly from Hedwig, but some also to her. And I have been able to speak to several people other than Anna who knew her or heard her play. My fascination with her and her life grew as I delved deeper.

Sketching out the main staging posts in Hedwig's life reveals some of the fortunes, and some of the upheavals, she experienced. She was born in 1907 in Jena, Thuringia, in Germany. Her father, Fritz Stein, was at the time the Musikdirektor[a] at the University; her mother, Margarete (Gretel), a proficient – possibly even talented – pianist who came from a well-to-do and highly regarded family in Heidelberg. Given the musical environment and contacts, Hedwig started the piano at an early age, and after the War, went to study in Berlin. There she quickly fell for – indeed, was utterly smitten by – a young Russian émigré pianist, Iso Elinson, who was of Jewish heritage (though not practising). In 1933, they left for England with next to nothing. Hedwig's father had raged about the liaison, she was pregnant, and in an acrimonious atmosphere and with the situation in Germany becoming ever more threatening for Jews, they departed with 12 bags and suitcases and a very small amount of money. They were stopped just before the border but managed finally to get through.

The two of them now had to start a life together in a completely unknown country with no base whatsoever, and almost no one to help them. Hedwig had no more than a smattering of school English, and Iso knew very little of the language. But what extraordinary generosity they encountered. People invited them to come and stay, first just for the odd night or even week, but then, during the War, for years; they helped to promote Iso's career by organising concert and recital opportunities; others, later, found ways of helping Iso and Hedwig to obtain teaching positions. They made many friends, some deep and long-lasting relationships, and had acquaintances and pupils galore. Despite Hedwig being very obviously German, they were welcomed with enormous warmth and kindness.

From London, where their second daughter Marga was born, Hedwig and Iso moved out to the country during the Blitz until the end of the War, spending most of the time in a tiny and picturesque village in West Sussex. Hedwig loved it, and Iso managed to find recital and concert opportunities across the country. They gave many lecture recitals together

---

a   Director of Music.
    Author's note: All translations from German are mine, unless noted otherwise.

16

in private homes, as part of adult education programmes sponsored by the Workers Educational Association, and in the deanery of Chichester. But all this provided for no more than a hand-to-mouth existence and when Iso was offered a position at the Royal Manchester College of Music, they had little choice but to move. Oh dear: the grime, the unsightly buildings, the poverty. Hedwig had to smother her dislike and get on with the quotidian duties she had set herself, the supportive wife of a highly ambitious but not yet widely recognised concert pianist and a mother, putting her own career in third place. Their friends seemed to find this unexceptional. There were moments, however, when Hedwig railed, to herself at least, against not being able to play.

Teaching piano was in no way the expressed goal, either for Iso or for Hedwig – nor did it do more than provide for a basic living, augmented by small injections of cash from Hedwig's inheritance in Germany. Trimmings to life were through their musical friends and acquaintances – invitations to this and to that special occasion, which usually involved Iso giving small concerts. Some of the trimmings were rather substantial gifts, such as the sponsoring of a concert trip to New York for Iso, and London concerts. The two of them spent many hours with dictionaries and a typewriter, writing hundreds and hundreds of letters, trying to get concert engagements for Iso to add to the few that came his way through agents. It was worrisome, but somehow it worked. Iso played with many of the leading conductors, including John Barbirolli, Thomas Beecham, Malcolm Sargent, and Adrian Boult; and Hedwig slowly built up her own, albeit in comparison very modest, concert opportunities. Always, she played second fiddle to Iso; from the outset it was accepted unquestioningly between them that he was the more gifted and better pianist. As a result, their world revolved around him.

But Hedwig's world collapsed when she received a call late one night in 1964 telling her that after playing Beethoven's *Moonlight Sonata* Iso had suddenly died, alone in his dressing room, during the interval of a charity recital at King's College in London. She was as devastated about what had been lost to music as about her own catastrophe. For nearly twenty years after that she was on her own, building her teaching position at the

College and taking on concerts wherever she could get them, while for a good number of years helping her daughters and grandchildren through problematic marriages. There were traumas to get through, but until the very end Hedwig kept her endless thirst for knowledge and ideas, and her commitment to enriching people's lives through music. She had written in the Diary, as early as 1956, that 'it suddenly seemed desirable – as an old woman, later – to live alone somewhere and perhaps mean something musically to some young people who would be less favoured!', after which she inserted a comment long after writing the Diary: 'I do! 1976!' Indeed, the circumstances became a reality, and Hedwig's openness and attitudes, on offer to those she got to know, attest overwhelmingly to the realisation of that long-held wish, as we shall see.

THREE

HEDWIG STEIN – A MUSICAL CAREER

When she played, it was as though an old 78 rpm record had come alive. Pure poetry.

NIGEL SIMEONE ON HEDWIG STEIN

Let us get straight to the nuts and bolts of the person who was Hedwig Stein, rather than the wife and mother, Hedwig Elinson: a performer and teacher. I thought it might be worth first finding out a little more about her own teachers: Richard Glas, James Kwast, and Frieda Kwast-Hodapp. And before we even get to them, there is the question of the early influences. Her mother Gretel clearly played a major part in Hedwig's grasp of piano technique and music literature. Hedwig's loving relationship with her godfather Max Reger, the musical illuminati she had encountered or heard about, the knowledge that people in her family had achieved positions of note, combined with her passion for music and conviction of her own abilities, must have reinforced her unquestioning assumption that she would become a pianist.

Fritz, Hedwig's father, of course played a central role. Knowing, however, that her parents were much bound by traditional attitudes and therefore particularly celebrated the arrival of Hedwig's brother Max (known in the family as Maertel) as the Stein 'heir', I wondered whether Fritz had devoted more of his time to Maertel. Hedwig had to contend throughout her life with her parents' seemingly greater approval of Maertel as a musician – though there were people who considered Hedwig to be the greater pianist. Whatever the case, Fritz was ambitious for both his children: they should each become performers and not 'only' teachers. Having studied with the conductor, organist, and composer Philipp Wolfrum, as had Gretel, he probably passed on some of Wolfrum's ideas and approaches, especially in the interpretation of JS Bach – though not Wolfrum's love for Liszt, which most likely came from his own teacher, himself one of Liszt's pupils. Fritz insisted Hedwig attend his lectures and go into the university in Kiel to copy out old manuscripts, and he did what he could to promote her as soon as she was able to perform as a soloist. Her first concert was when she was only 12 and still at school, playing a Mozart concerto with Fritz conducting.

Hedwig's first external teacher was Richard Glas, another professor and Fritz's colleague at the university. Glas was Austrian and had been a pupil of Leopold Godowsky, an internationally regarded pianist and composer. When she first encountered Glas, Hedwig described him as:

'...certainly the best teacher in Kiel... a very friendly, kindly, intelligent man, married to a Russian beauty whose inborn elegance and sophistication impressed us 'provincials'.

Programme from one of Hedwig's earliest concerts: 1923

I was unable easily to find out anything more about Glas and since Hedwig herself did not describe any aspect of his teaching or what she made of him as a teacher, I have no insight into any influence he might have had on her. Given that she kept in loose touch with him after she had left Kiel and during the War, including when he was interned, each presumably had a good feeling about the other.

We know a little more about James Kwast. He was Dutch-German and had been a teacher in Cologne and Frankfurt, and at two conservatoires in Berlin. He was already nearing 70 and not in the best of health when Hedwig went to him. He could boast of having had a number of students who went on to make names for themselves: the conductor Otto Klemperer (who followed him through three institutions) and the composers Percy Grainger and Hans Pfitzner being but three. In addition Kwast had played duos with Clara Schumann and was a good friend of Ferruccio Busoni, an Italian composer and true virtuoso pianist.

James Kwast (1852–1927).
Photograph reproduced with the kind permission of the University Library Johann Christian Senckenberg, Frankfurt am Main, Germany.

Hedwig was about 20 when she went to Kwast. At that time he was still teaching at the renowned Stern Conservatoire in Berlin, though shortly afterwards he instead held group lessons for pianists at his flat. Again, she does not say a great deal about his teaching, but Kwast:

'...kept to general remarks: 'bring out that line more markedly' in a Bach English Suite, or 'less pedal – more feeling', 'more period style' and so on. It was highly interesting but some time later Iso Elinson made me really listen and understand quite differently! For instance, both Herr and Frau Kwast never explained the importance of a flexible, 'adaptable', 'ready' wrist and the extraordinary crab-like positions the hands take on during many passages. In unison runs in Mozart's concertos or in Debussy's Toccata (first page where left and right hands join in unison) I always felt the wrists braked too much and stiffened, but I did not see clearly how to change this state. Once I wept and was led out of the room but I managed to return ten minutes later. Another time I fainted and fell to old Kwast's feet! It was quite a hardworking life for me with the other musical subjects I took at the Stern Conservatoire.'

As Kwast himself became increasingly infirm, Hedwig continued her studies with his wife and ex-pupil, Frieda Kwast-Hodapp. She had had a highly successful career as a concert pianist, touring Germany, Russia and many European countries before restricting her activities to teaching. There was a family link too: Kwast-Hodapp was very friendly with Max Reger and with Fritz and Gretel Stein, and she clearly ignited a spark in Hedwig. It is an irony that Kwast-Hodapp, who died in 1949, did at least make the odd recording, whereas Hedwig did not. When I listened on YouTube, what struck me so forcibly about Kwast-Hodapp's playing was its extreme lightness where needed, and the clarity, fluidity and certainty of line – features also of Hedwig's playing. One small anecdote Hedwig recounted reminded me very much of Hedwig's manner too – though not of her sartorial passions, which were rather more subdued, at least off stage:

'After having linked up a passage in one of Bach's mysterious Preludes from The Well Tempered Klavier with one of St Augustine's sayings, she might start talking about her trip to London and her purchases there (she then wore whatever was the latest craze and very very expensive things – a snakeskin coat or a gold lamé slip of a dress when fashion decreed skirts were to end at the knees).'

I cannot help but think Kwast-Hodapp's deep musical sensitivity coupled with her extravagant personality and very feminine attitudes were a powerful influence on Hedwig.

Both Kwast and Kwast-Hodapp were very much centred on the Austro-German classical and romantic repertoire, which fitted well with Hedwig's preferences. Both strongly encouraged Hedwig, and by 1930 she was no longer dependent on Fritz for creating opportunities for her to play in public. For a while she gave both solo recitals and orchestral concerts more or less every month in a number of cities in Germany – Kiel, Jena, Cologne, Aachen, Heidelberg, Berlin. She stuck largely to her

Frieda Kwast-Hodapp.
Photographs reproduced with the kind permission of the Max-Reger-Institut, Karlsruhe, Germany.

treasured composers – Bach, Schubert, Chopin, and Beethoven – but on occasion included something different, such as the Vier klassische Stücke,[a] freely adapted by Kwast from four composers. In 1930 she passed her Teacher's Examination in Kiel with Distinction – an event that stood out for her by the discomfort of having to start the day at eight in the morning with Beethoven's *Les Adieux* sonata, but was wonderfully celebrated afterwards on finding her room had been filled with pots of cyclamen from a few of the women who lived nearby. She was intensely happy with the way her life was working out.

We should probably not leave Hedwig's growth as a musician without a few specific mentions of Iso's influence:

'For a long time I felt that Mozart's music in particular was so difficult to get at. Little did I know then how important a flexible wrist is for the solution of a good 'jeu perle'.[b] It was only some years later that my dear Iso would solve these riddles, as if by magic!'

In a letter to a close friend from her school years, written late in 1933, she wrote:

'The Haydn D major concerto touches me deeply, even when I am practising. In that state, it is possible to lose oneself completely, whereas the Romantics, especially Chopin, force themselves ever more into your own emotions.'

And subsequently:

'I am working intensely on how to create the right tone – the most important thing for a pianist: to have at your command all the colours so as to achieve poetic freedom in your playing… That is

---

a   Four Classical Pieces.
b   Literally 'pearly playing': a technique used for semiquaver passages – in Mozart, for example – which give the sense of a light, sparkling thread of pearls.

crucial. And the ability to listen acutely to how one is playing. The Russian (Iso) listens to me touchingly often... I learned more by listening to Iso practising than from months of lessons.'

Throughout all their years together, Hedwig looked to Iso for guidance, both technical and interpretative. Yet as they worked through pieces, Iso was never condescending, recognising Hedwig's own artistic talent. Inevitably, the question arose in my mind of whether she would have achieved as much had she not had Iso, had she not had the conversations about music that they must have continued throughout their lives, and the exposure to Iso's practising and playing for thirty years. My sense is that yes, Iso had an enormous influence, but not a defining one. Hedwig had her own, very clear, ideas. But we jump ahead...

During her time in Berlin, Hedwig was learning to adapt to different conductors, sometimes in rather unusual ways:

'...I still went to Frau Kwast for some lessons and had even given a debut in Stockholm where I played a complicated programme which was warmly praised by the (then) critic and composer Kurt Atterberg (the man who won the world prize for finishing Schubert's Unfinished Symphony![a]). I included an amusing sonata by Carl Maria von Weber. I also had an engagement in Bielefeld, to play the immensely difficult concerto in C minor by Mozart, under Heinrich Kaminsky[b] (he was a fine composer and a character). The rehearsals at his home were unforgettable. He bypassed many of the smaller conventions: he had a thin, hypersensitive wife and eight children and was often dressed in

---

a   The prize was also for a symphony inspired by Schubert's *Unfinished*; Atterberg submitted his *Symphony No 6*, later known as the 'Dollar Symphony', recorded by Beecham and performed by Toscanini. *Wikipedia, 19.01.2020*

b   German composer, d. 1946. Kaminsky was professor at Prussian Academy of Arts in Berlin but his contract was terminated in 1933 with no renewal on the grounds of his political opinions; all attempts to re-establish his career came to nothing for the same reason. He was declared quarter Jew in 1941 and fled to France and then Switzerland. He lost three children in the War. *Source: Wikipedia, 19.01.2020* kneebreeches and a peasant shirt. He was surrounded by helpful female admirers... When I arrived I noted his fine 'Old Master' head. On this occasion he wore an Indian priest's gown, all silk and embroidery, and sandals, showing his fine, unclothed feet. To him every bar in the concerto had a special 'message', something bordering on mysticism (!) and he gesticulated to me and sang each phrase as he wanted it! These many new demands nearly robbed me of any peace at all. Moreover I had to play his own cadenza which did not in the least 'lean' on Mozart. However, the concert in the evening must have gone off without any sensational upheaval.'

The reviews from her concerts in the early 1930s show how Hedwig was starting to make a name for herself in Germany, even before she had met Iso in 1932. Expressions that were used were "a wonderful artistic talent"; "impressive virtuosity and technical ability"; "fine touch and expression of a wide range of colours of the piano"; "high degree of adaptability to the style and emotion of different composers"; "a clear sense of her defined and sensitive reading of the music"; "a young pianist in the top rank and with a most promising future". Interestingly, the critic on the Kölnische Zeitung[a] in 1933 described her playing of the Chopin E minor piano concerto as not in the style of chamber music, like many other players, nor in the manner of the 'salon', though nonetheless rather poetic and feminine. But the cadenza had been lacking in strength and bravura, and some passages remained a little flat. This particular critic concluded that while she was clearly a pianist worth watching, she would benefit from further study to sort out such problems. Unbeknown to him, it would be Iso who did this.

Hedwig herself felt that some of the reviews were too positive. Reflecting on the society in which she was living, I wondered to what extent she thought about being judged in part by people who were aligning themselves with the new Nazi regime. Might she have thought them less

---

a   Cologne Newspaper.

worthy, or their reviews tinged by the new attitudes? But as far as the latter was concerned, she was playing music that was foursquare acceptable, and it was widely known that her father was the esteemed musicologist Fritz Stein. Bizarrely, her solo debut in Berlin, in the Bechstein Hall, was on 23rd March 1933, the exact date on which the Enabling Act ("Law to Remedy the Distress of People and Reich"[a]) was brought in – an amendment to the Weimar Constitution that allowed laws to be passed without any involvement of the German Parliament, the Reichstag. It was passed only by excluding all potential objectors from voting, and it completed Hitler's takeover of all state institutions. This was a time when reviews of concerts started to reveal some of the unease felt by certain music critics as they sought – or did not, depending on their political affiliation – to adapt to the emerging politically driven cultural landscape.

After arriving in England, there was perforce a long gap in Hedwig's public appearances, but these slowly started again once she was able to

Wigmore Hall – a favourite venue for Hedwig and Iso.
Photograph reproduced with the kind permission of Kaupo Kikkas.

---

a   Gesetz zur Behebung der Not von Volk und Reich.

practise and her daughters could be looked after by friends. Her first Wigmore Hall recital was in 1946. For Hedwig, the Wigmore was and remained one of the most special venues, with its history displayed overtly through the many photos of celebrated musicians that hung in the Green Room – though they did not include Iso, despite his having many recitals there between 1933 and 1962. Her programme was mixed, covering works by Rameau, Wagenseil, Schubert, Beethoven, Chopin, Brahms, Liszt, and Debussy. She got a good press for it and now that she had her own students at the Royal Manchester College of Music, felt it was good to demonstrate to them that she was a performer: 'they like one to be in it, and not only be paedagogic'.

In one of the many exercise books that Hedwig filled with this and that, I found a list she had compiled of the works she had studied. The composers were not surprising: Bach, Beethoven, Brahms, Chopin, Mozart, Haydn, Schubert, and Debussy, with Schumann, Prokofiev, Liszt, Weber, Reger, de Falla, Ravel, and Bartók very much less represented. The works themselves, I felt, said a lot about Hedwig: these were in the main not bravura, but deeply reflective pieces. Not surprisingly, given the few openings that came her way for playing with orchestras, most were solo works. Some were incomplete: 10–12 of Schumann's *Faschingsschwank* and Études Symphoniques, 'about 20–24' of the Bach Preludes and Fugues, 'most of' Brahms Op. 118 and 119, 10 of the Chopin Préludes and 17 of the Études, and Book I (but not II) of the Debussy Préludes. None of the three posthumous Schubert sonatas was listed, but earlier ones were. And then quite a number of chamber works: Delius, Franck, and Brahms violin sonatas that she performed with Martin Milner, the Leader of the Hallé Orchestra; works for piano duo and four hands, and accompaniments to many Wolf and Schubert songs. The few concerti were by Haydn, Mozart, Mendelssohn, Chopin, and Beethoven. From Hedwig there were no grand offerings of entire cycles of works by Bach, Beethoven and Chopin, which Iso favoured. Maybe she wished not only to play those pieces that were closest to her, but also works that could be 'hers', consciously creating programmes distinctive from Iso's.

Hedwig may not have had the same sort of concert openings as Iso, but with time she too had occasional opportunities to play in venues such as Manchester's Lesser and Free Trade Halls. The St George's Hall in Bradford engaged her almost on an annual basis for a good number of years, and she played regularly for many smaller music societies and charities, mainly across the north of England but sometimes in the south also. She played the Chopin E minor concerto at the Bournemouth Pavilion under Charles Groves. There were concerts at the Royal College and Manchester University, and occasionally in Germany when her brother Maertel had arranged something. But overall, Hedwig's concert life was modest. What she felt about this – whether disappointment, resignation, pleased to have what she had – remains a mystery to me, despite all I have read. It was certainly nowhere near the heights that I suspect she dreamt of when she was embarking on her career. But she had the deep satisfaction of knowing that she had done everything she could to help Iso – musically, her 'god'.

I think she must have felt pleased too, on her own account, with all she achieved with her students – both privates and those at the College. Probably the most famous of Hedwig's students is Peter Maxwell Davies – Max. Max became a good and long-lasting friend of everyone in the family. He appreciated Hedwig no end. In 2009, Max, by then alumnus and Master of the Queen's Music, joined fellow composers at the Royal Northern College of Music for the New Music North West Festival. In an interview, Max said, "I studied the piano with Hedwig Stein, who was quite an amazing person, full of ideas… Hedwig taught me in German; I requested her to, so I could improve my German…".[a] From Hedwig's side, Max:

'…came often to us. He mentioned Huxley's books to me… We laughed together. For his final piano exam he played Beethoven's sonata Op. 110. He always seemed intellectually alert and keen on

---

a   Interview for alumni. *Published Royal Northern College of Music, 2009. © Marian Blaikley*

some funny German jokes too. (He learned German, Italian, and French well – on his trips etc.)'

When I went for one of my piano evenings, Hedwig recounted to me with some glee how she had seen Max earlier that day. 'Imagine,' she said, 'Max has just tried to persuade me that Orlando Gibbons[a] is comparable to JS Bach,' and she gave one of her all-embracing laughs – clearly not persuaded. As I learned later, however, Max was not alone: the pianist Glenn Gould was a champion of Gibbons and said his music moved him more deeply than any other sound experience, though he compared him to Beethoven rather than Bach.

Max felt deeply for Hedwig, and for Iso. After Iso's death, he wrote to Hedwig in most touching terms, revealing something too about Hedwig as a pianist:

"...I don't think you've ever realised just how much the contact with you and Iso helped in those first awful two years at Manchester University... The first lesson I had with you, you were playing Brahms (the E flat intermezzo)[b] when I came in – no exaggeration to say that the sheer sound of this – real music played by a real musician who loved it – was like water to a man dying of thirst. ...Nothing was more necessary than contact with people who breathed music and lived it without inhibition and without bitterness. That it was a hard life was also clear (though Iso never said so) – and to find someone who despite all that, was never joyless – even if full of temperament, thank God! – was the best lesson, at that stage. Unlike all the other teachers I had, you (and he) had no axes to grind, though your ideas – I remember particularly on Op. 110[c] – were very clearly defined and original..."

a   Orlando Gibbons (1583–1625), English Elizabethan composer.
b   Here Max included a sketch of the opening melody from Op. 117.
c   Piano sonata by Beethoven.

Through the closer associations that Iso built with some of his students and ex-students, and through Hedwig's deputising for Iso at the College when he was away on concert tours, Hedwig got to know other students as well as her own. I assumed that those who were mentioned in her Diary would have had especial significance and tried to track them down. I could not be certain that they would still be alive, or that I would be able to find them all; indeed, some proved tricky. Those who pursue or have pursued concert careers were the most straightforward as they had websites and were directly contactable. One such was David Wilde, who won the Liszt-Bartók competition in 1961. In email exchanges with me, he recalled:

> "For all her zaniness, Hedwig was a real charmer, and a very talented pianist indeed. I heard her play with the Manchester Mozart Orchestra [the concerto was by Mozart, too, but I can't remember which]. I was impressed. Her favourite pupil was the great composer and music educationist Max Davies, who spoke of her publicly with both affection and great respect, saying that he was lucky to have studied with her. I met Max in Manchester, too. I was her husband Iso Elinson's pupil at the time – and that wasn't so successful. For all his charm, huge repertoire, great musical background [he studied piano in St Petersburg with Felix Blumenfeld and composition with Glazunov] and immense musical and performing talents, he simply wasn't the right teacher for me..."

In casting around for others who might be able to help me to add some different colours to this part of my portrait of Hedwig, an encounter at Hurstwood Farm suddenly came to mind. The Farm was where my father had made me a surprise present of a Bösendorfer piano. I now remembered having heard Gordon Fergus-Thompson performing at the eponymous Music Club. Despite being a small venue where the 'hall' was no more than a barn, tucked far away up tiny Kent lanes, it attracted well-known pianists – maybe because of its unusual setting, maybe because of its passionate founder, Richard Dain. At a concert given by Gordon Fergus-Thompson, I noticed from the programme that he had been at the Royal Manchester College of Music at around the same time as Hedwig was there. I snatched the opportunity and spoke to him in the interval – at the back of the barn, pungent with the smell of mown hay which lay between the avenues of cobnut trees. I enquired, had he known her? "Most certainly, and rather well" was the response. We spent a few minutes exchanging stories about Hedwig before he resumed his programme. Now, wanting to glean what others thought of Hedwig, I thought he would certainly be able to help to fill out my picture. I traced him from his website, noting he had been Professor of Piano at the Royal College of Music since 1996 and had performed across the world. I found his telephone number and rang him. He was utterly charming and only too willing to talk about Hedwig. His opening words about her were "mercurial, highly intelligent, gracious and generous". As I listened to him, it was almost as if he was recounting *my* experience of Hedwig; she had made as big an impression on him as she had on me, and he too had been invited to evenings in Hedwig's flat in Platt Lane. Given that he was but an impressionable 18-year-old at that time, he was more of a listener than a participant in Hedwig's spilling-out of thoughts, and he remembered vividly how she might start with some talk about music but then abruptly switch to a recent finding in science before leaping to a reflection about art or literature. The way Gordon described it was "a polyphonic mind", her interests going far beyond music, ranging even into science. Her life, it seemed to him, had always been profound. Never had she been remorseful or sad or depressed, but she was always optimistic, almost quivering with a sense of anticipation, of things about to happen. Theirs, like mine, quickly became a special and trusting friendship and his encounters with her had been nothing short of life-enhancing.

This fascinating woman came to have an extraordinary influence, Gordon said. Students knew they would get so much more from her than most of their other teachers because she would take them into the world of musical philosophy. She might not have been the best for students searching particularly for technical help, but for people who wanted to understand and get to the heart of the music, and to see the wider context, she was unmatched, with the exception of George Hadjinikos.[a] What had also struck Gordon was Hedwig's sensitivity, and how perceptive she was. Her sixth sense about people, she being somehow able to see right into and understand them, had often smoothed things along at College. In a difficult situation between students, Hedwig would quickly work out exactly what the heart of the trouble was and how best to resolve it. It was no surprise that all those qualities had made her such a gifted teacher who really had helped young people and been much loved.

Gordon heard Hedwig giving recitals in College. She would also talk about the music – not in technical terms, but so as to give an audience a sense of what they were about to hear. Technically she was not top, but that did not matter, such was her ability to reach into and convey the music. "She was a wonderful Schubert player", he said, emphasising "wonderful, finding both the darkness and the poetry".

Through Gordon I contacted Alan Thorpe, who had studied with one of Iso's pupils. Alan was keen to meet and generously invited me to his house for coffee. In readiness, he had dug out from his hoard of old concert programmes all he could find from Iso and Hedwig. Alan was clearly an admirer of both, and of György Cziffra, and he lamented such notable musicians having fallen into the sump of the forgotten. He had been to a number of Iso's concerts with the Hallé Orchestra, and mentioned Michael Kennedy's obituary of Iso that alluded to his being erratic; not so when he had heard Iso perform Beethoven's *Emperor* and the Grieg concerti. To these reminiscences, Alan added having heard Iso, the dedicatee, giving the first performance of John Joubert's piano concerto with the Hallé Orchestra and George Weldon in Manchester's Free Trade Hall in 1959. Then, in a quite different tenor, Alan spoke of Iso's death, which had imprinted itself on his memory. The day after, he had gone into the College. Everywhere, there was a black cloud of

---

a   Greek pianist, conductor, and teacher at the Royal Manchester College of Music from 1960 to 1988.

mourning, reaching into the furthest corners of the College, enveloping all the staff and students.

Alan had heard Hedwig too, in recital. He remembered her as a rather large woman, dressed in a somewhat old-fashioned way – in brown, he thought, nothing flamboyant. She came across as strong and confident, and was quite stern-looking, without any sign of nervousness. Her playing had been effortless; no flashiness or throwing herself around the keyboard. One recital in particular, which had included at least two Chopin Études and ended with Debussy's *Pour le Piano*, he thought was wonderful. It had stuck in his mind. And he then picked up one of the programmes he had laid out, for a Hedwig and Iso duo: "It was fantastic! There was an obvious closeness which you could sense in the playing; you felt they knew each other so well, a real feeling of intimacy – but also enjoyment; they clearly revelled in playing together."

Christian Blackshaw, again an international concert pianist, was also a student at the Royal Northern College of Music (the old Royal Manchester College of Music) in the 1970s. He might have known Hedwig, I thought, and so I arranged to meet him in Southampton after a concert with soloists from the Berlin Philharmoniker Orchester in which they played, most movingly, the Mozart Piano Quartets and Schubert's *Trout Quintet*. Christian had been only sixteen when he had met Hedwig and had not had any contact with her after that, other than the odd wave. He recalled though that whenever he passed her room at College, she, rather than a student, would be playing (possibly because of the restrictions of living in a flat), and added that she had been much liked.

I had now been in touch with, or read about, the impressions Hedwig had made on several students at the College. They were similar. But these were not her own students. I wondered, would they have different views? Some were mentioned in the Diary – Hans Montanana, Nigel Simeone and Martin Bates – and Anna recalled someone called Sally, who I managed to find buried in Hedwig's address book: Sally Wilson. I hunted on the web, following leads here and there. Where I was able to find an organisation that mentioned one of them, I sent a message, hoping something would come back. And as I waited, I worried whether I had said enough, or too much, about myself and my 'Hedwig project'. Might I be encroaching on feelings and memories that were not welcome? My concerns proved to be entirely unfounded. I received interested and enthusiastic responses.

I was able only to speak to Sally on the telephone. She prepared me for disappointment; she would not be able to tell me very much because she had known Hedwig only as a child. Yet as we know, the brain is remarkable in recalling memory long thought to have been lost, and within minutes Sally found herself talking at length. The gateway had been to imagine herself at the entry to the Rusholme Gardens flats and then walking up to the first floor. From there she could remember the rooms exactly, could picture everything about Hedwig. She could almost smell the mothballs that Hedwig put into the pianos to protect the felts on the hammers, and recalled that while she had her lessons, her mother would sit in the long main room with its dark furniture and a table at the end, in front of the bay window overlooking the park. The words that came to the fore were warmth, kindness and happiness.

Sally was only about eight when she first went to Hedwig, having already tried two teachers who took her as far as Grade 2 but no further. Her mother, an ardent musician and amateur pianist like her grandmother, who had accompanied black and white silent movies in London, sensed there was musically much more to be discovered in Sally. It was the right move. Hedwig started not with any trial pieces, but by playing for Sally, singing all the while, and then getting Sally to play back to her what she had heard – and singing again. So it built up, Sally learning ever more about different sorts of music and how to play them, rather than spending the time on routines of technique and sight reading. Sally quickly and happily made progress and Hedwig formed something of a bond with Sally's mother. Before long, the Wilsons were hosting musical soirées at which Hedwig, and Sally and her friends, would play. After three or four years, Sally moved on to a more conventional teacher to accelerate her formal musical education and prepare her to get into Chetham's School of Music.

Sally was indeed successful and went on to study and to qualify as an accompanist, which she is still. Any compliments she receives are invariably about her musicianship, and she is convinced that is due to Hedwig's encouragement and guidance in unveiling it. But her heart is in her teaching, in trying to understand as completely as possible the ability and needs of each pupil and then moulding her approach, just as Hedwig had done. "So Hedwig's spirit lives on, and on," Sally concluded. "Looking back, those years with Hedwig were the happiest of my life."

My first response from Martin Bates, who I found through his choir, was by text: "She was an absolute inspiration to me. Looking back, she knew I was not going to be a great solo player but encouraged my great musical loves and was always keen to talk about my musical studies at the university." This was a good start, and we arranged that I would go to meet Martin and his wife Sue, who had also known Hedwig. I met them on a crisp October morning at Birmingham International Station. Recognising each other was not a problem: they were the only couple standing on their own at the ticket barrier, scanning the emerging passengers for someone who might match their ideas of how a person in her later years and musically interested might look. I immediately felt – and indeed was – embraced before Martin and Sue whisked me away to a nearby hotel where they had found a quiet lounge. On the way I had to keep stopping Martin from telling me this and that until I could record our conversation. Fortunately, it did not take long before we were perched on bar stools at a high round table in a remote part of the hotel. Sue unpacked the large silvery box she had brought, to display their wedding album. She turned to a particular page showing herself and Martin lined up with all the guests. One stood out: Hedwig, wearing a distinctive, stiff-brimmed and square-topped cherry-red hat (the only behatted person) and carrying a matching handbag. This was the 1970s, and the Hedwig of my memories. A fitting recollection to start our talk, and Martin's stories soon spilled out.

He had gone to Manchester University's Faculty of Music in 1969, and as part of the diploma he was also studying for, had had lessons in performance with Hedwig for three years at the Royal Manchester

College of Music – as he put it, a highlight of every week, regardless of how much work he had to do. Hedwig was quite unlike any of Martin's other tutors and a complete contrast to his previous piano teacher: she was a fully engaging, fresh and enjoyable source of insights and advice about how to approach and interpret the music rather than how to deliver a work as written. She did it by talking rather than demonstrating, and her particular love for Debussy, Brahms, Beethoven, Schubert, and Bach shone through. Martin has not forgotten how, early on, he had played one of the late Brahms intermezzi. Hedwig had said, 'Not bad. But Brahms would not have played it like that!' That pulled him up short. And she went on to relate how her grandfather had told her about hearing Brahms play some of his compositions at private gatherings in the countryside near Vienna.

Hedwig liked Bartók too and had fun with Martin studying the *Mikrocosmos*. When he told her he was studying Poulenc's *Gloria* at the university, she immediately asked him to relate everything he could because she wanted to know more. That thirst for discovery and understanding made a deep impression; Martin found her reaction "totally wonderful". Yet there were absences: no mention of Rachmaninov, and a reluctance to talk about Wagner or to attend any concert with his music, though Hedwig accepted his position as a composer of major significance. Martin still wondered why. Hedwig's troubled German history?

Hedwig and Martin worked through the programme for his Finals recital at the university: Beethoven Op. 90, a piece that was in his grasp. But wanting to probe Beethoven further, Martin opted to play Op. 101 for his recital at the College – a piece considerably more demanding. Without demur or attempt at dissuading him, Hedwig immediately set about coaching and encouraging him, in the same way as she had spurred him on with his composing. Martin told me too, with a grin, how he had been waiting for his lesson one day, trying out this and that on the piano, when Hedwig rushed through the door in a state of great agitation. 'I have been watching the pigeons,' she said (in her Germanic English). 'They have had babies!' It transpired that she had been observing their nest closely for some weeks but was unprepared for this and nothing short of thrilled. Then just as suddenly, she focused all her attention on Martin's playing. Such was Hedwig's compulsion to share whatever she had just experienced or thought as an abrupt interjection before returning to the matter in hand.

There had been few social interactions. Martin and Sue had visited Hedwig in her flat only once, when they were invited to dinner with one other pupil. While neither of them could remember the details of the evening or what she had cooked – after all, it was fifty years ago – the dessert stuck in their minds and caused a lot of chuckling. Hedwig had thought strawberries and cream would end the meal nicely. But not of the fresh Wimbledon tennis variety: they were not sufficiently sweet. Her guests were instead treated to several tins of strawberries – 'so much tastier'.

No doubt because all Martin's lessons were at the College, Hedwig did not share a great deal about her personal life with him, and he had not known until I contacted him that she had had two daughters. She had talked a little about Iso, however, and suggested that Martin get hold of his recordings. And by way of illustrating Iso's utter lack, indeed rejection, of any interest in himself, she had related how there had not been any mirrors in their houses. A nice little added insight.

I asked Martin how significant Hedwig had been for his musical development. Huge, came his immediate response. As he had always wished, his career has been spent in the classroom, and in addition taking private pupils and performing mainly as an accompanist and conductor of choirs. In each of these roles he makes a point of explaining the background to composers, the contexts, and the ways of getting into and revealing music, just as Hedwig had to him.

By now I was starting to wonder whether I would come across any dissenting impressions of Hedwig. Surely someone would have something less effusive to say, or have a slight reservation about this or that…

Next I travelled up to Witham in Essex to meet Hans Montanana, a cheerful, immediately welcoming bearded figure who was already standing and waiting on the pavement to greet me, smiling as I sought to fit my car into the space near his house. We spent a lively couple of hours together as he regaled me with stories. First, about his Spanish father who came from a politically leftish book-binding background, who had arrived in the UK as a Spanish refugee and, with the vital support of his devoted Danish wife, established a successful one-man antiquarian book dealership. Classical music was much listened to in their home, and his parents took Hans and his brother to as many live music and theatre performances as funds would allow. Hans then told me about people he had known or met at the College – Colin Horsley, John Ogdon, Harrison Birtwistle, Max Davies, and, of course, Hedwig. I posed my standard question about Hedwig's influence on him. The answer was the same as all the others: enormous. While she had not directly influenced his development and career, as she had Sally's and Martin's, what has undoubtedly remained and flowered is the way Hedwig helped to build and form Hans' musical approach to the piano.

The anecdotes poured out and Hans seasoned them with imitations of Hedwig and her pronounced German accent in recalled witticisms, disconcertingly close to how I remembered her. To him she had seemed to enjoy and live life to its brim, never dwelling on the negative, a decidedly strong character in every regard – a feature that Hans surmised might well have created problems for her daughters. Large in build, she had stature and a spring of constant effervescent energy, and was diametrically different to the conventional view of Germans at that time: not staid or over-serious, but very warm, effusive, maternal, and emotionally open – not unlike the picture Hans had built up of Clara Schumann. It was those qualities that had given Hedwig a reputation in the College for helping students and being respected by many of her colleagues, if regarded as eccentric in a fond sort of way.

Hans invited Hedwig to his 21st birthday party. Against his expectations, she came, dressed very flamboyantly – it was an event, after all – and carrying several bottles of wine. Never the snob, always open for fun, she sat on a beanbag and entertained the students with her stories for a couple of hours. They hardly knew what to make of her. It reminded me of when she came to visit me – completely unexpectedly – when I was seriously ill in hospital; suddenly the ward stopped as this unmissable figure strode in with a huge bunch of flowers and boomed out a hearty greeting. Neither staff nor patients had seemingly encountered anyone quite like her before.

Hedwig's musical loves, of the Classical and Romantic periods, were at that time (in the 1970s) out of fashion, Hans said, and her style of playing was decidedly of the old school, and ill-regarded by many. But it was precisely that approach that Hedwig had used to demonstrate how difficult pieces could be made easier by using the whole body, not by the mechanistic, bolt-upright approach then in vogue. When she herself played, here and there she would use a delayed, slower left-hand arpeggio. She was a "fantastic" Chopin interpreter, Hans said, recalling in particular a performance of the Chopin A flat major Ballade, and she would do themed concerts at the College, such as the Chopin Mazurkas: "It was riveting."

Before we parted, Hans suggested I try to talk to Nigel Simeone, who had also known Hedwig. He had no contact details, but said Nigel was on Facebook. I sent off a short note (fortunately the name Simeone is not common) and waited. And waited. I had all but given up when a notice came in from Nigel, enthusiastic to talk. I wasted no time but drove up to see him the following week, where he and his wife Jasmine gave me an astoundingly warm welcome. It seemed that here too, my opening the door to memories of Hedwig could trigger no other reaction. I discovered Nigel had been a flatmate of Hans and had taken lessons with Hedwig for a good couple of years. Having concluded that his musical life would not be one of performance, after graduating he had gone into music publishing at Chappell's and Weinberger's before running an antiquarian music shop opposite the British Museum for six years. Then came a postgraduate teaching qualification and posts at Nottingham, Bangor, and Sheffield universities before he returned to teaching A Level students at the English Martyrs School in 2012. Throughout it all, however, having relished writing about Janáček in his dissertation, Nigel had continued his own research on various composers and performers and had recently edited the letters of Leonard Bernstein and a book about the conductor Charles Mackerras. It was hardly surprising that he described himself as a writer, musicologist, teacher, and conductor.

We sat alone together after lunch. I turned on my recording device but did not need to ask more than the odd question. Nigel was brimming over with recollections and reflections, which he shared for the next hour and a half. He was unstoppable.

What kept coming to the surface was the acute awareness Nigel had had of Hedwig as almost the embodiment of the old Germanic musical tradition. It was early on in his time at the College – and before he had started lessons with her – that he and Hans had gone to hear Hedwig in recital. So deep was the impact that he still remembers much of the detail today. It was a marvellous programme, Nigel said – much Chopin, including the *Barcarolle* and the big C minor *Nocturne* – and the performance was captivating. Even though the piano was less than perfect, Hedwig drew out the best in it, finding burnished tones that she singingly phrased to the music. Yes, there had been aspects, technically, that one could easily have picked holes in, but that did not matter. What Hedwig had captured and offered her audience was a sense of humanity that Nigel found incredibly moving. The word he chose to describe her manner of playing was aristocratic. She had not simply walked on to the stage, but had made a grand entrance in a rather splendid dark evening dress, was obviously entirely at home performing, and she sat at the piano ramrod straight, with the air of a patrician.

Back in Hedwig's flat, however, where Nigel and Hans took most of their lessons, she was very much dressed down, usually wearing beiges and unadventurous greens; the only token to 'style', or her notion of it, was the immaculate hair 'done' by a local lady. Here there was nothing at all of any expectation of deference as one might have encountered in teutonic environments, as indeed I had myself in Germany from the Director of the Max-Planck-Institut where I did my research. No, here the serious artist who was Hedwig was overtly intertwined with the Hedwig whose face was intensely alert, reacting immediately to those around her and with a mischievous twinkle in her eyes which would invariably manifest itself in verbal quips or wicked jokes – jokes that were never intended to, or would, offend, but were always brilliantly amusing, spiced here and there with the odd Germanicism.

We touched on Hedwig's family. Nigel was in no doubt about the academic standing of Fritz Stein before the advent of Nazism and was admiring of the way he had pursued his passion for music and in particular (German) choral works. Hedwig had spoken to him about that, and about some of her early life, as she had to me, but had stopped at 1933 and her exodus with Iso, commenting only that Fritz had been the Director of the Musikhochschule in Berlin. Family loyalty, Nigel was convinced, would have stopped Hedwig from saying anything more. He could remember nothing of what Hedwig had related about her mother Gretel, and as for Maertel, her brother, she had always spoken fondly of him but without much detail.

As a teacher, Hedwig had been a perfect match for Nigel. Recognising and accepting his view that he was never going to be a performance artist, he was looking for pieces that were readily within the range of, as he put it, fallible fingers. Chopin Mazurkas fitted the bill: perfect miniatures, as Hedwig described them. They spent a long time working together on most of them, though Hedwig awarded a few the equivalent of Michelin stars – three for the best, her favourites (Op. 6 No. 2, Op. 17 No. 4, Op. 24 No. 4, Op. 50 No. 3); there was just one two star (Op. 30 No. 2); and to Op. 7 No.3 she gave a single star. As well as Chopin, one of Hedwig's other loves was Schubert. Student Nigel had ventured his opinion that Schubert was sometimes a bit long-winded. Hedwig's response was to say, 'Let me show you how wrong you are,' and she sat down immediately and played the small A major sonata D664, beautifully. 'You cannot possibly say that is long-winded,' she concluded. Nigel had been swamped with emotion soon after she had started. Any discussion from then on was only about the joys and depths of Schubert.

Nigel also chose to study the Beethoven first piano concerto, for a couple of reasons – presumably in addition to his love of the work itself: it was within his grasp; and also, for him at least as important, was that it would give him the opportunity to play *with* Hedwig on the two Steinways. They spent long evenings on it, Hedwig stressing the need for him to breathe with the music; that was the only way to get the phrasing right and the only way to impart the emotional sense and timbre.

Fingerings she could of course help with, but strictly technical aspects were not her focus. To make the piano sing and create a singing line was the goal. She made her students think about how they were playing while they were playing, listening hard to every single note and reacting as they felt necessary. She would introduce sophisticated concepts about how to perform really well, even though she knew that was not Nigel's career aim, but appreciating that he had a musical core that could respond and grow from inside. There was never any question of a 'Hedwig system' of teaching. No, each student was an individual to whom she responded fully, as a person, as a musician and as a teacher. She might gently curb the flamboyance of her wild and emotional students, and equally gently coax out of the less confident and technically secure students a playing that came to express their feelings. She was utterly opposed to the notion that one should deal with the technical features of a piece first and then graft on, as it were, the musical aspects. And as was to be expected from someone so sensitive, any criticisms Hedwig offered were dressed with tremendous charm, possibly augmented by her gloriously convoluted English. These were criticisms that inspired, not demoralised. To achieve the best for everyone, she gave unstintingly of her time, opening up herself and encouraging others to do the same. And she offered support not only through the lessons and evenings together, but by going to all the concerts and recitals that students gave. It was, said Nigel, quite something to be told you had played well by this pianist who had unwittingly assumed the cloak of the elder as far as the old German repertoire was concerned. Nigel's time with Hedwig was one of the longest-lasting and most profound influences in his musical development.

Hedwig's musical appetite was voracious. Apparently she revelled in her students taking along works hitherto unknown to her: Hans introduced her to a number of Spanish works which she loved, and she took delight in Nigel's discoveries about Janáček. They went together to a talk about Szymanowski, after which she joined him at the evening concert.

I asked Nigel, as I had asked Hans previously, if he knew how her colleagues and other students had regarded her. There were some true cheerleaders among the staff, he replied: two members of the faculty in particular, Maurice Aitchison and Peter Smith. Others thought she needed to practise more. But many of the students gravitated towards her, sensing that she would trust them entirely, and because Hedwig was almost a piece of musical history and someone who had lived a remarkable life.

As I watched Nigel's lecture on The Bernstein Letters at the US Library of Congress on YouTube, I thought how, had she lived long enough, Hedwig would have listened intently, and laughed with Nigel at some of Bernstein's exchanges with the composer Aaron Copland and conductor Serge Koussevitsky. Goodness, how she would have rejoiced and felt fulfilled at this development of one of her students.

Having spoken to all these people, I remembered that cry early on in Hedwig's Diary, the expression of a yearning ambition: 'How I wished we would one day get far enough to help young struggling musicians. We have scores of helpers in every corner; some people have none…' She did that in spades.

What a start to my story!

FOUR

HERITAGE, AND THE EARLY DAYS

I felt I should embark on Hedwig's life story by probing back a little in time. I knew from some of her stories that the family included some notable figures but was in the dark about any details. A few facts and anecdotes might, I thought, help to paint the general backdrop to my 'portrait'.

Before getting to her parents, Fritz and Gretel, it is worth casting an eye back to Gretel's grandfather Adolf Kussmaul, who was born in 1822. Even the name, which is Swabian, is rather startling: in English – 'Kissmouth'! Hedwig had told me about him with great glee: a doctor who invented a stomach pump (though it would be more accurate to say he modified its construction somewhat and, most important, used it as a treatment method). For the purposes of our story, a nice connection is that the paper he published about his results is thought to have had a profound influence on one Theodor Billroth's interest in gastric surgery – and more about Billroth shortly. That did not strike me as particularly interesting, but when Anna told me Kussmaul had published his memoirs and offered to let me see a copy, I thought it worth at least a quick skim. The book, in German, was bound in red leather, with a faded and crumbly spine, and had been given to Hedwig by her grandmother Luise; Hedwig had scribbled odd marginalia in pencil. But there was no way I could

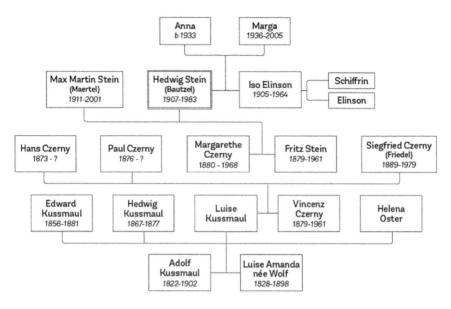

Hedwig's family

read this rather expansive tale: it was printed in the old Gothic script. I managed a few chapters, but then ducked out and resorted to a new and abridged edition in normal print.

'An Old Doctor's Memories of his Youth'[3] (the German title is much snappier) follows a standard chronological path through Kussmaul's life, the first half dedicated to his childhood and medical training, the second to his life as a qualified doctor and university professor. Of greatest interest, I found, were the stories from his time as a country doctor, when he would ride or drive one of his two horses for miles and miles through the woods and mountains to reach his patients, often in horribly inclement conditions and constantly sleep-deprived because there were so few doctors prepared to practise far away from towns. The conditions were truly appalling; two doctors, younger than he, had succumbed to the harshness and given up the practice after a very short time. Kussmaul thought it worth describing in detail his last visits before he became so ill that he too was forced to give up; it makes for gruelling reading. He suffered from consequential complaints, including lameness, for the rest of his life.

The two halves of his memoirs are bridged by a short section entitled 'The Engagement'. The summer after his studies, it seems it took no more than a tea at the house of his closest student friend for him to be swept away by his friend's sister. Returning to try to get a glimpse of her the next day, he saw she was about to board a bus. Distraught, he jumped on. Reaching the station, the same again: Kussmaul leapt on to the train. And then yet another bus, where the conductor spoke to them as if they were a married couple. At her destination, a landau was waiting to take the girl – she was only 16 – home. A farewell was now unavoidable. But Kussmaul had decided: Luise Amanda had to become his wife. Resolved, it came to be – though only a couple of years later, after he had served as a military surgeon during the 1848 Revolution. He obviously thought few further words on this aspect of his life were merited, other than to declare Luise's constant caring and love for him. But I mention it here because Kussmaul was not the only one in the family to take a rapid and unshakeable decision about his life partner…

Adolf Kussmaul, by Franz von Lenbach.[a]

---

a   German painter of well-known personalities from the aristocracy, the arts, and industry.

Medicine was not Kussmaul's sole interest, nor his sole claim to fame. He was an amateur naturalist, and composed a number of poems, some of a tongue-in-cheek nature, while working as a doctor. Later, with his lawyer friend Eichrodt, he published parodic poems under the pseudonym Biedermeier – the term that has come to be used widely to refer to the arts of the conservative middle class in Germany at that time.

Kussmaul is still known today: on the medical side, Kussmaul breathing, Kussmaul's sign, and Kussmaul disease, as the first person to describe dyslexia and to attempt gastroscopy, and in the names of a prize and medal awarded in Germany in the medical field. Aside from those, however, in Heidelberg, where Hedwig went to school for a time, there is a street named after him that she delighted in showing to her grandsons.

This, then, to the first illustrious member of the family. We do not have to abandon the older generations to find yet another. Luise and Adolf had a number of children, including a daughter, Luise. She was to become the wife of Hedwig's grandfather Vincenz Czerny. Like Kussmaul, his name is of interest, but in a completely different context: is he really related to Carl Czerny,[a] of musical fame? Vincenz relates how he was asked the question countless times; so many, in fact, that he set about trying to find out. His searches yielded nothing conclusive however, and the question mark still remains. Like Kussmaul, Vincenz Czerny also wrote his memoirs,[4] largely at the instigation of his colleagues at the University of Heidelberg. But he helpfully also included his life outside medicine, so I was able to put together a number of the pieces of the background jigsaw.

As I read these memoirs, I became increasingly interested in this man, and find it a little hard to restrict myself to the few words about him that are appropriate here. Vincenz was born and brought up in a small town called Trautenau, called Trutnov today, in Bohemia – now in the Czech Republic. The family had had a pharmacy for nearly a hundred years, and Vincenz's father was the dispensing chemist, which at that

---

a   Prolific Austrian composer of Czech origin, particularly known today for his books of studies for piano students.

time usually meant gathering herbs and plants from the surrounding mountains and countryside, and extracting various compounds to make up teas, powders, extracts, and syrups. Vincenz grew up speaking Italian, French, and English in addition to German and Czech, and had little doubt about embarking on a scientific education at university, which in time morphed into the study of medicine. While he was at university, having been brought up to appreciate music, he was keen to continue his piano lessons. But money was short, so he moved in with a fellow student who was similarly impecunious but did have a piano. Together they often went to the Vienna Opera, sitting in the gods, and afterwards they would sing for hour upon hour. The student was Adolf Barkan who later became Professor of Ophthalmology in San Francisco. He is of particular interest here not because of his singing, but because it was he who, after hearing an early concert of Hedwig's, became her benefactor and opened the door for her to move to Berlin by covering the costs of her further studies in piano.

After university, and despite his primary interest at that time in physiology, Vincenz was invited by Theodor Billroth to become his

assistant in surgery at Vienna University, where he stayed for nearly four years. Here Vincenz played every week in a trio and quartet, an activity he continued later in Freiburg. For us, however, most interesting is that Billroth took to inviting Vincenz to the convivial get-togethers at his summer lodge, where other guests included Johannes Brahms – already a

Vincenz Czerny, by Friedel Stein

well-known composer. A talented amateur pianist and violin player as well as concert reviewer, Billroth was one of Brahms' closest friends for thirty years, right up to the time of his death. Indeed, the relationship was so close that when Billroth died, many people wrote condolence letters to Brahms. They shared an interest in folk songs and with Brahms, Billroth worked through his ideas on what makes a melody beautiful (Brahms, it should be noted, remained unconvinced). He hosted countless soirées where Brahms would play, and he was the dedicatee of Brahms's string quartets Op. 51. Such was Brahms's respect for Billroth that he would often ask for Billroth's opinion on his recent compositions before sending them to his publishers.[5] No doubt this was a rather heady experience for Vincenz, creating strong impressions.

As a young but promising surgeon, Vincenz was offered a professorship in Freiburg. Shortly after his arrival, he received an invitation to a dance being hosted by Adolf Kussmaul. When he arrived, his eye was immediately taken by an attractive girl with long blonde curls – the youngest daughter of the Kussmauls. I need hardly say more. Vincenz took an apartment directly opposite the Kussmaul house, where he became a frequent guest. The engagement to Luise followed within just a few months, though the family felt it appropriate not to disclose it for a while and the couple did not marry until two years later – in pouring rain, "as though Heaven had opened the floodgates to pour its joy over us".

Kussmaul put in the odd good word for Vincenz, successfully, since he was offered a further professorship in Heidelberg. Here was a point of unexpected interest for me: Czerny had gone on to become a pioneer and leading light in the surgical treatment of cancer, and in 1906 founded the first Institute for Cancer Research. From my time at the Max-Planck-Institut in Cologne, I well knew of the German Cancer Research Centre in Heidelberg but had no idea that the founder of its forerunner was connected with my new friend Hedwig.

And so, to Hedwig's parents – surely a good place to start in trying to find out about the major influences on anyone's personality. And in Fritz and Gretel Stein, Hedwig had two very strong influences.

Gretel Czerny – short for Margarethe – was born in 1881, and Fritz in 1879. At the time they met, social norms and hierarchies were marked, and Gretel's and Fritz's relative positions in them were distinct. Gretel, as a Czerny, was part of a very well-to-do medical family in Heidelberg. In contrast, Fritz was brought up largely by his mother, who struggled to eke out enough for her five children after her teacher husband died. Although both families had roots in the Black Forest, by the time Fritz went to school his family was living in Heidelberg, as were the Czernys.

I found myself wanting to find out more about Gretel. Remembering this was around 1900, the expectation would have been for her to be a society lady – and dare I say, with the oft-associated blandness that goes with it. Far from it. Gretel had developed a strong streak of independence and will. She delved seriously into music, possibly encouraged by her mother Luise. But her father, Vincenz, seemed to me likely to have had the greater influence. Surely, I thought, given his own love of music, Vincenz must have spoken to his family about his encounters with Brahms and retold stories of Billroth's. It would be pure conjecture to think these helped to propel Gretel to music, but whatever the underlying trigger, Gretel went on to study with Philipp Wolfrum. Although his name has since been lost, he was fairly well known in his day as Generalmusikdirektor[a] and professor in Heidelberg. He was a conductor, musicologist and composer, and promoter of the works of Liszt, Bruckner, and Strauss. Wolfrum's standing was such that he would surely not have taken Gretel on unless she had already shown some talent.

Indeed, Gretel must have been quite a pianist. When the duo partner of the composer Max Reger was suddenly indisposed for a concert in February 1905 in Mannheim, Gretel stepped in with little more than 24 hours' notice and played the secondo part of his Beethoven Variations, Op. 76 – no mean feat. Reger was impressed and greatly appreciative, subsequently inviting her to play on many occasions and dedicating both his first sonatinas Op. 89 to her by way of thanks. Later, after a fruitless and frustrating period with a local piano teacher, it was Gretel who took over Hedwig's musical education. As well as giving her instruction, Gretel

---

a   Chief Musical Director.

Margarete Stein-Czerny (Gretel),
in her later years

played duets with Hedwig, demanding that she sightread the bass part of arrangements of classical symphonies (it was not unknown for the odd tear to run down Hedwig's cheek as she struggled with parts of a Haydn symphony); at other times, Gretel would sing Schubert and Wolf, with Hedwig accompanying. And when Gretel gave concerts for soldiers during the First World War, she would sometimes play together with Hedwig, then less than 10 years old. Whether Gretel was the main driving force behind Hedwig's love and dedication to the piano is unclear, but she undoubtedly played an important supportive and guiding role in Hedwig's musical development.

These were the days when 'Kinder, Küche, Kirche'[a] attitudes prevailed: women had their duties as mothers (and presumably as wives), belonged in the kitchen, and were to pay heed to the church. Yet here was a woman who pursued a long and serious musical education and performed in public, and who, under the name Margarete Stein-Czerny, wrote poems – including a couple of published collections, including one about Max Reger. Indeed, it was Gretel who decided on the poems for Reger's

---

a   Children, Kitchen, Church.

Kinderlieder Op. 142, published in 1916; on the cover was a photo of Hedwig and her brother Maertel, to whom they were dedicated. Like much of Reger's oeuvre, these do not get much of an airing today, but Anne Sophie von Otter has recorded one of them. Wondering further about Gretel's influence on Hedwig, I was excited when I came across Gretel's *Gedichte und Tagebuchblätter*,[a,6] published in 1936. However, I did not find anything like the entries of most diaries that one reads, with their details of a life, but rather a collection of short reflections, more or less in poem form, such as on the seasons and marriage, and on Reger – a walk with him, his improvisation on the organ, his love of children and the way he was as godfather, and an epitaph. Music is there too, and what surely was unusual for the time were Gretel's one-stanza poems about various composers – starting with Palestrina, Schütz, and JS Bach, and

Front cover of Max Reger's Five New Songs for Children.

Photograph is of Hedwig and her brother Max Martin Stein, reproduced with the kind permission of the Max-Reger-Institut, Karlsruhe, Germany.

---

a   *Poems and Diary Entries.*

ending with Brahms and Bruckner. Maybe influenced by the knowledge that Gretel's mother Luise was distantly related to the Romantic poets Schiller and Mörike, they are all very much in the German Romantic style, strongly evocative of the natural world, and of God's gifts and the eternal.

Good health was not Gretel's long suit. As she grew older, her eyesight deteriorated seriously, rather like Luise, who had resorted to learning braille to be able to continue reading. Gretel suffered always from hypersensitive hearing and tinnitus, and apparently found it intolerable on those occasions when she was disturbed at night by rowdy goings-on in the street, weeping and getting close to a breakdown. Added to all this were circulatory disorders and other chronic complaints. Again like her mother, she was seemingly in a constant state of anxiety. Throughout her life – and therefore throughout Hedwig's childhood and adolescence – she concocted all sorts of distressing possibilities in her mind: Could burglars get in by scaling a balcony? Might Hedwig convert to Catholicism? The impression I formed is of someone who was very loving of her children and close friends, yet somehow was not able to take life at all lightly or enjoy herself wholeheartedly.

Hedwig's father Fritz was born in Gerlachsheim, between Frankfurt and Nuremberg. When his mother moved the family to Heidelberg, he attended a 'humanistisches Gymnasium' – one of the more select forms of grammar school, which majored on the humanities, Latin, and Ancient Greek. He graduated in theology in 1902, with training as a pastor. By this time, however, it was clear that beyond all else, Fritz was a deeply committed musician who fervently wished to bring music to others. While the roots of his early musical education are obscure, he must have attained a good standard because he now gained a place at the university to study church music, organ, and conducting – under the guidance of someone we have already encountered, Philipp Wolfrum. Fritz's life had changed, and not only as regards music: Fritz gained entry to the Czerny household by being engaged as a Latin tutor to Gretel's brother Friedel.

Hedwig described the circumstances in which her parents formed their relationship as 'almost worthy of the clans of Romeo and Juliet in

Verona'. Fritz and Gretel struck up an intense relationship. Gretel took whatever opportunity she could to creep out of the house and go to listen to Fritz practising the organ in the local church – and no doubt do other things too. But every encounter had to be clandestine. After all, Vincenz and Luise were in the centre of the social and professional whirl of Heidelberg, and they were hoping for a 'good' match for their daughter. Fritz hardly fitted the bill.

But Gretel was smitten. And it lasted. People in town started talking. At some point it dawned on Vincenz that it might be better to accept the inevitable and make the best of it. To this end, and unbeknown to anyone else, Vincenz decided to support Fritz's music studies financially and, in Leipzig, Fritz continued his studies under the music theorist Hugo Riemann, the Hungarian conductor Arthur Nikisch, and Karl Straube, organist and cantor at Bach's Thomaskirche in Leipzig. In 1906 he landed the post of Music Director at the University of Jena, one of the oldest and most prestigious universities in Germany. News of Fritz's successes percolated to the entire Czerny household. After seven years of waiting, resistance melted away and Vincenz agreed to the marriage. In true Czerny style, it was a grand wedding, with a gala dinner of about five hundred guests, most, no doubt, from the Czerny family and posh Heidelberg scene. Fritz's mother can hardly have fitted in. The Diary gives the impression of a small old woman, alone, 'clad in her best black silk, a little hat on', no doubt feeling out of her depth among the accomplished and polished Czerny crowd that was well-used to such events and must have formed something of an in-crowd with little space for a stranger. She was not to become part of this scene; within a few years she died, despite the best efforts of Vincenz to operate on her cancer.

For the first little while, the Steins lived with the Czernys. Soon Gretel announced that she was pregnant, grounds for considerable excitement in the family and of friends, including Max Reger. At their wedding, Max, who indulged in eating caviar – by the spoonful – had persuaded Vincenz that it would be an appropriate expression of celebration if Vincenz were to send him five pounds of this luxury delicacy for the christening of any and every child. Vincenz no doubt understood; although fairly small and

Max Reger, by Friedel Stein

trim, quite in contrast to Reger, he too loved good food. Shortly after, Hedwig was born – on 21st October 1907. Express letters and telegrams bombarded the Czerny-Stein household: "Where is my caviar?" "I have been starving for the past three days. For the christening I want to be my usual portly self, but for that I need the caviar."[7] A man true to his word, Vincenz obliged for Hedwig and later for Maertel, though Reger clearly exploited other opportunities too: the extensive – and entertaining – volume of letters he wrote to Fritz over a decade[8] have rather frequent references to caviar.

It was around the time of Hedwig's birth that Fritz, pursuing what would be a lifelong passion for detective musicology, unearthed an old manuscript in one of the pubs in Jena, which he was convinced was an early symphony by Beethoven. What a coup! Most of the musicological world agreed with Fritz and the work was published by Breitkopf and Haertel in 1911 as the *Jena Symphony*. This part of the story was not then finished, however. We have to jump ahead to the 1950s when Fritz met the renowned musicologist Harold Robbins Landon in London. Through the watermarks on the manuscript paper, Robbins Landon established that the work was not by Beethoven at all, but by a minor Austrian composer, Friedrich Witt. Understandably, it was a blow for Fritz, then nearing the end of his life, though he accepted the evidence – at least "to 95%".

Anxious to start their own independent family life, by late summer 1910 the Steins moved into their own house in Jena, located appropriately enough on the Philosophenweg.[a] Reger was astounded: "I would never have thought that the Steins would have a house with such a respectable back… And if the back is so attractive, what must the front be like!" Hedwig remembered it well: 'Black and white, with a gabled roof, a veranda at the back, and a big garden with an old-fashioned pavilion in which we kept a square piano'. There they stayed, broadly content, for the next four years. In 1914, however, Fritz received a call to take up the post of Music Director at the Court of Meiningen held up till then by Reger, on his recommendation. It was an illustrious position: earlier incumbents had been Johann Ludwig Bach, Hans von Bülow, and Richard Strauss.

It was not to be. The outbreak of the First World War, which Fritz and Gretel heard about while on holiday in Switzerland, brought everything to an abrupt halt. Foreseeing the need for Fritz to become active in some way or another, they abruptly broke off their holiday and returned to Jena, where they closed up the house and then moved back to live with the Czernys, not knowing how long the crisis would last. Hedwig was too young to grasp the implications of war. She was told that the church bells rang when there was a victory, but did not understand what was meant by 'the enemy'.

For Hedwig, the move to Heidelberg was fun enough. Privations were felt in relatively small ways, such as being given hot semolina pudding with a little fruit syrup on top in the kitchen each and every evening. At lunchtimes though, things were very different: she joined the grown-ups in the dining room, which she recalled as being 'almost like a museum, hung with Persian carpets and copies of the Old Masters,

---

a   Philosophers' Way.

and good, carved furniture'. She went to a local school, crossing the river by the Old Bridge and walking along the river through the Altstadt.[a] For her, from the exceedingly grand and imposing Czerny house, she could hardly not notice the differences between her dress and that of some of the boys she passed playing in the streets; they were scruffy and barefoot.

In her Diary, recalling those years of the war when she lived with Luise and Vincenz, Vincenz emerges as a rather worldly man who had been sufficiently open and curious, as well as professionally recognised, to travel widely – not only to England, France, Italy, Spain, and Greece, but also to Algeria, Egypt, Tunisia, Turkey, the USA, and Russia – and Luise as a fairly strong woman with a streak of independence in her, at least for her time. But within a couple of years of Gretel and the children going to Heidelberg, Vincenz died. Hedwig was too young to be troubled by it. When asked by a neighbour how her grandfather was, Hedwig replied, 'Thank you, he is very well. He died today.' After Germany's defeat, Hedwig – then only about 12 – recalled seeing her grandmother setting off on most weekdays to go to her bank director. This was a time of devastating inflation and the family's capital was dwindling. Luise was terrified. How could the sizeable capital that Vincenz had built up possibly last very long when a litre of milk cost one million Papiermark?[b] And how could they manage the upkeep of the impressive grand house that Vincenz had had built on the banks of the Neckar river and opposite Heidelberg Castle? Luise would:

'stick one arm out as she walked, so as not to ruin her English tailormade coat (or if winter, her old sealskin jacket with a brown sable collar), on her head a smart, dark straw boater with 'arabesques' of tulle on it, at her throat her pearl brooch. She used bank envelopes to serve as inside soles, stuffing them into her sturdy, inelegant shoes.'

---

a   Old town.
b   German Paper Mark issued during First World War and period of hyperinflation.

Hedwig, not grasping the underlying seriousness, could not help giggling as she noticed the envelopes would sometimes poke out so that the addressee 'Ihre Exzellenz, Frau Geheimrat Dr Luise Czerny'[a] was there for all to read. Not that Luise herself was a professor or a doctor; these were still the times in Germany when a wife would assume the title of her husband – in this case Vincenz's celebrated status at the university.

With time, the war news got worse and worse, and the church bells sounded ever more infrequently. Food became scarce and 'ersatz' played a large part in their daily intake. Jam consisted not of wild fruits and sugar, but of carrots; turnips became a staple food; and tea was made from dried blackberry leaves. Fritz signed up voluntarily and was at the Front for the entire war, serving for the first two and a half years as a medical orderly before being assigned to the Telegrafentruppe.[b] He wrote letters to the family telling of train journeys so congested that he had to learn to sleep while standing up in the gangway between the masses of exhausted soldiers. By the end of the war he held the rank of Unter Offizier/Vizefeldwebel.[c] He received three distinctions for his service: a Red Cross Medal, awarded for service to the sick and injured; a medal from the state of Baden-Wuerttemberg; and an Iron Cross II. Hedwig mentioned the last of these expressly in her Diary, and I had assumed it represented an appreciation of especial valour – but then found out that about five million were awarded during the course of the war. That, I surmise, was in any case of little significance for Fritz. Much more important was that for the entire duration of the war and on his own initiative, he had founded the 'Kriegsmänner Chor,[d] Laon' which he took up and down the Front, conducting concerts for the soldiers and musical vespers in large French cathedrals for the wounded. In her collected poems, Gretel included two that it appears she adapted from the Händel oratorios *Deborah* and *Joshua* which were played in these concerts.

---

a   Her Excellency, Eminent Professor.
b   Telegraph Unit.
c   Vice-sergeant.
d   Soldiers' choir.

Fritz had thought for some years, as no doubt had most Germans, that they would win the war. Yet he was personally well-disposed towards England, having enjoyed a visit there as a young student and having studied in Leipzig together with several young students from the USA and England. Hedwig recalled the last months of the war only as memories of:

> 'horses, as thin as Don Quixote's mare, being lodged in our big, unused garages in the Heidelberg house and sad, wasted soldiers coming back to the town. My mother continued with small concerts at the hospitals for the wounded, and I, aged 11 by then, helped her by playing little Schumann or Mozart pieces to the soldiers.'

Quite how Germany's defeat made its mark on Fritz's future attitudes is of course unknowable. As we shall see, however, there are indications that it had a major impact.

By the end of the war, reality for the Steins was fraught. The Court of Saxe-Meiningen was bankrupt and unable to finance the position Fritz had been promised. He now urgently needed to find a job. By a stroke of luck, or judicious intervention by someone, the Kaiser's brother Prince Heinrich, who had heard Fritz's choir, strongly recommended him for the post of Professor and Musikdirektor at Kiel. It was an attractive offer: the town had a large university and Fritz would be able to pursue his interests in choral music and to conduct. In 1918, Fritz paved the way for the family move by first going to Kiel on his own to see how things looked. The timing was hardly the best: it coincided with the Kiel mutiny by sailors and workers that led to the widespread German revolution, the abdication of Emperor Wilhelm II and the monarchy, and the formation of the Weimar Republic in 1919. Fritz found himself in physical danger several times, with street fights just outside his lodgings in the heart of the town. Also, his slightly mad landlady took rather a shine to this young man. But Fritz put a gloss on it all. Writing to the family in Heidelberg, he portrayed Kiel in its best colours: "the lovely harbour, the salty sea, the steamboats, the good air".

The family packed up and left Heidelberg to join Fritz, first staying in his flat for some months. 'Dostoyevsky or Gogol-style scenes' abounded almost every day. The landlady, her eye on Fritz, resented the appearance of Gretel, going to endless lengths to make things unpleasant for the family. Gretel found everything, and especially the noise outside in the street, irritating and was constantly on edge. All this troubled Fritz only lightly. He was indefatigable, and single-minded in building up his domain at the university: as organist of the St Nikolai church he went hunting donors to help to get the organ vastly improved; he conducted all the symphony and other concerts; he had his university Collegium musicum; he gave lectures – where he seems to have been popular with students; he organised festivals dedicated to Bach, Händel, and contemporary composers such as Honegger, Hindemith, and Hans Gál; and he rehearsed three choirs every week, one of which is still active today.

But Gretel's distress could not be pushed to one side. Fritz spoke to her mother Luise who, after some considerable protestations, agreed to open the family purse so they could look for their own house. They found exactly the right one in a peaceful location close to a park outside the centre of Kiel. It had a small garden where Gretel could keep chickens, and there were 'many pleasant pieces of furniture in the house, and some good pictures on the walls'. Here the Steins adopted a lifestyle not dissimilar to that of the Czernys in Heidelberg, though more of artistic activity and probably nowhere near as lavish. They hosted dinner parties for musicians and students. At 'musical teas' they crammed scores of people into their best rooms, and Hedwig and her brother Maertel would play two-piano works or Fritz and Gretel would play adaptations of symphonies. Fritz was known for his bonhomie, sense of fun, and extrovert nature. Unlike Gretel, he could never have too many visitors, in spite of his many duties, and every year he insisted they open their house for a huge party.

Fritz was not bound by convention. He horrified Gretel when he came home with several pink silk shirts from the sales, or with an old farmhouse clock with very buxom mermaids painted on it – a "bargain". A visit by the Lord Mayor of Kiel was in his books nothing particularly out of the ordinary. The mayor might indeed sport a silk hat and all that goes with it, but that was no reason to be bothered when the family Dachshund hopped on to the best red saffian armchair. And mislaying the key to a cabinet in which all the best silver and glass was kept just before one of their house concerts was hardly cause for Gretel to panic: all that was needed was an axe to force the door open. Fortunately, though she had to swallow hard at times, Gretel was at one with Fritz in spurning fine society; academic interests and good art counted for more than refinement, even if she did now have to forego the newest Paris fashions from the Heidelberger haute couturier and all the other exclusive things that had been part of the normal Czerny family life:

'My mother was 'schöngeistig'[a] all her life – in fact she was such a believer in what seemed great or real or genuine or 'worthwhile' that anyone who told her he liked Goethe (or Bach or Bruckner) would have had some advance sympathy from her.'

Gretel was strongly Protestant, though she appears not to have pushed Hedwig unduly in religious matters. There was continuous exposure to sacred music through Fritz, and Hedwig's early education:

'consisted of prayers said at night – and a good knowledge of Bach's chorales and the Matthew Passion… Then the confirmation instructions began and I started to be very interested in religious themes such as the Trinity or Last Judgement.'

But Hedwig never memorised the set catechism. Far more important to her was her concert in Jena where she was to play Mozart's A major concerto (K488). Though confirmed at sixteen,

'the Arts and especially music had taken largely the place of organised religion… I loved the discipline needed to try and get a fine musical piece right!'

---

a   Aesthetic.

Fritz and Gretel were apparently happy to go along with this.

Politics, too, appear to have played only a secondary role in the Steins' lives. They simply got on with making the most of wherever they were and whatever they saw should be done. Nor was overt affection on display. As a couple, Fritz and Gretel adopted the norms of the time as far as their children were concerned; they were mainly to be seen and not heard when there were celebrated guests for dinner, and the goodnight ritual for them consisted of going to Fritz's study and kissing him on the top of his head. But for all the high-minded sobriety, Fritz was also an inveterate fun-seeker – a characteristic that Hedwig adopted in full.

As Hedwig entered her mid and late teens, Fritz took on an increasing interest in her musical development. Although she left school when she was 16, without the Baccalaureate, Fritz insisted she go into the University and copy out Bach cantatas, in old clefs, and attend all his concerts and many of his lectures (which she thought 'excellent') as well as singing with Gretel in one of Fritz's choirs. Fritz certainly had a name by this time. Special people would visit the Steins at home: Albert Schweitzer was 'a big impressive figure with a walrus moustache. They talked of old European organs and Bach, my father and he'. Little could Hedwig have imagined that much later on, she would become friendly with someone who had worked closely with Schweitzer in Lambaréné.

'Wilhelm Furtwängler came too, and had lunches with us. I well remember his highly cultured speaking voice and his animated conversation with my parents (we just sat in silence, naturally!)'

Life in Kiel continued much along the same lines for the next seven years for Fritz and Gretel. The family took one holiday each year, in the summer, sometimes at Pellworm, a North Sea island, or visiting places of their interest such as Passau, the graves of Schubert and Beethoven in Vienna, and Bruckner's coffin under his organ in the chapel in Linz. All was going sufficiently well for them to be able to have a family treat in 1931: a trip to Italy to celebrate their silver wedding and Maertel's Abitur.[a] They took

---

a   German high school matriculation examination.

advantage of a special deal that required – or, better expressed, enabled – them to visit certain cities and sights: Genoa, Florence, Rome, Naples, and Palermo, Taormina, Syracuse and the temples in Sicily. This first trip abroad made a deep impression on Hedwig – one that stayed with her and, to a certain extent, shaped her for the rest of her life – and it reflects Fritz's interest in experiencing culture outside Germany and introducing his children to it. Here is Hedwig's description of the trip:

'Genoa, the typical harbour-town, with narrow, smelly streets and bloodthirsty-looking little butcher's shops and the washing hanging across the lanes, pulled up high. One could see right into people's bedrooms, the enormous lace-faced pillows. In Florence we spent a night and saw the beautiful surrounds – the cartoons by Raphael. Great stylishness, and lovely looking people! Of Rome I remember Monte Piuccio where elegant, sensuous-looking young husbands carried their dressed-up babes on their shoulders – the children in white – like doves; the street with the early Christian burial chambers, the marble arches and statues, the gigantic colosseum, the elegant shops and dark haired beauties, the poor in St Peter's where I noticed dozens of peasant women kissing his big toe; the cafes with the bitter and refreshing brew, the gay men looking anyone up and down; the holy processions in the streets (it was Easter!); and I thought I had never seen so many fine and expressive men's faces assembled as here!

'We visited Naples, were followed by the little boys who dived after pennies thrown into the pond, and saw the 'Blue Grotto'. We went to Palermo where the very special Dome glitters with its gold and frescoes and we marvelled at the strange exotic flavour of it all – magnificent cloisters, gaily festooned ponies drawing carts painted all over with naively fanciful wedding scenes. We admired the severe style of some of the buildings and the tiny chapels and the mimosa and oleander and the huge cacti on the dusty roads of Sicily, growing taller than 6 feet... And the heat! And the white goats nibbling yellow weeds around the Temple of Paestum (a foretaste of Greece!), the Girgentium[a] on the vast and lovely landscape, and Syracuse with its Plato Theatre where hundreds of tiny lizards crept or flitted over the stairs… And the oddity: 'The Ear of Dionysos', a crack in the mountain with the funny echo! And the impossibly beautiful Taormina – a garden of millions of flowers, big hotels and orange trees, in fruit and in flower! And the sea in turquoise-pinkish tints. I met a dark-skinned Sicilian schoolmaster, a friendly man, who played us ancient lullabies on his guitar (he said the words had still some Greek 'remnants' in them). We bathed in the jewelled sea. Much poverty could be seen too, if one had a mind to see it (in the back streets of Palermo particularly), but also many semi-humorous scenes and people with the gift for improvisation – which is to me very markedly Italian!

'Once we travelled 3rd class, amid peasants with their chickens. It was stifling and hot and I shut my eyes. Gently a (wonderful looking!) little youth's hand crept into my dress-pocket to take some sweets out from there! I did not disturb him. As if to make up for lack of 'good style' he later offered me to drink from his dirty bottle of wine which I declined. But he took it well. He was more perfectly shaped than youths in the Northern climates!

'In Naples I once went about alone, to post some letters. Immediately the taxi-man and horse-cab men shouted: 'Bravo – bella – bellissima!' It was funny; all I had that I thought could be the reason was a pair of nice young arms that showed in the sleeveless yellow-silken summer frock! So my brother joined me when I went out on future walks. My mother was hunting out the many museums. She could sample an immense amount of 'Art', truly enjoying it – but not quite so much for me! 'Ah, I shall probably never again see these wonderful things,' mother said (quite correctly).

'A kind of craze befalls me. I am on Italian ground. It's no good trying to describe the feeling. One lives fully to the brim, I

a Ruins of Jupiter's temple.

feel! What is the smell of garlic, or a little bit of cheating, or the great heat to the enjoyment of what this fantastic race has left us and 'done' for us!

'It was such a good idea of my dear parents just once to have gone really south. My father could not easily get away from all his duties in (then) Kiel. So we were most grateful to them. I kept my sketch of Etna, smoking into the blue, thin air. Yes, we paid it a visit: the little Etna smoking and belching down below our feet – bubbling like Shakespeare's witches – a cauldron! – slightly frightening is the noise and physical feeling of unrest. The earth looks crusty and hard and ancient under one's feet and there are thousands of little cracks in it.

'We saw Pompeii and the touching monument: the runner fleeing from the approaching disaster... This tour prepared me for the delicious joys we encountered in Greece nearly 30 years later! Bravo, bravissimo, dear Papa and Mama!'

It is already quite clear that Hedwig was not from any 'ordinary' family. Her grandfather and great-grandfather both had considerable reputations in the medical profession. Other people in the family had professional titles and published academic and other works. In Heidelberg, Vincenz and Luise hosted and were hosted at countless dinners for visiting doctors and surgeons, and during Hedwig's teenage years in Kiel, Fritz's growing reputation meant that there too were countless comings and goings of interesting people. Hedwig's godfather, after whom she was named – Maximiliane – was Max Reger, by now an internationally renowned composer, conductor, and pianist. And Hedwig had heard about her grandfather's friend Theodor Billroth and Vincenz's encounters with Brahms. The family had a distinctive history and circle of contacts. Once exposed to that sort of life, it is almost impossible to contemplate any form of insularity or parochialism. Later, Hedwig's daughters Anna and Marga would face the same situation.

Backing up the intense musical environment provided by her parents, Hedwig's lifelong interest in pictorial art was no doubt sparked by visits as a child to Gretel's brother Siegfried, known as Friedel – 'a very good looking, sensitive man'. She observed him closely in his studio, heady with the smell of turpentine, as he struggled to decide which background colour to choose for his portraits – olive-green behind a sitter? or a Persian rug? Friedel was a dab hand at copying the old masters and followed them in his own paintings. After his years at the Front during the First World War, Friedel returned to his passion and became a professor at the Karlsruhe Academy of Art. Hedwig continued a good, warm relationship with him for the rest of his life.

Hedwig grew up used to being in impressive homes – the Czernys', for starters, which was known throughout Heidelberg as the Czerny Haus. Built in white sandstone, it had a classical Greek design with numerous loggias, set in a garden full of flowers. Inside there was a grand hand-carved cedar staircase (Hedwig could forever remember the smell of it) ascending from a large hall with an 'English' open fireplace. The kitchen had a modern 'English' grill with a bell that rang when the meat was cooked. There was a library – sufficiently large to require a stepladder to reach the upper shelves. A few servants helped Luise to run the place. Vincenz also bought part of a vineyard and a large park on the hill near their house, which they called the Wiese.[a] It was all well-meant, but the reality was a bit different from the concept. Like many things tackled by Luise, disappointments ensued. The dog chased and injured deer, there were swarms of mosquitoes in the summer, and the children kept getting hurt by the spiky horse chestnut cases. In a fit of trying to do something good, Luise decided to throw the Wiese open to people from the neighbourhood and to give them tea. This was yet another misadventure; despite signs with polite requests to respect the garden, fences were broken, trees uprooted and fruit plundered. The experiment was not repeated. For Hedwig, however, it was overall a time of considerable fun, and at that age she was not particularly conscious of the privileges. Her normal way of life even included visits during the war to Gretel's best friend Else von Löwis at Schloss Mauren:

---

a   Field.

'...an ancient knights' castle which, to us, seemed paradise on earth... it was a very simple large square house with 4 little turrets, near Böblingen. Everything seemed wonderful: the flower alleys, with immense clusters of phlox, columbines, pinks and roses, and the little pond with a tiny fountain. I loved the country smells of hay and field flowers. Even the terrific noise of geese seemed to add spice to life. There were large forests nearby, with mushrooms of every type, and mushroom 'tours' were organised by the ladies of the house. Oh! – that fine odour of decaying shrubs and mushrooms in the undergrowth or the Steinpilze[a] and golden Pfifferlinge[b] which we had stewed for supper. We picked forget-me-nots along the brooks and saw dragonflies sitting on whatever they liked for the moment. We made little exhibitions of dolls' hats from large leaves, pinned them together with fir needles, adorned them with little flower ornaments, and charged halfpence for the exhibition, all in aid of the Red Cross. I played pieces by Bach in the 'blue room' on a wheezy fortepiano of walnut, or we did drawings of trees and the large houses. Once I even managed a long poem in praise of Mauren! The family lived in a very simple way. They spoke well and read good books.'

In Heidelberg, Hedwig encountered at least one other girl who was growing up in an arts-saturated environment not unlike hers. Lilo (nickname for Lieselotte) Buzengeiger was the granddaughter of a landscape and impressionist painter, Friedrich Kallmorgen, one of the founders and first president of the Grötzingen artists' colony. The two of them hit it off and would spend hours together, often playing with Lilo's puppet theatre, when Hedwig would play or improvise suitable accompaniments to whatever Lilo decided to put on.

For the children at the small private day school that Hedwig attended

---

a   Porcini.
b   Chanterelles.

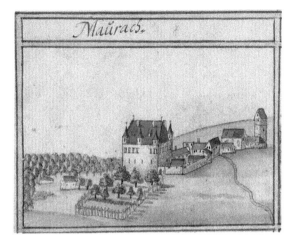

A Place for Holidays: Schloss Mauren

a) Painting from 1681. Vorlage und Aufnahme: Hauptstaatsarchiv Stuttgart: Mauren, BB, H 107/3 Bd 10 Bl 7

b) Photograph from 1938, reproduced with the kind permission of the Krohmer family.

in Kiel, however, she was nothing short of odd, always dashing away to get to her piano, and on occasion being allowed to miss school because she was performing somewhere. Although she wrote of herself 'I may have been a little prig', the other girls seem not to have found her so. There was no serious dislike or resentment: 'Such was the real respect for the arts in Germany that I never experienced any quarrels or difficulties with the other girls'. Maybe so. Or maybe just a reflection of the attitudes in families that sent their girls to a private school.

Even as a child, Hedwig heard world-famous musicians and those who came to play, often under Fritz: the pianists Walter Gieseking, Edwin Fischer, and Artur Schnabel; the coloratura Maria Ivogin; and the violinists Adolf Busch and Carl Flesch. Many of them took time to sit and

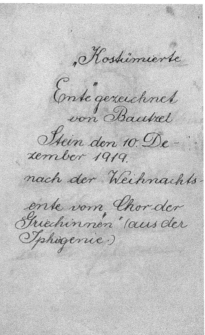

Drawing by Hedwig (aged 12). Reverse side reads: 'Costumed Duck by Bautzel Stein,[a] *the 10 December 1919, after the Christmas Duck from the 'Chorus of the Greek Women' (from Iphigenia)'.*

have a glass of wine with Fritz after the concerts, and although Hedwig was surely not allowed to say very much at all, she must have absorbed a great deal from the conversations and become familiar with the way in which people in such circles interacted.

Fritz, we know, was ambitious. He was also ambitious for his children and so Hedwig's own conviction from an early age that she wanted to forge her life as a pianist was entirely congruent with Fritz's.

Aside from the musical envelope to Hedwig's life, her parents apparently set great store by the notion of German 'Gemüt' or 'Innigkeit'[b] (words difficult to translate), as expressed in many of the finest Schubert or Schumann songs, and Hedwig grew up wondering whether other

---

a   Bautzel was Hedwig's nickname
b   Gemüt – soul, character; Innigkeit – intimacy, ardency, warmth.

'European people possibly had no Gemüt!' Her (typical) response was not to leave the question hanging, but to go and look for the answer: she devoured literature from all sorts of authors, German and international, and lapped up whatever she could from other cultures:

> '...the elegant ease of expression, the art of living, and the sensuous enjoyment of smells, tastes, and colours as expressed by the French Impressionists (painters and composers).'

The thought of a hot climate she found intoxicating, and in later years she would revel in trips to southern France, Italy, and Greece.

As she moved into her teens, Hedwig encountered a passionate artist rather more of her age than Uncle Friedel, who was to have a strong influence. This was Georg Döring, known by all as Görli, who was pressed by his father into studying law but who wished only to be a painter. They met at a fancy dress gathering to which she had gone as Princess Brambilla:

> 'Behind my tastes and probings stood the figure of Georg Döring (later a solicitor), my first real friend. At a slightly Bohemian party of Frau Ada Adelmann, painter and friend of young people, I appeared in the costume of Princess Brambilla (after ETA Hoffmann). Though Görli obeyed his father and was pursuing law, his inward hope was to paint in life. He did lyrical scenes of the Holstein Schweiz – the small lake district near Entin and Lübeck, idyllic lakes, connected by canals, dreamy cows grazing or the dragonflies flitting about – and they achieved a sensuous loveliness with a minimum of line-drawing or painterly effort (the late Turner was his ideal). He was mainly self-taught and was still trying to find his way. His childhood had many ups and downs – the death of his beloved mother when he was a child which was a huge blow to his father. And relatively speaking, they were poor. Görli's intellect fascinated me; he was not what people call a nice person. No, he had the chameleon's capacity for

being many different 'characters' and he had a marked love for his interesting 'self'. Like Narcissus he meant much to himself but had also the capacity to be a friend to many chosen people. He liked to dominate a small party by his interesting and often careless talk. He would talk about Plato and homosexual love, Balzac, David Caspar Friedrich – the fine Romantic painter from North Germany, and the painter Runge – and he could talk somewhat viciously against the bourgeoisie!

'My interest in Görli alarmed my dear parents. Here was a young man with a fine head, good, deep blue eyes and dark brows and black thick hair (with a chic, silvery streak running across it from the forehead to the back), of middle class background but with very little money to spend, who dressed shabbily or strangely, and who saw their Bautzel [Hedwig] often and as they later confessed might have frightened away other young men! As Görli was very careless in his talk and my young brother particularly good-looking, a lad of 13 or so – they must have been worried that he might be a bad influence on both of us. They rather had their eyes on the young Kurt Thomas, a composer whose first major work, performed by my father's a capella choir at the Deutsches Tonkünstlerfest in Kiel, made the European critics sit up: they all wrote 'here was a young man of genius!' Physically K.T. seemed to my mother descended from the angels (at least the Gothic ones, done by the masters of that time!). She well may have had secret hopes that 'the spark' would fly between us. We even played piano duos in his flat in Leipzig where he worked, but the spark did not fly. It was Görli's ideas, my music and general studies of books and people and nature that occupied me fully for the next tense years.'

It was not the romance of Hedwig's life. In this first blush of a special friendship, only hesitantly and a little obliquely did they get to talking about where their relationship might be heading, marriage being the obvious possibility. But there were the contraindications: Görli was not at all musical, he was in poor health, and he clearly tended towards homosexuality. Although Hedwig did not seem to feel uneasy about homosexuality in principle, it certainly did not accord with her view of her own future life. (She obviously thought it worth recording in her Diary if a friend or acquaintance – only male, however – was, or was thought to be, homosexual. In the family these people were referred to as WB – warme Brüder.[a])

Writing in her Diary all these years later, Hedwig summed up her then-feelings – through a prism of nostalgia for the excitement of the first might-be romantic love:

'My friendship to Görli – though we felt very tenderly for each other – did not develop into love. It could not have done so; there was that strain in time that pulled mysteriously in other directions. Yet I remember one kiss which had significance: he had given me a lovely naively painted rose (in watercolour), done when he was only 12, saying: 'Keep it. You'll marry, you'll be like an apple tree in Chekhov (!) that bears fruit.' – that was direct indeed! I did not take it easily, this semi-fatherly pose! But it cleared the air. Görli had suffered from TB as a youth and his health was never robust. He aged before his time. I shall always think of him in deep gratitude, in spite of the many Dostoyevsky-coloured upsets he caused us all. He gave me a ring with a large turquoise which his young goldsmith-friend had made for me, at 16!'

Hedwig treasured this scarab ring. She wore it often. There were even scratch marks on her Manchester Steinway from it, and I remember the ritual of her taking off her rings, including the scarab, before she started to play. Overall, I wonder whether Görli did not implant some significant ideas that remained with Hedwig: his anti-bourgeoisie attitudes were much more explicit than any that Hedwig had encountered before. While Fritz and Gretel paid little attention to material aspects of life, I have no impression that they were principled about it, as I think Görli was.

---

a   Literally, 'warm brothers'.

Later he probably had to walk something of a tightrope as the Nazis' grip tightened.

Görli remained a good friend to Hedwig for the rest of his life.

FIVE

INDEPENDENCE, ISO, AND LOVE

It became clear where Hedwig was heading when a wealthy friend of the Czernys came over from San Francisco and heard her play at a concert. This was no less than Adolf Barkan, the student friend of Vincenz Czerny. 'Could he be allowed to be a little useful? And pay toward expensive lessons in Berlin, or something like that?'. Fritz and Gretel jumped at the offer, and it was agreed she should go to Berlin to have lessons at the well-known Stern Conservatoire under Professor James Kwast. Fritz was clearly in no doubt about Hedwig's budding talent.

For her part, Hedwig was not daunted at the prospect but typically opened her arms wide to this sudden explosion of her world:

'The new life shook me greatly! I fell under the spell of the old Professor, who though nearly 70, had much charm for the circle of admiring students. He had wavy silvery hair (like my father!), smelled of Eau de Cologne and spoke a very distinguished-sounding German (he had produced some great players when younger!). His wife was the famous Frieda Kwast-Hodapp, a legend in her lifetime, as far as my family was concerned (though she did not aim at international fame). I was over-ready to fall under the spell of these 'new' people. To leave Kiel every 2 weeks and enter a totally different 'climate' was a joy! The metropolis was swayed by big artistic events. If one had the time and money one could see Pavlova dance one evening, Nijinsky another, see Alexander Moissi, the Austrian actor, do 'The Living Corpse' by Tolstoy and a Reinhardt play – or Laban's dance group – or Kurt Weill's 'Dreigroschenoper' might be performed again or one could go to the Blaue Vogel – a first rate cabaret (after my heart!), or to the Wintergarten where particularly Apache and Spanish dancing took my fancy... There were the regular Furtwängler concerts with the 12-year-old Yehudi Menuhin playing Brahms's violin concerto like a young god! The Don Cossacks excited. Elisabeth Bergner gloried in a play by Gerhardt Hauptmann... I was frugal in my spending but saw and heard what I wanted.'

It must have been thrilling: Hedwig was in her early twenties, following her star of being a pianist. She had the background to appreciate the classics in music, theatre, and art that were on offer, as well as a curiosity for the avant garde. Berlin at that time was the magnet and cultural crucible for artists from Germany and well beyond. At the beginning, for her fortnightly visits, she stayed with a sister of her grandmother's in the centre of Berlin (no doubt Fritz and Gretel thought this a prudent move). Unattached, Hedwig was able to take advantage of all that was on offer, although her piano studies – soon to be with both James and his wife Frieda Kwast-Hodapp in their 'comfortable, lovely flat in west Berlin with around fifteen young students assembled for half a day for communal lessons' – were very demanding. Any approaches by young men were spurned and Hedwig focused instead on mastering her piano technique and musical understanding, in which she was tutored solely by Frieda after James became very ill. Frieda was not only 'the high priestess of great music' for people such as her parents but also for Max Reger, who dedicated his piano concerto to her. Hedwig liked and got on with her. But she responded also to Frieda's flamboyance and wit, lapping up her tales of going to London and buying extravagant and fashionable clothes, and enjoying the parks, and seeing the old gobelins[a] in Brussels:

---

a   Tapestries.

'She adored jewels and had a big collection of them. The elderly Duke of Baden was one of her admirers and had given her some fine specimens. By now – 1930 or so – we knew she was great friends with a multimillionaire, a German businessman[a] who lived in style near Weimar. (Kwast's feelings about it were not known to us.) Frau Kwast cuddled her Pekinese far too much (he was bathed in Eau de Cologne – she had no children!) and much of her time was spent at the friend's Rittergut[b] near Weimar where also the Adolf Busch Quartet often stayed. This friend had had the good sense to buy many Impressionist paintings (a collection which, I believe, fell largely into Russian hands after the War). Her husband died soon after, greatly mourned by us. My parents thought it a little daring that Frau Kwast and her friend shared the house so often. Once she asked some of us students to spend a weekend with them. I was among them. A lovely property, and kept rather in English style. We played to her and had our lessons but also champagne (!) and I even counted 2 little Renoirs (original ones) and one small Degas in my bedroom! (This news went to Kiel – on a postcard!)'

Commuting between Kiel and Berlin soon proved troublesome – it was, in those days, a lengthy journey – and Frieda laid down a condition: "From 1st May you have to live in Berlin. This current arrangement will not work in the longer term." By a stroke of luck, Hedwig's friends from Heidelberg, the Adelmanns, had gone to live in Berlin, and with time she became their paying guest. The act of leaving home was difficult for Hedwig: she sensed her commitment to a career as a pianist meant she would not return for a long time. She said goodbye to her closest friends at the Kiel Carnival the night before, and four friends came the next day to the station to wave her off. Gretel and Maertel accompanied her as far as Plön. Then she was on her own. Arriving on a beautiful day in bright sunshine, Ada Adelmann, her husband Leo, and their three children

---

a   Though Hedwig was coy in the Diary about disclosing his name, we know this was Dr Otto Krebs.
b   Rittergut – manor house, hunting estate, here named Holzdorf.

welcomed her almost as a member of the family. Hedwig went up to a room on the top floor that faced south and had a view of the green in front of the house, a church and its cemetery. She could see vast expanses of sky through the large windows. It would be ideal for painting, she thought, and most important, she would not disturb anyone when she practised. Living with the Adelmanns proved easy, and through them opened the most significant door in Hedwig's life: an introduction to Iso Elinson.

Hedwig's life was changed completely by Iso. It would be impossible to write about her without also talking about Iso. But how? There is so little to go on other than Hedwig's diary entries, a handful of recordings, and a few reminiscences from his family, and people who heard him play and who he taught. So Iso Elinson, this person who fundamentally shaped Hedwig's life, is rather an enigma. But let us get as close to him as we can.

He met Hedwig in the early 1930s. Adolf Diesterweg, a music critic in Berlin who was related to Ada Adelmann and had written a positive review of Hedwig's performance of the Mendelssohn piano concerto, rang to ask if she would like to hear "a fantastically gifted young Russian pianist". She and Ada's daughter Renate went. Iso played the Schubert A major sonata, D959. Hedwig was struck by Iso's:

'thick black curls, marble-white forehead and very strong compact-looking hands… His outer hand had tremendously developed muscles and his thumbs and fifth fingers were far stronger in action than those of other players I knew (his fingers were not long or tapered). He liked to look at his hands and disliked the least little scratch or blemish on them.'

Renate cut out Iso's photo from the programme and hung it in her wardrobe. But it was Hedwig, donned in her Russian hand-embroidered blouse brought by her father from a World Exhibition in Moscow, who caught Iso's attention at a coffee and cake afternoon at the Diesterwegs' home shortly afterwards. 'This time Elinson's hair seemed even longer. He squinted a tiny bit and teased the host in a childlike way.' Iso asked Hedwig to play. She decided on the Chopin E minor concerto, despite knowing that she had not yet solved many of its problems. Consequently she grew rather hot and bothered. Iso's comment at the end was memorable: "Well done, Fräulein Stein, you really are very talented, but your tone sounds just a little constipated!" Hedwig's reaction was equally memorable: 'I was intrigued, not upset! Yes, this was a splendid way of putting it.'

Each was no doubt drawn to the other by their intense musicality. By this time, Iso had already had considerable successes, not only in Russia but also with tours through Scandinavia and South America. Unlike Iso, Hedwig had not been singled out as a child prodigy, and was still only just embarking on her professional career, but she was as dedicated to music and developing as a public performer as he. Each probably held out the suggestion of something unusual for the other. For Hedwig, Iso was truly exotic: a Russian, an exile, interested in little beyond piano music, and striking in appearance with his head of thick black curls and distinguished hands. He brought alive her fascination with Russia and the Russians which had been sparked by reading the classical Russian literature and hearing stories from her grandfather Vincenz. She wrote how much she liked to study different types of Russians: some, like Horowitz, struck her as worldly-wise and sophisticated; Iso was possibly the exception in that, she thought. For Iso, Hedwig was a budding pianist who was as passionate about music as he, and the daughter of a well-known musician and musicologist with good contacts in the German musical world; added to that was her innate and deep-seated inquisitiveness, her unbridled enthusiasm for the arts – and her humour.

It is obvious from her Diary that Hedwig thought and felt very much in the context of what she had read and seen, which included Dostoyevsky and Tolstoy, and the German classics and philosophers, especially Schopenhauer. I wonder whether she thought Iso embodied genius in the Schopenhauer sense, through his pianism and musicality. Schopenhauer had held that those with a high degree of genius could be taught to communicate their aesthetic experiences to others. Such a view certainly fits with Hedwig's descriptions of Iso's playing, which she felt enabled audiences to lose themselves in the essence of any particular piece. Much later, when he performed, 'gloriously', Chopin's Op. 10 Études at the BBC Studio in London, she wondered whether the many invited friends who were listening realised his 'enormous inborn gifts'.

From then on, there were many meetings: walks along the canal, concerts, evenings at Ada's. On one occasion, they paced backwards and forwards along the canal after Iso had played to some friends. Hedwig went with him to the underground station, Iso then went back half the way with her, they then returned to the station... all the while – Hedwig claims, at least – discussing how to keep the wrist flexible, how to ground technique by playing the five notes from C to G in slowest bel canto legatissimo with gradations of tone, and then in pizzicato, staccato or in a detached, heavier style 'so important for the playing of Bach and much of Beethoven, or Brahms'. Iso would advise Hedwig about fingering – maybe on a walk in the countryside.

> 'We all were under the spell of this immensely gifted and humorous young man who used his own brand of eccentric German. ... I now played all works in slowest tempo – like a slow-motion picture – but with expression and pedals. This was a revelation as I studied Chopin's Study in F minor Op. posth, making the part of each hand comfortable. Iso was so patient and happy to pass on wonderful pianistic bits of fingering.'

Surely, though, there were also exchanges of a rather different kind...

Hedwig heard that Iso had been born in 1905[a] in Mogilev (now in Belarus), but his ancestors may not have been Russian. Once, when Iso was performing in Göteborg, the town councillors at the concert told him that the Swedish General Elinson had fought at the Battle of Poltava in 1709 and had been taken prisoner by the Russians and probably stayed on in Russia. A forefather? Possibly.

I have been able to find out precious little about what shaped Iso: his parents and siblings, let alone his wider family, or his friends; his awareness of St Petersburg and the world surrounding it; his early relationship to music; his love or otherwise of the city and of the countryside; the influence on him of the arts more generally. We do know, however, that his family

---

a   There is some uncertainty about the exact year; Iso might have been born in 1907.

Iso Elinson's parents, Marie and Yossip.

was well-educated. In the first decade or so of the 1900s, Iso's father had established himself as a successful lawyer, holding a position equivalent to Attorney General. The family was comfortably well-off, with a holiday place at the Black Sea. A story Iso apparently liked to tell – and the sort of story that pleased Hedwig – was of his father's encounter with Tolstoy.

> 'Elinson (senior) was a student, Tolstoy an old writer of world renown… It was in a railway carriage, and the young man said: 'Have I the great honour of seeing Count Tolstoy?' The other: 'Well, I am a writer of fairy stories!"

Music was an integral part of the Elinson family life, and from the age of three Iso was taught piano by his mother, who as a young girl had been taught by Anton Rubenstein, the founder of the St Petersburg Conservatoire. At six, he was invited to go to study at the Conservatoire. Here he distinguished himself in both performance under Felix

Blumenfeld – himself a protégé of Anton Rubenstein and influenced by Liszt – and composition under Alexander Glazunov. It is likely that by this time the family had moved to St Petersburg because of Iso's father's work, or as a result of this invitation. Iso mastered the piano literature very early on and played Chopin studies in public at the age of only eight. After one recital, Scriabin held him up to 'show him off' before the public. He won a grand piano, and had concert tours across Russia, one of which went right to the Chinese border – a journey of almost two weeks.

'The old photos show Iso in very carefully planned clothes, fit for a prodigy: stiff, white collar, a classic little dark suit, leather booties, side-buttoned – and inside them a very serious boy, with an indrawn look in his eyes; in one picture he studies a score of Beethoven Sonatas on his knees, while in another, he plays what seems to be a papier-mache small piano (!) at the photographer's; on another he holds a pistol, dressed as a little soldier, but with dreamy eyes, and completely absorbed in something else – a look of utter detachment (which later on he often had when people talked in a 'womanish' way!). His teacher taught him every day of the week, and they finished the sessions by each eating an 'Anton' apple (a type now extinct in Russia). Apples played a big part in Iso's life!'

Blumenfeld was "an opinionated and critical teacher who wasted little time on social niceties… accepted very few private pupils and only those he considered technically advanced and extraordinarily talented".[9] Like him, Iso appears to have been somewhat short on the finer points of social intercourse – they simply were of no importance to him. His way of getting by socially was using his innate charm and sense of humour, and playing the piano for people whenever he had the opportunity, almost regardless of the circumstances.

Let us join Hedwig in her recollections of what Iso told her about his time in Russia:

'The students at the Conservatoire were taught rather like those of Bach's St Thomas Church in Leipzig. He knew much of German literature (translated into Russian, I think) but did not learn English or French. His mother mystified him by words like 'pince nez', guipure (lace!), cache nez[a] and she hid a magnificent pictorial edition of Balzac's Contes drôlatiques when she noted his interest awakening. His composing began early. I have a touching Russian printed copy of 'La Filleuse' by Iso Elinson, with his dressed-up photo on the cover (on the photo he looks about seven) – a simple little piece with a middle-part in minor, obviously influenced by Chopin.

'The shadow of the Revolution appeared: on May 1st of each year all the students paraded on the big open place, together with thousands of other people. Iso did not want to take part and excused himself with tummy pains. The times began to get more difficult. Food was scarce and the principal teacher of harmony and counterpoint, a sensitive old gentleman, went habitually round in the canteen, saying: 'Excuse me, if you have any herring heads or tails you don't want, I should be so grateful...' When a celebrity died and the horses for the hearse too weak (like Don Quixote's), then the favourite students had to step in.

'There is a certain gap in my memory: the next 'picture' flashing before my inner eye is of the mob smashing up the Elinsons' grand piano – (that is, thrown out of the window into the square below) and cutting up Iso's father's edition of Shakespeare and using it for WC purposes. Or tragi-comic incidents in the old Palace,[b] in deepest, coldest winter, when one floor was abandoned and designated for lavatorial purposes. Iso told me too how an ex-General used to meet old Princess Varwara;[c] no one cared any more... Iso often had to walk 1–2 miles just to get water from a pump.

---

a   Muffler.
b   The Winter Palace, official residence of the Russian Emperors up to the Revolution.
c   Possibly Princess Varvara Ilynichna Turkestanova – a Russian noblewoman of Georgian origin, known for her affair with Tsar Alexander I. *Wikipedia, 19.01.2020.*

'Iso had some interesting concert experiences during this time: Chaliapin[a] and he shared a tour of concerts for the sailors and were paid in kind, such as sacks of flour. 'Chopin's Nocturnes are far too soft for our boys,' said the organiser – after Iso had begun! 'Give them meaty stuff!' Well, 2 Liszt Rhapsodies came handy and went down very well! Then there was the night when Glazunov and Iso were sent to gaol. In despair, as there was so little fuel for the forthcoming Tchaikovsky concert at the Conservatoire, both had searched for wood among the abandoned houses and found several old doors. Yet the police objected and put them into a large room where they held the real criminals. The musicians were greeted in an alarming manner: 'Hey – you with your white hands, you are not of our class.' Somehow they managed to extricate themselves. On another occasion, Iso had to play the Rachmaninov C minor concerto. He possessed only one pair of evening trousers so when he aired them on the clothes line, he left a notice: 'These are my only pants – respect them. I play Rachmaninov in them tomorrow evening.' It worked!

'Times got worse and worse. Iso and one of his brothers (he had 9 siblings) were 'cut off' from their parents by the Revolution. They lived in a room let by a landlady who said she could not give them coal in winter. To demonstrate their anger the brothers demonstrated by splashing water on the floor – it froze, and the two boys skated in the room! Iso slept on his big grand, with only a thin mattress separating him from it. He had to practise with one hand at a time while he warmed the other in the pocket of his trousers. One day a red-bearded 'Commissionaire' arrived: 'Comrade, we need your piano for the children in White Russia,' whereupon Iso fought him – 'a good staccatissimo!' He kept his piano.

'When Iso saw his parents again, his father asked him to barter a gold watch for meat. Iso went to the country by train

---

a   Feodor Chaliapin (1873–1938); Russian opera singer, well-known internationally.

(journeys were now free, but the trains frightfully over-crowded) with a large rucksack on his back, containing some of the family treasures for bartering: 'We've got 20 clocks, my boy, 15 gold watches, 11 top hats (!) and even 10 small upright pianos,' said one farmer. 'But for this silver-dish I'll give you 3 pounds of good meat!' This was arranged and Iso ran for his train back to town. Alas – an equally hungry dog followed him, sniffing, barking, and jumping up behind him until part of the expensive meat was bitten off the rucksack. Iso was sorely tried by this episode and looked crestfallen when talking about it, even many years later.

'Iso's studies at the Petersburg Conservatoire went on until 1927, 3 years after Lenin's death. This was also Beethoven's Centenary year. Iso played all the 32 sonatas in Moscow and St Petersburg. He had passed brilliantly at the Conservatoire, his Diploma signed by his principal, the composer Glazunov:

"This is to certify that Mr Isaac Elinson entered the Conservatory in 1911, having displayed a musical gift of genius. Under my tutorship in the years 1917–1919 he thoroughly studied all the musical literature. He graduated brilliantly in composition in 1920. He possesses both a remarkable and skilful technique in piano playing and a genius for artistic musicality. In the might of his talent and performance he is truly a follower of Franz Liszt. Therefore I consider his musical education to be complete.'

'Iso remained at home for another 3–4 years, usually practising for 8–9 hours a day as well as giving concerts. Then he left for Estonia and Berlin. These were times full of struggles for food and any comforts. His parents seemed to advise his going to Germany – come what may. Iso did not like the political creed and had given hundreds of concerts all over Russia and was eager to 'conquer' new territory. I believe his trip started in Riga where a great lover of music – the owner of a large men's outfitters – showed his artistic admiration in a truly realistic manner: he begged to be allowed to give Iso a complete outfit of best blue suit, shirts, shoes, coat and so on for future travel occasions! Of course Iso accepted gratefully – he saw the fun of it, too!'

'His father accompanied Iso to the German border, to deliver him 'in person', so to speak. The visa for Iso was only made out for a 4 weeks' stay in Berlin. All I know on this point is that Iso overstayed these 4 short weeks with the approval of his parents. (A grim decision to have to make. Did they guess it might be goodbye forever?)'

As with Hedwig, it was hardly surprising that Iso made for Berlin. Berlin during the Weimar Republic lured all manner of artists and intellectuals. They made the city spin. Academic institutions had been opened up to Jewish scholars, and a number of them received Nobel prizes during this time, including Albert Einstein. Here were Georg Grosz, Jean Arp and avant garde artists of the November Group, Mies van der Rohe and the Bauhaus movement, novelist Christopher Isherwood, poets Stephen Spender and WH Auden, film director Billy Wilder, and the theatre of Berthold Brecht and Max Reinhardt. Radicalism was alive and thriving in art and culture. And there was an avid audience to appreciate what these people were saying and doing. The German middle class had expanded significantly because employment had risen with the growth in the number of entrepreneurs, businesses and commerce since the end of the First World War. Berlin, as the capital, was unquestionably the hub of new thinking.

Iso was of course not the first artist, nor the first pianist, seeking a new life outside Russia. Blumenfeld's favoured pupil Vladimir Horowitz and Iso's senior at the St Petersburg conservatoire (though there is no record of them having met) had also gone to Berlin but ahead of Iso, in 1925. Hedwig had heard him from the front row in a concert, and admired him:

'The young Vladimir Horowitz made an oddly fascinating impression on me. I … could observe his very breathing. It was the Rachmaninoff in C min (with this, the Tchaikovsky, and Liszt's A major he had his greatest successes in Germany). He gave these works the exotic flavour they need and I thought of a fine racehorse

when I saw Horowitz's delicate profile and quivering nostrils...
He was in his early 20s and had arrived in Germany with a huge,
totally non-musical-looking special manager and much preliminary
propaganda! (So different from Iso Elinson who left Russia with an
'allowance' of only £10 in his pockets as he was expected to return 4
weeks later, and who was not 'very worldly-wise and sophisticated'.)'

But later when Hedwig was married to Iso, she was tantalised forever by
Horowitz's ability to command rave audiences and huge fees, especially in
the USA, while Iso struggled constantly on both those scores. And at the
very outset of her relationship with Iso, when Iso was trying to bring round
Hedwig's father from opposing the marriage and said he thought he would be
able to provide for a wife in England, Fritz Stein had thrust Horowitz in Iso's
face: whereas audiences 'tore themselves to pieces to get to hear *him*', it would
hardly be the case with Iso. His words were in many ways to ring true.

The parallels with Iso's experience are notable. Both pianists were
lauded in Russia, both had studied with Felix Blumenfeld, both had
had concert tours across the country, and both had gone on tour with
Chaliapin. Both found themselves at odds with the impact of the political
direction on the arts in Russia, particularly its closing in of options for
pianists, the scarcity of good pianos, and the overall lack of sophistication
on the musical scene. Both decided to leave the country. Both found it
difficult to be able to do so. But whereas Horowitz managed to get a
six-month visa, allegedly to study with Artur Schnabel in Germany, Iso
managed one for only four weeks.

"Many years later, Vladimir vividly remembered the evening of
his escape. 'At the border, I was nervous and white. I thought
they would stop me with the money hidden in my shoes. When
a soldier at the border examined my passport, I began to tremble.
He looked at me for one long moment. At this point, my heart – I
don't know where it was. The soldier looked into my eyes and said:
'Do not forget your motherland.' It was very touching.[10]"

Quite possibly Iso went through something similar – with the added heartbreak of the goodbye to his father at the border.

Horowitz apparently found Berlin a huge contrast from Russia. Here, standards were higher and audiences much more discriminating, and to some extent he felt daunted. Did Iso feel the same? All the indications are that he did not: he was assured and confident that through his hands he could offer audiences a special musical experience.

Iso's life in Berlin before he met Hedwig had included an 'adventure' during a concert tour in South America, where he spent some time in Rio de Janeiro. There he got to know the Professor of Harp at the conservatoire. She was Spanish, an 'elegant beauty', and she had a daughter called Isolde Bach – even the name was bound to arouse Iso's interest. He set about learning some Spanish. 'Romantic feelings developed, and Isolde and Iso got engaged, celebrating the occasion by Iso playing three concertos in each of three public concerts under a well-known conductor.' The time came for Iso to return to Berlin and the romance continued through letters and postcards. But after some time, the girl – she was a mere 16 – wrote to say she felt too young to leave her mother and live in Berlin. That was the end of the escapade, and Hedwig noted in her Diary that she was pleased that Isolde had not returned the (very expensive) ring.

We are then brought up short in trying to get any closer to Iso and his background. Having disclosed his past once, early on in their relationship, Iso seems then to have become almost completely silent on the subject. Here again there are parallels with Horowitz, whose:

"break with his family in 1925 proved to be a permanent one. In interviews over the years, the pianist declined to discuss details of his family's life in Russia, and close friends felt he had attempted to erase from his memory much of his early life... When success and public curiosity finally made it necessary to discuss his background, he sometimes invented an idealised family... Russia, he felt, had scarred him. 'I have no desire to return. I don't like the Russian approach to music, to art, to anything. I lost all my family there. I never want to go back and I never will.'"[11]

Iso probably did not quite share all those sentiments, but he never returned to Russia.

Hedwig confided with her old schoolfriend Lilo her thoughts about her training and concerts, and then meeting and getting to know Iso. The two of them were close, young girls emerging into the world of adults, slowly discovering themselves. They knew each other's families and had been to stay with each other as often as they could manage it. Hedwig wrote in 1931:

'I am not at all surprised at your thoughts about the 'relationship' between the soul and the living and the dead. Various experiences in recent times have led me to new revelations about my inner self. Before that I was in the main very cheerful and optimistic, self-confident, and focused on my career and so on, until last year I discovered a completely different spirit in myself. I cried nearly every day – often provoked by tensions with my friends and my parents... as a result, Berlin, where I have been living since 1 October, offers a refuge. This whole experience has not changed me. Rather I am now clearer what it means to be altruistic... I now have an old Steinway. That alone makes me abundantly happy.'

Having emerged from this dark place, Hedwig was upbeat about her playing. She performed the Chopin E minor concerto in Aachen and for the Kölner Rundfunk,[a] and had the prospect of another public concert in which she was to perform the Haydn D major concerto. In 1932, she was deeply affected by the silence from Lilo, which she put down to a troubled soul. And there was the question of Lilo's book-binding business, which she thought 'will be going badly' – possibly a reference to the difficulties of starting a small business, or maybe the increasingly troubled situation in Germany. Hedwig tried her best to help, sending Lilo money whenever she managed to put a little aside from the slender allowance her parents sent her and earnings from teaching piano. She asked Lilo to bind some

---

a   Cologne Radio.

of her music – and to send the bill immediately – and encouraged her parents to send some of their most valued music to Lilo, though she admitted this was not likely to yield very much. Fritz, she confided to Lilo, was experiencing on all sides the effects of the 'dismantling'[a] that was going on. Even with the dual position of professor and conductor, his income from the latter was the lowest in Germany and he was not flush with money. On the receiving side, Hedwig would write about how much she had enjoyed the eggs Lilo sometimes sent, taking them when she went away for a weekend with the Adelmanns. Or once, that they had meant she could save on lunch and so, with the money and some extra from teaching she had put on one side, she had been able to buy a Plaster of Paris replica of the mask of Tutankhamun she had seen at an exhibition; it looked very good against the blue walls in her room, she wrote. It could hardly have been more exotic and spine-tingling for Hedwig, who so viscerally responded to places and events, to see such artefacts only a few years after Carter had first walked into the king's tomb in Egypt.

Hedwig and Iso grew closer and closer, and by 1933 they had decided to get married. Hedwig was in a state of exhilaration – that time of newly discovered love when the world constantly looks radiant, feet do not touch the ground, emotions almost expel thought, and any separation from the beloved feels interminable. Whether Iso drove most other thoughts from Hedwig's mind, whether she was in a permanent state of excited anticipation, whether she could think only of potential scenarios and futures, is hardly mentioned in her Diary. But towards the end of my writing, Anna suddenly found another batch of letters, all in German and written in 1932 and 1933, mainly from Hedwig to Iso during the times they were apart, which were frequent and often fairly prolonged. They tell everything. What is more, Hedwig had reread these letters in the 1980s, and in her usual fashion, scribbled odd comments on them. These give an insight into any discrepancies between her later memories and judgements and the spontaneous gushing of emotion that the letters contain.

---

a   Abbau – Hitler's take-over of state institutions.

The earliest letter was a New Year 1932 letter from Hedwig, not to Iso but to the Diesterwegs, who had been so instrumental in introducing her to Iso. She wrote:

> '...I feel I have to tell you how very much you have enriched my life by introducing me to Iso Elinson. I am grateful to you from the depths of my being. When he plays, the music stands entirely on its own, beyond his person, and he combines soul and spirit with a remarkable talent. Even more for me though is his utter dedication to his art, which he possesses more than anyone else. Over the past weeks the Adelmanns and I have experienced in ourselves a renaissance as we sat and listened to him, whether playing the Wohltemperiertes Klavier, or Haydn sonatas, or the earlier or late Schubert sonatas, or Chopin works.'

She wondered how she might give the Diesterwegs some pleasure, and decided upon a letter from Clara Schumann to her (Clara's) friend, Frau von Herzogenberg – also an esteemed pianist, which she thought would be a fitting mark of her gratitude. A later comment to this particular gesture was an enigmatic 'oh, oh!'.

I was intrigued to see that well into 1932, Hedwig was still writing to Iso using the formal address 'Sie', even though she called him 'Isolein'[a] and signed her letters with her own nickname, Bautzel. But by July, she had dropped it. They had spent a night together in – appropriately named – Freiheit.[b] Iso was living mainly with a close friend in Langenau in southern Germany (why so far from Berlin is unclear), while Hedwig was primarily in Berlin and Kiel, making occasional visits to Timmdorf, which lies halfway between the two and at the edge of a lake. 'How can one possibly live in the city?' she wrote. 'There is something divine about the countryside.' All the letters to Iso are peppered with poetic descriptions of her surroundings, the landscape, the weather, her mood. She told Iso what

---

a   Diminutive of Iso, often used to reflect a fondness.
b   Freedom.

Iso

piano works she was studying – the *Davidsbündlertänze* and *Kreisleriana* by Schumann, and various fugues from Bach's *Das wohltemperiertes Klavier* – and what she was reading (which included a book of 17 questions and answers by Clara Schumann's father about what audiences want). At this stage they were still keeping their relationship a complete secret. Iso thought they should not write about their feelings and should destroy their letters once read. Hedwig paid no attention to this. Her letters give full rein to her despair at being separated from Iso; how she imagines herself with him in Langenau, going for long walks; remembers their trip to Czechoslovakia, how painful the parting from him was; and she talks time and again about how on journeys all she does is daydream or read music, and how very often she thinks of him. And she says how very loved and cared for she feels, how she imagines kissing his 'Lockenkopf',[a] how she wishes she could listen to him playing. Every time Iso had a broadcast, she and the Adelmanns would be sure to listen, often going to a friend

---

a Head of curls.

who had a superior radio. She mentions how she is taking care of his precious jam, which he loved to have with his tea – a Russian custom. She asks him to give her warmest greetings to his parents. She talks about looking at a lock of his hair – which for her contains Iso, and with that the treasure of his music. What came through so powerfully to me was the sense I had had even before reading these letters: that for Hedwig, Iso was music, and music was Iso – the two inextricably and completely bonded.

She told Lilo:

'He is a genius, more than anyone else I've met. And a true genius. He creates music out of a very great warmth and sensitivity of

Hedwig's Easter greetings to Iso, 1932

feeling while being able to inject demonic forces when needed – utterly captivating and powerful. But as a person, there is none of that or anything of what one might think of as 'Russian'. He has a very natural manner yet is so sensitive and has an enormous affinity towards people. On top of this, he is a creation of God's in the way he radiates emotion as an artist. The Adelmanns and I listen to him for hours every day when he is here.'

Undated in this Hedwig-Iso collection of letters, I came across one with a small peep of a wrinkle – though no more than in the early stages of any amorous relationship. I was unable to decipher the odd word, but the sentiments are clear. Hedwig writes:

'…You must not doubt me, dear Iso. It is as though a blossoming plant suddenly has no more air to grow. We have together had so much that is good; life is short and difficult, and happy if, apart from living the arts, one has someone who only wants the best for one. If sometimes one doesn't manage to do the right thing, the other must understand and excuse it.

'I so dislike what is called 'adventure', and know that you too can be very trustworthy. One of your good traits is that you demand a great deal from others. Only in this way can there be a meeting of souls that will endure. But to be as brusque as you are, when you are disappointed… you must try to understand whether the cause of your disappointment truly is what you think it is. In the case of love (or friendship) a time will always come when one is disappointed; in spite of that one carries on if at all possible. That for me is the right thing to do; not to say, in passive resignation 'I always knew it would be so.'

Although she was only 25 when she wrote this, it remained an unchanging core belief.

SIX

BERLIN – A STAGING POST ONLY:
CLOUDS BLACKEN

Iso moved to Berlin and after some uncomfortable, if entertaining, experiences with various landladies, became a guest of a gynaecologist, Dr Mainzer.[a] The significance of Mainzer in Iso's life was the circle of artists and intellectuals he mixed with. That circle included Albert Einstein, who loved to play the violin. Iso would accompany him – all the while aware, no doubt, of Einstein's eminence, of this scientist who was lauded throughout the West after the publications of his theories of special and general relativity. Iso told Hedwig he 'half-pretended to understand the high-flown talk on physics across the dinner table!' Einstein finally left Berlin in March 1933 – presumably an action that Iso, himself of Jewish descent, noted.

Around this time, Hedwig wrote to Iso about her travel to Stockholm to give a broadcast concert, delighting in signing herself 'soon-to-be Frau Bautzel Elinson', and about the concerts she was giving throughout Germany. She mentions she is to play the Beethoven C major concerto

---

a   Possibly Ferdinand Mainzer, who, because of an injury, gave up surgery and followed his interest in numismatics and the ancient world. Associated with anti-Nazi resistance and later fled to England. *Source: Wikipedia, 19.01.2020.*

in Bielefeld under Kaminski, whose contract was abruptly terminated a short time afterwards on the grounds of his political views; he was later forced to flee. Yet the shadows appear nowhere at all in these letters; there is no mention of the insidious and infiltrating political developments – those are restricted to odd comments in the Diary. Maybe she and Iso were too frightened and wary to include anything remotely political in case the letters were intercepted. After all, these were times when they would soon need exit papers.

1933. By now, alarm bells were ringing loudly. In March, federal elections were held after Hitler had been appointed Chancellor the year before. Despite the activities of the SS[a] and brownshirts,[b] the Nazis did not secure a majority. Nonetheless, Hitler was able to pass legislation shortly after the election giving him overwhelming powers that he then used to dismantle most of the state's arrangement of checks and balances. All parties other than the Nazi Party were banned shortly afterwards. Hedwig wrote:

'My parents were bound to be apprehensive [*about Hedwig's relationship with Iso*]. Hitler's shadow loomed large on the wall. As I had lived in a closed circle – friends, books, music, nature, I had never gone to hear one of his speeches, but from time to time we heard alarming tales.'

In Kiel, Richard Glas, who had not only been Hedwig's teacher for a while but was also soloist in many of the symphony concerts, lost his position. When reviewing Iso's concerts, the German press was still very positive,

'...but we had no illusions. I do not think Iso was then asked for one engagement for a concerto with orchestra. The Hitler ideas were penetrating to agents and committees.'

---

a   Schutzstaffel – major paramilitary organisation under Hitler and the Nazi Party.
b   Members of the Nazi militia.

The rhetoric and action from the Nazis were penetrating all sorts of institutions and communities. The Deutsche Studentenschaft,[a] dominated by the National Socialist German Students' League, launched its 'Aktion gegen den undeutschen Geist'[b] and on 10th May, students, egged on by Goebbels, burned untold numbers of books that they considered to be un-German – books that were not only by Germans but also by American, British, and French authors. This continued throughout Germany over the coming months. Certain artists, scientists and intellectuals were forbidden to work and to publish. Berlin, the magnet for the avant garde, was no more.

And yet, at another level, life for Hedwig and Iso up to this time seemed to be bringing some riches. Iso was starting to make his mark in Germany. Blüthner, the well-known maker of pianos, financed a series of Elinson concerts in Berlin and Leipzig, where Iso played Bach's *Das wohltemperiertes Klavier* to acclaim by the press. The critic Alfred Einstein had written in the Berliner Tageblatt:

"Here is a pianist of truly unusual calibre. He played the 48[c] with remarkable rigour, intensity and clarity, yet with deep sensitivity, and the posthumous B major sonata of Schubert in a rare combination of lyrical improvisation while not losing the structural framework."

And the critic on the Allgemeine Musikzeitung thought:

"Iso Elinson is a pianistic phenomenon, as witnessed through his unique approach to playing Bach. His playing was utterly compelling in its immediacy and intensity. The ambiguity of the work – phrasing, tempo, dynamics – was here resolved, and one revelled in his ability to unveil the piece."

---

a   German Student Union.
b   Action against the Un-German Spirit.
c   Bach's *Das wohltemperiertes Klavier*, often referred to as 'the 48' since it consists of 48 preludes and fugues.

Hedwig too was moving forward, albeit at a different pace:

'After passing the State Examen for music in Berlin with
distinction, I felt I ought to give a public debut in Berlin. One
in Heidelberg had gone extremely well – all the relatives came
to hear me. I 'sailed' under the flag of the Kwast School but in
reality Iso Elinson had taught me the most valuable things.

'My parents and Görli arrived in Berlin and Iso sat at
my recital too, quite in the background. Edwin Fischer and
Wilhelm Kempff were there as well (Fritz Stein had invited
them). I played a very difficult programme but all went very
well. My inner tension was great, though not about playing. I
knew this coming together of Iso and my father would cause real
difficulties. Prior to this concert my parents had only heard Iso
privately, at Ada's, when my father arrived hungry and tired after
the long journey from Kiel to Berlin. Iso had some marvellous
'guns' ready for him: Chopin's tempestuous Scherzo in B minor,
which Iso played with a tigerish attack. My father had listened
in the darkened room while secretly munching a liver sausage
sandwich, smuggled in for him by my well-meaning mother.
Well, this was remembered by Iso for years; it symbolised for him
an unpardonable offence – B minor Scherzo and Leberwurst!
And here we were, now no longer discussing mainly the best way
of producing 'portamento' touch and so on. No, Iso and I were
resolved to marry, come what may.'

Fritz and Gretel were still in the dark about the proposed marriage, but
with every week bringing new troubling developments and Hedwig's
pregnancy confirmed, the news would have to be broken. There was a
complication. On the recommendation of Wilhelm Furtwängler:

'my father was approached from Berlin: would he consent to take on the Director's post of the famous Berlin Hochschule für Musik?'[a]

By this time, critics were hard-pressed to continue with their laudatory reviews of Iso's concerts; opportunities were drying up, and shortly afterwards, in his inaugural address at the Hochschule für Musik, Fritz said: "We do not want to educate artists, but rather *German* artists, who see their profession as a sacred and spiritual, an ideological and national, cultural calling" – a sure sign of the times.

We might ask what the discussions between Hedwig and Iso and their close friends must have been. Had they worked through whether there was any option of staying, and in which case what the possible consequences might be, or was it by now glaringly clear that Iso's Jewish family connections ruled that out? It seems they did not spend much time weighing things up:

'We did not sit to analyse our situation but behaved like two grand, foolish optimists for whom things were bound to work out well in the end! It was not all joy and laughter. No – I remember those nights spent on reading and answering letters – always to my father who was severely against our marriage.'

The 1932–33 letters reveal the drama around Hedwig's visit to her parents to tell them of her decision to marry Iso and leave Germany. She wanted to write to Iso before the 'pistol letter' from her father arrived. It was an apt adjective: Fritz had raised a question about whether Iso would be faithful and said that if he breached that, he (Fritz) would shoot him. In her letter Hedwig begged Iso not to do anything – but not surprisingly, he wrote an angry reply. Ironically, it was only a month later, and after they were married, that Iso apparently disclosed something about a woman admirer who followed him after a concert he had given in Finland. Hedwig was

---

a   The Berlin College of Music had had the internationally famous violinist Joachim as its director up till 1907, when it gained its reputation as one of the best in Germany.

not angry; it was natural to feel that way, she said, given how Iso was able to reach out to audiences with such emotion in his playing. She ended one letter:

> '...I have only one thought and intention: that I will do everything to make sure that our life together is good. I will remain true to you.'

She did.

Later, she remembered the very bitter correspondence between Iso and her father in 1933. 'These letters were destroyed by me – they smelt of the 'new' German ideas'.

> 'My father 'composed' his very long letters with a desperate zeal. But they fell on stony ground. I lived through many very difficult days. The Diesterwegs were on 'our' side. So was the lovely old Frau von Bülow[a] who called us her 'fairy-story children!' The Adelmanns rallied round us and my dear brother was in constant touch. Just then my father's Hochschule appointment was confirmed. A Russian son-in-law with Jewish blood was an enormity, then. I spent many hours and long evenings discussing things with my dear (and now so stormy) Iso. It would be best to go my own way and I would tell my parents so.'

Hedwig duly set off for Kiel, on her own. Everyone was at pains to be extra kind to each other. Her message was nonetheless clear: she and Iso would marry and leave Germany very soon. And probably she also disclosed that she was pregnant – surely the final straw. When she left, Fritz said she should come back if she needed help. But Gretel knew her daughter: "Ah, Bautzel would rather become a public lavatory attendant

---

a   Née Marie Schanzer, stage and film actress, who became Hans von Bülow's second wife in 1882. She was a great organiser of soirées in Berlin over decades, attracting the most celebrated of musicians. Hans von Bülow was a great friend of Brahms, and also a pupil of Liszt, giving the first performance of his B minor sonata in 1857.

than do that." Hedwig's resolve was indeed unshaken. Germany had become a nasty country.

'The world was open to us, a world in which there would be no disgraceful and yellow benches, or old men having to scrub the Vienna streets because they were Jewish.'

We can do no more than surmise what lay behind Fritz's opposition to the marriage – for it appears mainly to have been his, rather than Gretel's, though she probably felt the stigma that would be attached when 'people' got to hear that Hedwig was already pregnant. Whatever the reasons for Fritz's position vis-à-vis Hedwig and her intended marriage, there was no ambiguity about his decision that she would have to find her own way, without any help from him. When she said goodbye, not one of them could have been able to conceive that they might not see each other again for years.

The immediate consequence was that Hedwig was cast adrift, without any support from her parents:

'Financially our position was precarious, more so than Iso knew or cared to analyse. I had a little money left by my grandmother after her death. Iso had some in his bank, but he thought his riches were in his mind, in his strong, marvellous hands, and in all his big favourite volumes of Bach and Beethoven and the Mikuli Chopin edition and so on. All these and hundreds of musical programmes of his recitals and others he valued so much.

'Görli, who was ready to send us monthly instalments from my inheritance to England, invited us to Timmdorf for an all-round farewell, to which also my dear friend Frau Hilde Holstein came for a day. While Iso played the Händel Variations by Brahms on the old pianino at the pub, Görli did a pen-drawing of him. And as before, the mice squeaked at night and the floorboards creaked. Next day, the ancient horse-drawn carriage took us to the tiny country station. Iso sang the theme of Schubert's great B flat sonata to all the friends! And off we went, to Berlin – to get married.'

Here there was a hitch:

'The very difficult and highly bureaucratic officials in Berlin ('Heil Hitler') required an Ehebefähigungszeugnis (a testimonial from Russia that Iso was not yet married). His old father wrote to that effect – there was no wife! – but his letter got delayed.'

It was a nailbiting time. When, at long last, the formal marriage became possible, it was just in time: strong moves were afoot to bring in a law prohibiting German nationals from marrying foreigners.

Strictly, the start of a marriage is of course the wedding day, often planned for and anticipated for some considerable time in advance: selecting a venue, deciding on invitations, choosing witnesses, finding a dress and so on. Nothing so elaborate could be conceived for Hedwig and Iso's wedding; they faced the imperative of needing simply to get the job done. Accordingly, the marriage ceremony was low-key and a total contrast to the grand ceremony of Fritz and Gretel's wedding with its gala dinner for the high-ups in Heidelberg. Any money that could be saved had to be for the express purpose of getting to England and could hardly be spent on the frivolities of a single day, and Fritz had made abundantly clear he was not going to stump up.

The day itself was one for umbrellas. Hedwig and Iso went to the nearest Register Office, Hedwig doing her best to look as smart as possible but certainly not in white; Iso did not even have a hat. The sole nod to the magnitude of the occasion was a rose in each of their buttonholes. In a tastefully decorated room with painted walls and lit with candles, they were married 'with great sensitivity and charm'. Maertel was one of the witnesses, the other Herr Adelmann. As soon as it was over, they headed out to a restaurant before the wedding party gathered at the Adelmanns' flat in the afternoon. Many close friends came. Sigurd Raschèr, well known as the only saxophone artist for classical music, came and played.

The main room was decked out with roses, and while Hedwig and Ada Adelmann hastily buttered bread, cut cakes, and whipped cream for strawberries, Maertel got Iso to give him a lesson on how to play Chopin, since in his view, Iso was a master in generating depth of tone on the piano. It was, in other words, a wedding in true Hedwig style: off-centre, simple, fun, with just a few people she was fond of, and much music. 'That was what I loved! I never felt for formal celebrations!'

Hedwig made no great mention, either in the Diary or in a letter describing the day to Lilo, of how she felt that her parents were not there – other than that it was very good of Gretel to send through Maertel a very nice diamond ring that had originally been her grandmother Luise's, with 'wishes and a written little prayer on the back of a small Italian St Francis "that all may go well"' – a hint possibly of at least Gretel's disquiet about the rift.

The next weeks were filled with collecting information and advice from friends. The basis for their decision was pretty straightforward. Now came the question of where to head for. Switzerland, a possibility politically, was too expensive. Iso had been thinking for some time, however, of going to England, and Hedwig at least had her school English. For them, England appeared a free country and had been for hundreds of years, and it was now politically acceptable. It offered tradition and fair play, and there was a strong musical scene in London. The decision was taken rapidly: London it was to be. A few of their Berlin friends had contacts and wrote letters of introduction for them. Did they consider the possibility of war, and the likelihood that they might become embroiled in a war with the country they were about to flee? That surely was more likely with England than with the USA. Or was it that they felt the USA was too far away? Or simply too much associated with Disney and brashness? No letters shed light, and nor does the Diary, though Anna thought that they would have found it too hard to break away from Europe and their familiarity with its culture.

'I had to earn now; every Mark counted. Iso had no great resources in his bank (finances played the least part in all our dramatic exchanges!). I now profited from the fact that I had never taken 'luxury' for granted (as so many young ladies of the 'upper' class seemed to do). I was no puritan but found it easy not to wish for too many good things; besides, Germany had lost the *first* War!

'Berlin had plenty of 'dens of vice', as the book by Christopher Isherwood, 'I am a Camera', shows. Yet we music-minded people were rather removed from this sort of 'entertainment', save for good or interesting novel films or 'real' dramas, or even circus performances. Frau Marie von Bülow invited us to her charity concerts more than once.

'In spite of my work in preparation for England, I managed to practise. Two difficult works: the 'Les Adieux' sonata by Beethoven, and the Weber sonata, with the virtuoso last movement and funny theme which Iso called 'Bier vom Fass'.[a] (I learned more by listening to his [Iso's] practising than from months of lessons.)'

They were not alone in leaving Berlin around this time. Many were feeling extremely uncomfortable and anxious, and as violence became ever more evident and personal safety endangered, more and more people decided to chance it. Not all had happy endings. Some departures were thwarted; some who managed to leave found a new beginning much, much harder than they had imagined; there were even returnees who must have felt the world at large held no refuge for them.

Whether Hedwig encountered returnees we do not know, but in any case she appears to have been immune from external opinions, other than Iso's, and for Iso the situation had by now become blindingly stark: he was seriously threatened. Choice hardly came into it. It would be the second time in his life that he would be taking the step into exile, each time emerging from behind a curtain, first of the Russian Revolution and now of the Nazi movement. Was this decision in some

---

a   Literally, beer from the barrel, i.e. draught beer.

ways therefore easier for him than for Hedwig? I suspect so. Probably the greater decision, and the one that now faced Hedwig, was one he had taken only a few years earlier, that of leaving the country of her birth. But whereas Iso had had the full understanding and support of his parents, Hedwig had the added anguish of knowing her parents were totally opposed to the move. I asked myself what it was in Hedwig that made her view her position with such clarity and resolve. Neither Fritz and Gretel, nor her brother Maertel, were showing any inclination even to contemplate a radical move. Yet she appears not to have hesitated for a second.

Implementing their decision was not only a question of having the necessary papers to leave Germany, but also of acquiring permission to enter England, and to stay. There were people in the UK who were willing to help – in this case, a surgeon's wife from the north of England who had heard Iso play. She offered to act as guarantor, and made all the arrangements with the Home Office, though it was only shortly before the day of departure that she became aware that far from being alone, Iso had a wife and would shortly have a baby. She was undeterred. Iso's conviction that his hands and his playing would see them through seemed to be correct. The time to leave soon came.

'We lost no time with mournful analyses but packed up our belongings. The Adelmanns were sorry to lose us. We had spent much time in their flat in Lankwitz; my lovely large room easily took two! Görli Döring came one day and the photos show us all visiting a little zoo nearby. Our food was simple but good. Of my pregnancy, I remember next to nothing – except very good feelings indeed! It must have been easy. I was young and was unable to imagine that something might go wrong: our target was London!

'Twelve pieces of luggage were ready at last. I believe the limit for taking money out of the country was then (1933) 100 Mark only. Iso, never too keen on bureaucratic restrictions, 'risked' hiding another 20 Mark – a tiny sum.

'My memory lands me in a train, leaving Germany for the Dutch Frontier. All seemed to go very well. At the last German station the train halted a little. It moved on. It stopped again, and then 4 or 5 travellers were suddenly picked and asked to get out, including us. 'Kontrolle!' 'What check?' we thought. 'How terrible!' flashed through our minds. We were put into a Customs Room for up to 7 hours, with all our luggage piled up around us. Nazi officials (with the fat 'beer necks' one saw so often) in dark shirts searched us for anything not quite right but all they found was quite correct. A lady felt my 'Plautze'[a] and believed me when I said that I was pregnant! Odd, grotesque scenes followed. Our love letters were with us: 'Mein gutes Pferd'[b] read one from Iso to me (a 'chiffre'?[c] they wondered! A Russian Communist, a spy?) I could have burst out laughing! Another, a postcard this time: 'Heil, Schumann – my lovely little Bautzel!'[d] Worse was to come! But first they held little harmless boxes, filled with needles, against the light, further toilet articles, old and new socks, plenty of music by Scriabin and Schubert, huge and valuable volumes of Bach, hundreds of old programmes of Iso's... But then they stopped: 'What's that?' A letter by Albert Einstein,[e] a beautifully composed message in his small scientist's handwriting: 'Open all doors to Iso Elinson and do not be suspicious about his passport. Look rather in his pure, happy and childlike face. Accept him as one who has been blessed by God, *signed* Albert Einstein.'[f] 'Hey, look at this – what is it?' said the fat one to the small guy. Both went into the neighbouring room with the note.[g] How did

---

a   Bump.
b   'My good horse'.
c   Chiffre – a code.
d   Heil, Schumann, mein gutes Bautzelchen –in the diminutive form.
e   Einstein had left Berlin just a few months previously.
f   Öffnet Herrn Elinson alle Thüren und seht nicht argwöhnisch auf seinen Pass, sondern in sein reines, fröhliches Kindergesicht und nehmet ihn auf wie einen, den die Götter gesegnet haben, *signed* Albert Einstein.
g   'Du, schau mal – was ist das?' sagt der Dicke zu dem Kleineren. Beide gehen mit dem Schreiben in ein benachnartem Amtszimmer.

we survive the next 20 minutes?? Einstein was then the blackest name on the Nazis' list! 'If they won't let us go on the child will be born in Germany,' flitted through my mind. Iso meanwhile was active in another matter! Luckily so far the searchers had not detected the secreted 20 Mark! Very secretly, without my noticing anything, Iso crumpled the note up into a tiny ball inside his hand and managed to put it gently into the office waste paper basket! (Of this I heard later on.) His physical movements, right up to 1962 or so, were very relaxed and natural, be it walking, running, bending or going upstairs in a hurry... (He seemed to walk loosely, from the hips.) Well, luck was on our side. (Did they possibly think: 'Damn it, why should we burden ourselves with these people?') So, one hour later, after some Palmgren,[a] Gretchaninoff,[b] and Chopin's Mazurkas were 'searched', the fat man said, in a not unfriendly manner 'You can proceed!' – and gave us the Einstein letter back (which Einstein had meant for any situation in which Iso's passport needed renewing). Did they perhaps not know it was THE Einstein?

'Our joy was terrific. Forgotten were the worries (and cost) of getting a full 24 hours too late to London (there was no other train on that day)! We hurried out of the hideous office into the fresh air to get a Dutch taxi to Venlo, the first little Dutch township across the border. 'Bravo, bravissimo,' Iso said. 'Look here, Bautz, what I got!' Out of his hand came a little paper ball – the 20 Mark he had rescued from the waste paper basket after the all-clear, quite unseen! (Deftly managed, this! It would have been a real crime, had they seen!) We went into a Dutch Konditorei[c] and had an orgy of rich Dutch cakes, with and without cream, and the strongest of coffees and felt like small happy children! (No complaints like in England where such cake is considered 'too rich'!) We were young and sugar,

---

a   Finnish composer, pianist and conductor.
b   Russian Romantic composer.
c   Konditorei – cake shop.

surely, is the thing to make up for great mental strain! It was unforgettable.'

'After more than 31 years I see us munching and laughing and talking in presto-style! (I forgot about the Channel crossing. No matter how I then felt!)'

And so, to London.

But before we get to that, there arises the vexed question.

SEVEN

THE VEXED QUESTION

Es gibt keine patriotische Kunst und keine patriotische Wissenschaft.
Beide gehören, wie alles hohe Gute, der ganzen Welt an und können
nur durch allgemeine freie Wechselwirkung aller zugleich Lebenden
in steter Rücksicht auf das, was uns vom Vergangenen übrig und
bekannt ist, gefördert werden.[a]

JOHANN WOLFGANG VON GOETHE,
WILHELM MEISTER'S WANDERJAHRE III

It was inevitable that one of the threads running through my explorations would be the relationship of individuals to political and societal shifts, particularly in the context of Nazism and the Second World War. My sensitivity to the issue had in any case been aroused by my sojourn in Germany, and as I dwelt on Hedwig's story, one recurring thought came: what *was* Fritz Stein's attitude to the Nazi regime, and what exactly had he done, how had he behaved? Subsequent questions might of course arise in response to the answers to these. While the portrait here is of Hedwig

---

a "There is no patriotic art and no patriotic science. Both art and science, like all the great good, belong to the entire world and can be furthered only through universal free exchange between all those alive, having in mind what is left and known to us from the past."

and not Fritz, his thinking and actions cannot help but have had some impact on her, even though she did not write about that, to my knowledge at least. Let me say at the outset that I approached this part of the story with considerable apprehension. It is one thing to write and think about someone you admire; it is quite another to start probing into recesses that you know from the outset will throw up deeply disturbing questions.

To recap: in early 1933, in addition to the irons Hitler was successfully chaining around German institutions and society, a momentous event of a quite different nature occurred – the offer to Fritz of that pinnacle of positions, the directorship of the Berlin Hochschule für Musik. It must have been a cherished prize after his extraordinarily diligent efforts over the years to get himself noticed and to have the prospect of realising his ambitions for music. He was now highly regarded as a musicologist, as President of the Max Reger Society, and as a member of the Swedish Royal Academy and the German Academy. Hedwig said in her Diary:

'After many years of hard work in Kiel (where he had built up an excellent musical tradition) he felt this post would suit his combined gifts to perfection. He was admired as a great organiser of remarkable energy and foresight and as conductor of a chamber orchestra, and in Berlin he would use his gifts as a 'practical' musician.'

She leaves it at that.

We know Fritz was set completely against Hedwig's marriage to Iso. I ruminated on the possible underlying reasons. Maybe it was simply concern for his daughter, heading out with a Russian pianist who she had not known for very long into a more or less unknown country where it would be far from certain that they could make a go of it. Or might he have had uppermost in his mind that having a Russian and Jewish son-in-law would be viewed far from favourably by the new Nazi forces which were making themselves quite clearly felt in the world of music by banning 'unacceptable' compositions and performers – and with what consequences? Was it possibly that, having been recommended by no

Fritz Stein in the 1920s or 1930s.
Photograph reproduced with kind permission of the Schleswig-Holsteinische Landesbibliothek, Germany

one other than the great Wilhelm Furtwängler, he felt he could not do other than accept the offer? Or was there some sympathy, to whatever degree, with Nazi doctrine and what it promised – maybe specifically its highlighting of the role of *German* classical music culture in society? Hedwig and Iso's decision to marry and to leave Germany now created enormous personal, as well as political, turbulence in Fritz and Gretel's lives.

Many musicians in Europe today do not expect politics to cut deeply across their lives, or even their behaviour. Their 'calling' is to the furtherance of this most special of art forms, and the only impediments are the challenges of reaching their ideals in performance or composition, the constant search for openings to reach audiences, and, inevitably, financial survival. That was all true in Germany in the 1930s also. But as we know only too well, the radical changes afoot across the entire society put that first set of considerations not quite into an eclipse, but at least meant that any of their actions would be judged across a set of emerging and quite alien criteria. Even keeping your head down would not necessarily mean your life could simply centre on music. And in any case, artists of any ilk *need* to interact publicly. In our quest to find out about those closest to Hedwig and who surely influenced her, what, we must therefore now ask, would Fritz and Gretel do now? Hedwig, in her Diary, offers some insights but these understandably are from the perspective of a daughter. I wanted to look elsewhere in order better to understand the bigger picture.

For this, the focus has to be on Fritz. While she might have been relatively independent-minded, given concerts, and written some poems, Gretel was not the one pursuing a career. She was primarily Fritz's constant and loyal companion. The path of her life was entirely determined by what Fritz wanted to do and was able to secure by way of employment.

At this point, I found it illustrative to step back a little to look at the relationship between Fritz and Max Reger. There can be little doubt that Reger was a giant figure for Fritz for the entire duration of their friendship. By the time they first met in 1906, Reger was an accepted composer, conductor, and performer. Their personalities and passions matched, and Fritz soon found himself charged by Reger with the arrangements surrounding many performances of his works, putting up with his temperamental and mercurial friend, his impatience, and his fastidious musical and other demands, expressed in unequivocal 'you must' terms. But Reger offered Fritz a great deal too: ever-deepening friendship and trust, reflected in the confidences Reger shared with him; professional recommendations as Fritz sought positions for himself; love and kindness towards Fritz's family; and even financial help on occasion. Reger's letters to Fritz[12] reveal an almost avuncular relationship. Throughout, Reger addressed Fritz by his first name (though he always signed himself 'Reger'). He was unsparing in expressing his gratitude for whatever Fritz did to help him and in recognising Fritz's own talents. Having a number of characteristics in common, they each mixed the serious promotion of Reger's music with a great sense of fun, underlined in Hedwig's diary and

Reger's letters. Later, Maertel even compiled a small book of anecdotes to illustrate Reger's humour.[13] As Reger said of himself: "As beloved God dealt out humour, I yelled out twice: here, here!".

Aside from their obvious shared passion for music, it seems fair to say that both Reger and Fritz were rather ardent nationalists. In Fritz's case, this may have been partly because of his experiences in the First World War and the defeat of Germany. He simply could not countenance anything other than victory in the Second. I imagine this was a widespread sentiment.

Fritz and Gretel were devastated by Reger's early death, though they must have known all along that his lifestyle, heavy drinking and temperament meant he was sailing close to the wind. Fritz was indefatigable in continuing his promotion of Reger. He gave countless talks about Reger and his music – he was one of the very few remaining who was able to give his personal impressions – and completed a biography before going on to carry out a painstaking collection and cataloguing of all of Reger's works. Despite serious differences with Reger's wife, Elsa, about the appropriate location for the Max Reger Achive, which Fritz did all he could to keep private, he supported the Archive, financially as well as by donating books and records and other documents. For Fritz, the friendship with Reger was the most precious of his life.[14] It is fair to ask just how much Reger would have secured his position as a composer had it not been for Fritz. Reger might have remained on the periphery instead of holding the firm, if not prominent, place in the canon that he still has today. The story of Fritz's friendship with Reger is a clear demonstration of his loyalty and commitment. It is therefore important in thinking about the person who was Fritz and who played a central role in Hedwig's life, and who now stood before some highly appetising – and at the same time, some deeply distasteful – decisions.

In the early 1930s, Fritz's star was rising, and although he may well not have described himself as a political animal, it seems he was very much alive to what was going on and at the very least played safe. Or maybe it was more a case of seeing that the changes might just offer opportunities for him…

Gretel and Fritz Stein with Max Reger at the Martinsbrunn Sanatorium, 1914. Photograph reproduced with the kind permission of the Max-Reger-Institut, Karlsruhe, Germany.

To dig deeper, I consulted various books and publications, and also made enquiries at the very helpful Bundesarchiv,[a] as a result of which a wodge of papers arrived one day. While they do not give a full picture, they provide insights into the people and circumstances Fritz was dealing with. Together they cover the period 1933–1947, most being from the early days. It was interesting to see what was going on in Fritz's professional life at the time Hedwig was becoming friendly with Iso, and during August and September 1933, when they made their plans known and prepared to leave Germany. It was also chilling to read letters signed by Fritz that ended 'Heil Hitler', even knowing this was the conventional ending of many formal letters. Equally so were the recommendations for the reorganisation of the Hochschule as regards dismissals (surprisingly not dated), with their stark words for the reasons given: Jewish, incompetent, cultural Bolshevik, inadequate command of the German language (for a Pole), adherent of Kestenberg[b], and mean-spirited nature.

---

a   German Federal Archives.

b   Leo Kestenberg was an influential musical and cultural innovator during the Weimar Republic and advisor to the Prussian Ministry of Science, Art and Education, carrying out major musical educational reforms. He was forced out by the Nazis and fled Berlin in 1933.

Fritz had joined the Kampfbund für deutsche Kultur[a],[15] in 1932. The aims of the organisation were to support the Nazi ideology, and particularly the forces rooted deep in German culture and civilisation, through its activities in the cultural sphere; it was expressly against the efforts of those supporting liberalism, which it considered were inimical to that culture. And it was anti-Semitic. Some enemies had already been named: Thomas Mann, Bertolt Brecht, Emil Nolde, Paul Klee, Georg Grosz, Arnold Zweig, and Lion Feuchtwanger, to mention but a few. Stravinsky and Hindemith were no longer to be performed. By May 1933 Fritz was already in post in Berlin (he was Acting Director, having only taken leave of absence from Kiel University) and was presidial counsellor in the Reichsmusikkammer.[b] Fritz had also become involved with the Confessional Church, which was seeking to restore pure Lutheran sacred music and to restrict it to the liturgical confines of the church. Given his early education as a Lutheran pastor, his standing as a church music scholar, and his positions within various Reichs music groupings and the Hochschule, it is hardly surprising that Fritz was ordered by Hans Hinkel, the Staatskommissar[c] charged with the removal of Jews from cultural positions and influence, to bring order to the turf wars between the Confessional Church and the German Christians, both of which were open to Nazi doctrine.[16] And as the leader of the 'Interessengemeinschaft für das deutsche Chorgesangswesen[d] he became responsible, with others, for the 'Gleichschaltung[e] of all choirs into one umbrella institution – significant because it resulted in the dissolution of many of the former communist workers' choirs.[17] In July 1933 he became the head of the music chapter of the Kampfbund. On 30th July, he submitted an application for accelerated membership to the NSDAP,[f] signing a declaration: "I can truly confirm that I have been, with all my heart, an admirer of the

---

a   Militant or Combat League for German Culture.
b   Reich Chamber of Music.
c   Special State Commissioner.
d   Community for German Choral Music.
e   Coordination or consolidation – the process by which the Nazis ensured total control of the policies and activities across institutions – in this case, the choirs.
f   Nationalsozialistische Deutsche Arbeiterpartei – the Nazi Party.

'wonderful movement' of Adolf Hitler for many years." There was nothing unusual about this. As far as many people were concerned, and maybe especially those who had felt humiliated after the Treaty of Versailles, Hitler embodied the sense of hope and regained pride. He had notched up untold successes and achievements that people were only too ready to applaud. Sebastian Haffner, a historian, is eloquent on the topic.[18] In support of his application to the Party, Fritz underlined his Aryan heritage: on his father's side, the family was traceable back to 1660; the Steins had been farmers in Kaiserstuhl; and on his mother's side, his grandfather was a teacher and her forebears were craftsmen and could be traced back to a similar time. His application was not immediately accepted because the Party had a ban on new members between May 1933 and 1937; gaining membership for Fritz took until March 1940. By then, even if he had had second thoughts as it became more and more obvious what the Nazis were doing, rescinding that application would have had major – and possibly, in this case, truly fatal – repercussions. According to this view, he had got himself into a spider's web; flies do not get out.

Yet once he was in Berlin, there was not a straight line running through what he did: Fritz retained Hindemith, whose work he had championed over the years, at the Hochschule though only until 1935, and we should bear in mind that Hindemith was an admirer of Reger – a fact likely to have influenced Fritz in this. He also "obtained an honourable discharge for other teaching personnel unacceptable to the Nazi regime",[19] offered a position to the composer Carl Orff, and expressed his support for the well-known music critic Karl Holl. He gave a public and celebratory speech about the harpsichordist Wanda Landowska, who was Jewish, and arranged for a grant to be awarded to a Jewish musician – both of which were noted by the regime, negatively.[20] By 1936, Fritz was obviously feeling sufficiently confident of his position that he wrote to Hedwig and Iso, holding out an olive branch. They were happy to take it, each responding in a joint letter. As a result, Gretel paid them a visit in London. Yet on the other hand, Fritz had a clear-out of a number of the staff at the Hochschule, leading the action to relieve harpsichordist Eta Harich-Schneider, one of Landowska's protegées, of her professorial position. Whether this was for musical or political reasons, we do not know. And beyond the confines of the Hochschule, he publicly made disparaging remarks about one of the well-known music critics.

Throughout the War, Fritz worked closely and consistently with the Commissioner Hans Hinkel. He enjoyed success after success, always seeking Hinkel's approval before taking major decisions. Fritz was responsible for musical events at the Olympics in 1936; and in 1939, on his 60th birthday, was awarded the Goethe Medal, presented by Robert Ley – later indicted at Nuremberg – and received the Kriegsverdienstkreuz 1 Klasse.[a] Finally, during the end game of the War, in March 1945, he took up the position of the head of the Staatlichen Instituts für deutsche Musikforschung[b] (probably in addition to his Hochschule position), from which it is reasonable to conclude that Fritz at the very least had not blotted his copybook as far as the Nazis were concerned. It seems to me that he had trodden a very skilful path through the various competing and antagonistic cultural and political groups within the overall organisation of the Reich and, given his undisputed scholarly achievements, might well have emerged with something of a reputation had the War ended differently.

Along with many others, Fritz was denazified in 1948 – a process instituted by the Allies to eradicate Nazism from all forms of culture, the judiciary, the press, society, and politics. I was somewhat taken aback that there were no official papers detailing Fritz's specific case – at least in those I received from the Bundesarchiv. I have no explanation. But it is unsurprising that he had to go through a formal process, given that he had held such senior positions while the Nazis were in power.[21] Fritz had been in a completely different situation from that of 'ordinary folk', such as Brunnhilde Pomsel, Goebbels' stenographer, whose disclosures were recently brought vividly to theatre audiences in London through Maggie Smith in Christopher Hampton's *A German*

---

a   War Merit Cross, 1st Class.
b   National Institute for German Music Research.

Life. Pomsel could, and did, choose not to concern herself overly with what was going on around her, to select what she paid attention to and what not, and to exercise selective amnesia. For the professional classes, it was different. Sebastian Haffner[22] writes compellingly of what it felt like as a young lawyer in the Berlin of 1933, and of the impossibility of not noticing what was going on; his story closely maps chronologically on to Hedwig's and I read it compulsively. But while Fritz probably did not know the full extent of Hitler's actions until during the War, there can be no doubt that he knew exactly what the aims of the regime were. As we know, the Kampfbund für deutsche Kultur was set up precisely to eliminate Jewish influence on culture, and Hinkel's brief was to excise all Jews from institutions. We are still no wiser, however, as to what Fritz's personal views were and whether, deep inside, he felt clearly aligned with one position or the other. What is incontrovertible and undeniable is Fritz's lifelong passion for music and his interventions to promote works and composers he loved and respected. At the top of this relatively short list, and separated from the others by a huge margin, was Max Reger, from the time Fritz first encountered Reger and his music as a student, until shortly before his (Fritz's) death. That impulse seemed to me to be a major feature of Fritz's character.

All that notwithstanding, Fritz had supported the Nazis from 1925, but secretly. At that time he was Director and Professor of Musicology at the University of Kiel and it was forbidden for anyone holding public office to support any extreme group, which at that time the Nazi Party was;[23] he would have risked dismissal had he done so openly. By the end of the War, Fritz was one of 8.5 million Germans who were members of the NSDAP. While those who had held senior positions in the Party – police, members of the SS and civil servants – were removed from their posts by the Allies and subject to 'automatic arrest', there is no mention anywhere of Fritz having been arrested or interfered. The process of denazification was carried out diversely in the various zones. The most elaborate procedures were instituted in the United States zone, where individuals being investigated were required to complete detailed questionnaires about their personal histories and to appear at hearings before panels of German adjudicators. In the British and French zones, however, denazification was pursued with less vigour because the authorities thought it more important to reestablish a functioning bureaucracy in their sectors. As it happened, the Hochschule für Musik was in the British zone, close to the Kurfürstendamm and the Kaiser Wilhelm Memorial Church.[a] Fritz, with others, was therefore probably picked up by the British, having spent the last days of the War living in the basement of the Hochschule. They had subsisted on potato peels and presumably anything else they could lay their hands on. How must they have felt when, finally, the bombing ceased? The building had been bombed, and there were no window panes left. But this was not devastation while securing victory. Once more, people like Fritz, who still carried the defeat in the First World War and the Treaty of Versailles in their bones, were confronted with the unpalatable: Germany's humiliation. It was indeed a defeat of the nation, but also a defeat felt closely by individuals. For some this was the start of a long process of analysing what had happened, what their role had been, and what the end result said and meant; for others, it was a time of suppression of past reality, for whom any coming to terms with or resolution was out of the question, and it produced a sense of resentment. Much has been written about the guilt, and many on the side of the 'victors' – at least on the American and British side – were deeply divided about whether it was the German nation that was guilty or individuals. Wherever one stands in relation to that question, I found it strangely moving to go through the process of finding out more about what had happened to Fritz and trying to work out where he had stood.

There was little by way of post-War documentation in the Bundesarchiv but the few communications to various authorities felt to me to be written in a very different manner from when Fritz was at the Hochschule. It felt as though his conviction and self-confidence had been lost and it brought directly home to me how, from one day to the next, the rigours of the new order required survivors to adapt their attitudes and to recognise the new

a   Known as the Gedächtniskirche, a memorial that stands against war and destruction.

realities. A couple of documents seemed to me of particular interest, each one a statement made by a person who had known Fritz well. The first, from Walter Rumpel, concluded that while Fritz had not had any innate sympathies with the Nazis, he had always behaved in a cowardly[a] fashion, seeking every opportunity to conceal the fact that he had a Jewish son-in-law; he had also expressed in ugly terms his views about the origins of jazz. The second statement, by Mark Hendricks, stated that while he (Hendricks) had been in England and studying with the exiled violinist Carl Flesch, he became friends with Hedwig and Iso. This was during Hitler's time in power. Flesch had written to Fritz requesting that he help Hendricks on his return. Fritz said in response that he would try, but that as Hendricks knew, he could not really effect anything. And he begged Hendricks not to tell anyone about their correspondence. Hendricks' view was that Fritz had taken every opportunity to gain from his position, and that he had been cowardly. In his statement, Hendricks requested not to be called as a witness because of his friendship with Hedwig and Iso. It is possible therefore that these two statements concern the denazification process, but I cannot be certain.

Michael Kater, in his book *The Twisted Muse*, looks in detail at the relative and interweaving nature of the roles of music and politics in the Third Reich. Fritz is one of the musicians he talks about, and he does so in a masterly and even-handed fashion, on the basis of painstaking examination of the evidence:

> "...if a musician proved to possess artistic talent and loyalty to the regime in more or less equal measure, then professional success could be virtually guaranteed... As a National Socialist academic Fritz Stein went further than most of his ilk, providing more than sufficient proof of his loyalty to the dictatorial regime. But perhaps his Jewish son-in-law also caused him to have a bad conscience, for occasionally he suppressed the Nazi side of his personality for the benefit of his politically less sheltered colleagues."[24]

---

a   Another possible translation would be 'craven'. Either could be the case.

Kater shows convincingly that at the end of the day, the public face of music could not be divorced from politics.

Although I have placed the focus on Fritz, we should not completely overlook Gretel, who seems to have gone through considerable anguish, not so much about the establishment of the Nazis but more about the cost to her personally. Here Gretel's poems allowed me to get a little closer to her. One is entitled *Trennung*.[a] All we know about the date is that it can have been written no later than 1936, the date of publication. It offers no direct reference to who the separation is between, but inevitably I wondered whether it was expressing Gretel's grief that Hedwig was no longer close to her. In just a few lines, she expresses the agony of the separation, given that water now lay between the two of them, how happily they had walked hand in hand – but how now the page had turned. Gretel also composed several poems around the theme of 'Heimat'.[b] The first is an unequivocal expression of the centrality and constancy of her love for her homeland, followed by a marching song written in August 1934 and one praising 'my Germany'. The last in this section of collected poems is also from 1934 and is called *Lied der Arbeit*,[c] extolling the pleasures and rewards of working 'as the Führer asked' to ensure the 'empire of the new times'. These are quite probably expressing no more than many Germans felt at that time: the patriotism and conviction that what was being done was in the best interests of the nation. In utter contrast, Hedwig's Diary for 1932 and 1933 contains entries that are unequivocal about the despicableness of what was going on at that time and her revulsion at it. Although these were entries written significantly post hoc, I have no reason to consider that she had taken any different position in the early 1930s. Her actions alone attest to that.

As the action to rebuild education and to start teaching at the Hochschule started in the winter semester of 1945, whoever was in charge would need to embark on a completely fresh start. Fritz was out of the question. The reputation enjoyed by the Hochschule before the

a   Separation.
b   Home.
c   Song of Work.

War – both national and international – had entirely crumbled during the Third Reich. Even if Fritz had been of an age where, in theory, he might have continued as director, it is inconceivable that he would have been allowed to pick up the reins again. But in any case, Fritz was by then nearly 66, and presumably the question never really arose. Whether he resigned or was pushed is unclear.

Fritz's situation cannot have been particularly unusual. He had believed in the strength and values of Germany as exemplified by its traditional composers, but had ended up backing the wrong horse. He had not, it seems, considered whether to follow Hedwig before the turbulence of the immediate pre-War times broke out. The lure of big possibilities for himself and the glory of the music he almost worshipped was too great. And in late middle age, moving countries is an enormous gamble and desperately uncomfortable – and not necessary if a once-in-a-lifetime opportunity is offered on outstretched hands and with no hint of what the outcome – or the lead-up to it – might contain. We should also not forget Fritz's humble beginnings and therefore the enticing prospect of such lauded professional recognition. Overall, it seems to me that Fritz was an arch tactician. He might not have belonged, in his inner core, to the Party, but he certainly knew how to pull the right levers to his advantage – and to what he clearly felt was a laudable aim of the Nazis: championing German classical music.

But in reality, that – the glorification of German music – was of course not the aim of the Reich. Rulers have forever been aware of the power of music, and Hitler and his propagandists were simply looking to exploit that for their own ends. Put together with the deep-seated need people have to belong together, the conditions that can so devastatingly lead to fervent expression of nationalism were provided. I wonder if this reality struck Fritz at some time, and whether he might have felt a sense of betrayal, a sense that he had been courted and then used as a pawn.

In 1945, Fritz had to confront the question of how to forge his life in the new – and for him, alien – environment. Added to that, how would life be now that he and Gretel could once more live together? Quite early on in the War, she had moved out of their large flat in Berlin to a farm in Eckernforde in Schleswig Holstein because of her poor health and eyesight. Maertel and his family of four had joined her and they all lived in one room, subsisting largely on potatoes, bread and macaroni, but at least there they were out of the line of sight of the Russians. They had even managed to squeeze in a Steinway so that Maertel could practise.

The prospect of a reunion with Hedwig must have been sweet. It had been a long time coming. A short message through the Red Cross had allowed all of them to be in touch, and Hedwig was impatient to make a visit. In 1946, she returned to Germany on her own, first to see Gretel and Maertel. Maertel met her at the station and took her in an old landau through the Suffolk-like landscape. They talked throughout the night. A few days later, Hedwig left for Berlin to meet Fritz.

She travelled through Hanover, in the Russian zone. Fritz did not meet her at the airport because her plane landed earlier than he had expected. Alone, she set off for his flat next to the Liezensee. How did it feel for her, going back to the city she had known well, and of such heady memories? She does not say, other than to remark on the visual impressions. Her emotions she surely shared with Iso later, and through her communion with the piano. She was appalled at the destruction; every third house had been bombed. She thought, 'this will take a hundred years to put right'. The rubble women, however, desperate for fat rations, were already hard at work. It was they who would ultimately expedite the rebuilding of Berlin.

When Hedwig arrived, she found Fritz taking a nap in a chair. His hair was no longer red but silver, and first she kissed his head. He had been close to starvation for some time and was painfully thin. What did they say to each other? How could they bridge those thirteen years, each with the broad knowledge of what had happened, yet in the dark about what the other had been through and how they each felt? What reservations were there for each of them? Did they stick only to the events that had led up to Hedwig leaving so abruptly with Iso? And most important, were they able to understand each other's positions and actions? Hedwig writes nothing of these.

There were external diversions which no doubt helped to smooth things over. Already, within a year of the War ending, works banned by the Nazis were starting to be performed and Fritz, who had assisted Hindemith at the beginning of the War, took Hedwig to the first performance of his Mathis der Maler at the opera house. 'The applause was deafening and went on for at least 20 minutes.' He also took her to meet some of the people who had helped him to survive, most notably his secretary, Rita Redlich. Professional life had more or less ended for Fritz, but he found one or two decidedly modest jobs, such as teaching in families he knew and playing for the Christian Scientists on Sundays, which at least allowed him to play a Blüthner piano. And in time, he became president of the Verband für evangelische Kirchenmusik.[a] Nonetheless, what a plummet. Did he feel a victim, that he had only been doing as best he knew to further music, and had simply been pulled along by events? Or was he aggrieved that once again Germany had been defeated? I suspect – without any grounds of certainty for being able to do so – that it was a confused mixture of both.

Whatever he felt, somehow Fritz came through. He and Gretel took advantage of Hedwig being in England and visited often, sometimes for protracted periods of time. They went on family outings and holidays together. They even arranged a family concert, hiring Chelsea Town Hall and an orchestra so that Fritz could conduct once more. Hedwig, Iso, and Maertel each played concertos. Fritz could not get enough time at the British Library – a veritable refuge where he could exist in the bubble of anonymous shared concentration, divorced from all else, and in the direct company only of archives and ideas. It allowed him to indulge his lust for playing musical detective and seeking out and poring over old manuscripts, thinking that surely here, contained within all the bits and pieces gathered from old estates and houses, was at least one hitherto undiscovered gem. Had he not, after all, discovered the Jena symphony? (The dénouement with Robbins Landon was yet to come.) In this he remained empty-handed, but forever loved the experience.

---

a   Association for Evangelical Church Music.

CHELSEA TOWN HALL
KING'S ROAD, S.W.3

The R.B.A. CONCERT SOCIETY presents

TWO ORCHESTRAL CONCERTS

on

Monday, February 18th

and

Wednesday, February 27th

at 7.30 p.m.

by the

LONDON MOZART PLAYERS

Conducted by Professor

FRITZ STEIN

Soloists:

ISO ELINSON

HEDWIG STEIN   BARBARA HOLST

MAX-MARTIN STEIN

——————— STEINWAY PIANOFORTE ———————

TICKETS for each Concert: 7/6, 5/- and 3/-
Obtainable at BENTLEY'S, 267 King's Road, S.W.3 (FLAxman 0335); CHAPPELL'S
50 New Bond Street, W.1 (MAYfair 7600), and usual Ticket Agencies; and at
CHELSEA TOWN HALL on concert nights only

Concert Direction:
NICHOLAS CHOVEAUX, 28 Bury Walk, S.W.3 (FLAxman 7010)

C.L.J. (1951)   NOTES AND PROGRAMMES OVERLEAF

Professor FRITZ STEIN is well known on the Continent for his work as a conductor and musicologist. He was Director of the "Berlin Staatliche Hochschule für Musik" for many years and has edited a great number of works by German composers of the 17th and 18th centuries, including Bach's sons, Telemann and Bruhns. He discovered the so-called early Beethoven "Jena" Symphony which he edited and published in 1907.

Stein was a great friend of Max Reger and did much to make his music popular. His biography of Reger is one of the standard works in Germany.

For many years Stein conducted his own chamber orchestra in Berlin, giving regular concerts there as well as in other parts of Germany and abroad.

This is his first appearance in London.

HEDWIG STEIN, his daughter, is the wife of Iso Elinson. She has made many appearances abroad and in this country, where she has lived since 1933.

MAX-MARTIN STEIN, his son, is one of the leading pianists of the younger generation in Germany. This is his first visit to England.

ISO ELINSON, his son-in-law, is well known in this country by his frequent appearances as soloist under leading conductors and his many recitals, which have included series of Bach, Beethoven and Chopin in London and the provinces. His name is equally familiar on the Continent, where he gives regular annual tours.

BARBARA HOLST has studied privately with Iso Elinson since her training at the Royal College of Music. This is her first public appearance in London.

MONDAY, FEBRUARY 18th, at 7.30
PROGRAMME

Symphony in C, K.200 . . . . . Mozart
  Allegro spiritoso — Andante — Minuetto, Allegretto, Trio — Presto

Piano Concerto in A, K.488 . . . Mozart
  Allegro — Andante — Presto
  Soloist: HEDWIG STEIN

INTERVAL

Piano Concerto in C minor, K.491 . Mozart
  Allegro — Larghetto — Allegretto
  Soloist: ISO ELINSON

Piano Concerto in C, K.503 . . . Mozart
  Allegro maestoso — Andante — Finale: Allegretto
  Soloist: MAX-MARTIN STEIN

WEDNESDAY, FEBRUARY 27th, at 7.30
PROGRAMME

Sinfonia in E flat, Op. 9, No. 2 . . J. C. Bach
  Allegro — Andante con sordini — Tempo di Menuetto
  (Edited and published by Fritz Stein)

Piano Concerto in E flat K.482 . . Mozart
  Allegro — Andante — Allegro
  Soloist: BARBARA HOLST

INTERVAL

Piano Concerto in B flat, Opus 19 . Beethoven
  Allegro con brio — Adagio — Rondo: Molto Allegro
  Soloist: ISO ELINSON

Symphony in E flat, No. 55 ("The Schoolmaster") Haydn
  Allegro di molto — Adagio ma semplice — Menuetto — Presto

Programme from Chelsea Town Hall concert, 1952

125

On one of his early visits, Fritz re-acquainted himself with Margarete Grünfeld, who had come to see him after one of his concerts with the Berlin Chamber Orchestra but who had had to leave Berlin for England at about the same time as Hedwig and Iso. It soon became very much closer than acquaintanceship. Margarete was wealthy and much attentive to Fritz's desires whenever he came, arranging to hire a Rolls Royce to take him to the British Library, and then collect him, promptly, whenever he had finished. She would provide accommodation in London for him, and for Gretel if she wished, and would order the car for the Elinsons to be driven by her chauffeur to various places for concerts and for picnics. Hedwig described 'ardent feelings' between Fritz and Margarete – causing Gretel much grievance. But Gretel tolerated it, forever the loyal companion.

Margarete Grünfeld died in London in October 1961. Just two

Hedwig, Fritz and Iso
in the 1950s

months later, Fritz had a heart attack. Hedwig went to Berlin and stayed until he died ten days later. When it came to sorting things out, including Fritz's papers, Hedwig threw away all the correspondence between Margarete and Fritz. They had known each other for nearly fifteen years. 'I felt a little disturbed by this…' wrote Hedwig. But she did not say why or what was in those letters. One can conjecture.

For Fritz, this last period of his life was calm – superficially at least. He had his friends and family, and music, even if he was no longer at any helm. What remains in darkness is how he might have looked back over his life and actions. Gretel survived him by a number of years until a severe heart attack in 1968. Hedwig flew out to see her. Communication was hardly possible, but she recognised Hedwig and smiled. On the advice of the doctors, Hedwig returned to Manchester and was not there when her 'beloved Mutter' died a couple of weeks later.

Quite how Fritz and Gretel influenced Hedwig as a child remains difficult to pin down. While I have little sense of an intimate early family life, they clearly provided a strong artistic and intellectual base that resonated with Hedwig and from which she took a great deal. And so, despite the harsh break forced upon each of the players by Nazism and the War, both Fritz and Gretel in their different ways provided the springboard for Hedwig's musical career, and so for her entire life.

As for the vexed question about how Fritz *really* felt, we are no further: it remains just that.

EIGHT

INTO THE UNKNOWN

...to London.

I find it hard to imagine how Hedwig and Iso must have felt as they drew into Victoria Station, somehow having to manhandle their twelve bags. Neither of them had ever been to England, and they knew no one at all in London, or even in the country, who one or the other of them had been friends with or had met in Germany – or in Russia. They had no concerts arranged, knew of no teaching openings, had more or less cut off all connections with their families, and were soon to have their first child. Nor could they rely on meeting many others in a similar situation or have any idea of how unusual they were. At this time, the numbers of émigrés coming into the UK from Germany were very much smaller than later: only about 2000 entered during the first 15 months after Hitler had seized power.[25] What Hedwig and Iso did have, however, was the name of the nephew of the clothier who had fitted out Iso after hearing his concert in Riga. A fine start! This 'Jack', a Pole, met them at Victoria Station – quite probably raising an internal eyebrow at Hedwig's get-up of a cat-grey velveteen long dress – and took them to a boarding house he had arranged for them.

'That evening I had my first, more private, impression of things 'English'. I was fully prepared to like it all, if possible! But naturally everything was so different: the bright red letter-boxes and buses (and the Doppeldecker – doubledeckers!). The formal and slim and tall look of the policemen, the special gadgets in the boarding house (in the bathroom: 'Visitors are politely asked to clean the bath after each use!'). Those mysterious containers marked 'Vim'[a] … The dining room with artificial flowers in little vases. And the menu: 'Haddock' and 'Poached eggs' – 'Kedgeree' (?) – 'Trifle' (?) – 'Raspberry jelly'. My school English seemed useless now but I managed to make some adequate noises to the waitress, and said many 'thank yous'.'

Through a contact and with Jack's help, they found a doctor who could help with the birth. Dr Zimbler and his wife were not only well acquainted with Russia but Zimbler even knew Iso's family and had often danced with one of his sisters. Immediate bonds were created, and Iso revelled in their first invitation 'out' to dinner, when they were treated to pickled herring, bortsch and all kinds of Russian sweetmeats. As always happened, Iso played afterwards: much Chopin. And then the Zimblers asked Hedwig if she would teach their daughter. It was an unexpectedly propitious beginning.

The Elinsons' entry papers stated they could remain for four weeks – only. This was standard. And one of the conditions was that they were to stay for one to two weeks with their guarantor. Not daring to leave anything to chance, Iso left for Leeds, where he was the centre of attention and looked after no end. After that another benefactor stepped in who helped to arrange for the permit to be extended, though only by a further two to three months. The boarding house was already proving too expensive, and Hedwig and Iso moved out to a family in Cricklewood where they could get full board for £3 a week. It seemed to Hedwig like a doll's house after all the places she had lived in up till then, but at least it

a   An almost ubiquitous bathroom abrasive in English homes for many years.

was in a leafy side street and had a small garden. Its big attraction, though, was the baby grand, and Hedwig was able to indulge in hours of Bach every day.

Life then changed fundamentally with the birth of their daughter Anna. Picture Iso, in his anxiety grabbing his special edition of Bach piano works for good luck, before they rushed into a taxi and sped off to the hospital. As Anna appeared, he had to adjust his expectations from a fully-fledged beauty to the tiny, no doubt wrinkled, immediate post-birth baby that he finally saw. Hedwig, on the other hand, simply savoured the simultaneous relief, exhaustion, exhilaration and joy. They did not celebrate quite alone, though; despite having been in the country for less than two months, Iso already had a small circle of admirers, some who visited and many of whom sent congratulatory bunches of flowers.

Shortly after Anna's arrival, and once they had received the necessary permits from the Home Office, the well-known concert agent Harold Holt arranged Iso's London debut. It was at the Wigmore Hall, *the* venue for performers of note. It was billed as 'Iso Elinson, The Celebrated Pianist – His First Appearance in London': three of the Bach Preludes and Fugues, the last Schubert sonata, three works by Schumann, one of the Chopin Ballades and four Études, and the Valse oubliée and *Mazeppa* by Liszt. Hedwig somehow managed to squeeze herself into the gold lamé gown that she had worn for her own Berlin debut and did not feel out of place with the velvet-cloaked ladies who graced the first few rows of the hall. Even though the press gave Iso an enthusiastic reception, the concert could not serve as a promotion for paid concerts: as immigrants, Iso and Hedwig were not yet permitted to earn. However, almost as good was the offer from the piano firm Blüthner of a good instrument for Iso, to be delivered to their third-floor flat in Maida Vale. Invitations flew in. They now had just what they needed: a piano, a place to live, opportunities for Iso to perform, and a small income from Hedwig's inheritance from her grandmother, Luise Czerny, which her faithful friend from Heidelberg, Görli Döring, sent each month and was just enough for them to manage.

How was life for Hedwig? A reading of her Diary is like a breathless whistle-stop tour of places and personalities, with descriptions of daily routines that had to fit in around them. Survival required success along many axes: finding out who best to contact about concert opportunities for Iso – indeed, even finding out *how* best to contact them, improving her and Iso's English, discovering the dos and don'ts of English society, meeting people and growing friendships, making sure they could stay in England, and managing their restricted finances, all the while keeping Iso happy (not entirely straightforward), taking care of all the household duties, and looking after Anna.

Wherever they turned, they encountered open arms and generosity. Benefactors appeared – after a concert, or through a contact, or from an encounter. Many of them would remain friends – and supporters – for years. Some were especially active in helping exiles, which Iso was twice over. Other friends included many of the illustrious musicians and artists of the day. Hedwig does not paint expansive portraits of them but she does offer vignettes from time to time, and I found myself hunting for a few facts about this pot pourri of artists to display alongside Hedwig's portrait. These are not just names; they are varied and intriguing personalities, and all are part of the immensely rich and colourful world of creativity that the Elinsons became part of.

One of the first people to take Hedwig and Iso under her wing was Lady Swaythling. Her husband had been a prominent member of the British Jewish community and a Liberal politician. She herself publicly opposed the Balfour declaration on Palestine and co-founded the Anti-Zionist League of British Jews. Maybe that was partly why she did whatever she could for Iso, helping to get concerts and interest critics. Lady Swaythling was a great hostess, holding many private dinners and parties in her Kensington home, around the corner from the Royal Albert Hall. The first encounter Hedwig had with her was very soon after Anna was born, when she invited Iso to play for a private audience in a setting Hedwig described as a 'rokoko and stucco golden music room, actually removed from a Parisian Palais'. A good number of similar occasions followed over the coming years, including cycles of Bach and Chopin;

and during the War, Iso would stay there when he was performing at the Albert Hall, Hedwig joining Lady Swaythling in her family box. At one reception Lady Swaythling hosted for King Prajadhipok of Siam, the king requested a nocturne by Chopin. He clearly had a particular one in mind. The guests, ladies wearing tiaras and evening dress, had to stand and listen – no shuffling – as Iso played his way through most of the 24 preludes until, finally, the king said, 'That's it!'

From a golden music room to a large Victorian house in Buckhurst Hill: Leslie Linder and his sister Enid, whose family had run a business of ship's chandlers, approached Iso after his debut Wigmore concert, inviting him and Hedwig to what proved to be a gargantuan dinner for only five of them – two chickens, lavish sweets and pints of cream – presided over by Leslie and Enid's silver-haired and moustached father, almost enthroned in an over-sized Victorian chair. Disregarding all the hand-carved furniture, Iso espied and played all three of Leslie's pianos – a Bechstein and two Steinways, one of which had been made for Baron Rothschild in Paris and was a Baroque-influenced instrument with five legs which almost sagged beneath its gold embellishments. Leslie and Enid remained staunch supporters for years, not only organising many private concerts for Iso and attending his big public appearances, but also inviting him to go with them to Budapest, and providing financial help to the family over many years.

There were sculptor friends too. Hedwig and Iso went for suppers to Henry Moore and his Ukrainian wife and model, Irina. They lived very simply, even though by this time Moore was receiving numerous commissions and exhibitions of his works were fairly frequent. In contrast, the regular Sunday receptions at Jacob Epstein's house brought together:

'...a medley of mankind, exotic people – models, youngsters, children racing around, old wise men, his (then!) wife, huge and redhaired, pouring out tea from the big pot into an assortment of sometimes-chipped china cups, smiling beatifically. Femmes fatales who I could not identify swanned around. Epstein himself, exuding the impression of a great creative artist and dressed in a thick jacket, trousers bespattered with clay, shook people by the hand, in a heavy, honest, and almost peasant manner.'

Epstein came several times to Iso's Wigmore recitals, always in the same tweed jacket. And the family often went to his home. All their conversations, said Hedwig, were in *allegro con brio*[a] and Iso would play Epstein's Blüthner. Once, this produced a stern rap on the door. There stood Winston Churchill, complaining about the loud noise. I doubt Iso would have been impressed – maybe Epstein neither. It is a measure of Epstein's regard for Iso that he expressed a wish to model his head. Though the idea floated around for years, somehow they never managed to put the arrangements for sittings in place and it remained no more than an aspiration. Epstein died in 1959.

Some members of the London Group of painters, such as Arnold Auerbach and John Cooper, became good friends. Ivon Hitchens was one of the closest, often inviting the Elinsons to his London home, which was just a short walk away, and then, after it was bombed in 1940, to his studio caravan and tiny cottage in a birch wood just outside Petworth in Sussex. Hedwig warmed to the single-minded Hitchens and his 'decorative' wife, and Iso was not too proud to play on their ancient grand piano. While I was writing this, the Pallant House Gallery in Chichester put on an exhibition of Hitchens' works. As I wandered round I wondered which, if any, of the paintings from the 1930s, and then his more abstract works from the 1940s, Hitchens might have shown Hedwig and Iso. Had Hedwig, possibly, been Hitchens' inspiration for his picture of the piano player? A fanciful thought, in all probability, but it lent an additional frisson to the exhibition for me. Anna subsequently told me of how, when Hitchens was working on his colossal mural at the London headquarters of the English Folk Dance and Song Society, he had also sketched Iso playing.

---

a   In musical terminology: at a spirited and fast tempo.

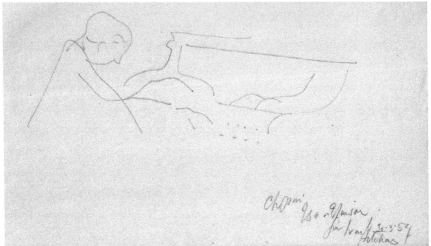

Sketches of Iso by Ivon Hitchens, 1959

It was not only musicians, sculptors and painters who swam into Hedwig and Iso's life but literary people too, such as AP Herbert, the novelist, playwright and Member of Parliament. JB Priestley invited them over for dinner and was kind enough to ask if he could help them in some way. Iso played some Brahms before they went up on to the roof of Priestley's Hampstead house to look at the panoramic view over London. As I read the Diary, knowing this had taken place not too long before the Blitz, I could not help but recall the stories in Elisabeth Bowen's *The Heat of the Day* about fire wardens standing on roofs to watch the skies for incoming bombers, and Graham Greene fire-watching on the roof of a garage, where he and his lover Dorothy Glover saw "the flares come slowly floating down, dribbling their flames: they drift like great yellow peonies".[26]

At a big party they met the poet John Drinkwater and his then-wife, the violinist Daisy Kennedy, with her 'reddish flaming hair, in Wagner style'. Daisy's former husband, the pianist Benno Moiseiwitch, also appeared. Then suddenly Iso found himself being scrutinised by an elegant, white-faced, sophisticated lady wearing long black gloves, leaning on a shooting stick and holding a fine cigarette holder: the pianist Harriet Cohen – obviously something of an eccentric. Quite what each made of this particular encounter Hedwig did not say, but no sparks were ignited, no friendship developed, and when they noticed Cohen in the audience at Venice's La Fenice opera house years later, neither Hedwig nor Iso made any move to make contact.

There must have been quite a chain of people in London, like Lady Swaythling, who hosted young performers in their homes. One such was Evelyn Suart, herself something of a pianist and the wife of Commander Cecil Harcourt. They lived in a rather grand antique-filled house in Chelsea, where Evelyn held Sunday receptions at which she always had good performers to play, tempting them with the promise of securing purchased tickets for their next recital. The old Mrs Harcourt, in black silk with a lace collar, would pour out the tea ("Oh dear Mr Elinson, you already had six," she said to Iso once) and the smiling Commander would hand out the cups. Mrs Harcourt, at the proper moment, urged people to stop chattering, and might sit on the carpet on a cushion near the open fire with her two exquisitely dressed daughters. One of the daughters, Diana, became a ballet dancer and the wife of the violinist Yehudi Menuhin; the other, Griselda, married the pianist Louis Kentner. Iso revelled in this sort of atmosphere, knowing that this was not simply a group of the social élite; a good number were true music-lovers who fully appreciated the music and his playing. As at all such gatherings, it was not altogether relaxed for Hedwig, who worried that she and Iso might commit some social blunder or other, not knowing exactly how to behave, or who people were – indeed, sometimes not even being able to distinguish between a guest and the butler. But any indiscretions must have been minor, for they were invited again and again. Hedwig's irresistible smile and enjoyment and Iso's playing no doubt helped to carry them through.

In a rather different sphere was Marga Deneke. She was born in the 1880s into a wealthy German banking family that moved in a circle of musicians, including Mendelssohn, Brahms, and Clara Schumann. The circle also included the violinists Jelly d'Aranyi and her sister Adila, great-nieces of the renowned József Joachim.[a] As well as being a musicologist, chosen by the Mendelssohn family to take care of a collection of his manuscripts, Marga herself was a fine pianist and pupil of Eugenie Schumann,[b] and a close friend of the pianist Paul Wittgenstein, brother of the philosopher Ludwig. She was politically aware and a strong supporter of women's rights. With the private income she inherited with her sister, Marga lived in a Gothic villa in Oxford which had a large separate music room built by her parents. In this she would host many concerts of the Oxford Ladies' Musical Society, today the Oxford Chamber Music Society. It was the sort of place Iso liked to perform in, with its signed photographs of Brahms looking down from the walls.

'A personality of great vigour! She invited us: 'Bring tiny Anna with you – for a weekend! I have a little bamboo cradle, a present from Lambaréné where I helped Dr Schweitzer with nursing…' Well, the idea was so kind but these were some of the worst nights because Anna measured several inches more in length than the cradle allowed for!'

A musical party at the home of the German philanthropist and music supporter Robert Mayer set the scene for what was to become a central friendship for Hedwig and Iso. Rosamond Stutchbury happened to be sitting in the audience next to Iso and as he turned his head, his long curly hair brushed against her face while they and the other guests, many of whom were German refugees, were waiting to hear the Busch Quartet.

---

a   Hungarian violinist, conductor, and composer, and close friend of Brahms.
b   One of Robert and Clara Schumann's eight children.

The incident made Ros look more closely at her neighbours. "One could have guessed at once that he was a musician", she later wrote, and she noted how both Iso and Hedwig (who was "very fair and typically German-looking") were interested "in everybody and everything – but perhaps most of all in a wonderful sideboard loaded with fruit and sandwiches and good things on sticks". When she tried speaking to them, "Iso looked blank, and said 'Spanish?', though he was talking to Hedwig in broken German." Ros, whose mother was German, was easily able to continue the exchange and then used the interval to ask the host Robert who these people were:

> "He is a Russian Jew who escaped via Riga to Berlin where he made a name for himself immediately. He won the heart of the daughter of a pillar of the German musical establishment who forbade the marriage. She too is a very good pianist. Unfortunately they had had to flee from Germany and nobody knows them in this country." [27]

An introduction and further exchanges followed, in German, Hedwig and Iso all the while devouring the goodies "like hungry children". Enough interest was sparked on both sides that Ros contacted them a few days later with an invitation to go down to her house in West Sussex: a violinist, a Viennese lady, was visiting her and since she, Ros, played the cello, they might make up a trio. Ros was even sufficiently sensitive to offer a fee of five guineas – no doubt a cause for an Elinson celebration of tea and buns. Hedwig and Iso jumped at the opportunity. It was to be their first outing outside their London circle of friends and acquaintances. Very quickly the question arose of what they should wear, in hot June, in the country. Sartorial adviser Jack came to the rescue. For 'special' people, he said, a black striped suit and Iso's large Continental black artist's hat would be appropriate. And to match that, Hedwig donned a silk hat with an eye veil. Ros met them at the station, surely with a raised eyebrow and twinkle in her eye as she saw them. She was in her old maroon corduroy jacket, ordinary flat shoes, and with no hat.

Ros Wycliffe was just over ten years older than Hedwig, and had married Mervyn Stutchbury, a wealthy mining engineer, in 1918. Both had gone into the arrangement with their eyes open and were honest with each other: Ros did not love Mervyn, who had written to her beforehand: "I don't want you to try to love me because I happen to love you. There have been many who have loved you and there will be ever so many more who will do so."[28] One of the wedding photos shows them each looking rather grimly straight into the camera. But they found a way of living together that each could enjoy. They had children and each probably had the odd affair. Their last child was rather certain she was the daughter of the Russian cellist Igor Piatigorsky. No matter. Ros was able to lead an unencumbered life: Mervyn earned the money and she spent it, all in ways of which Mervyn seems to have approved. And so she was able to be extraordinarily generous, in monetary terms, when Hedwig and Iso were still finding their feet in England.

Coming from a half-German background and having had a German music tutor, Ros was probably well-disposed towards German artists. She was one of a circle of people who gave whatever assistance they could to German émigrés. But in Hedwig and Iso's case, the relationship was to go much further and deeper on all sides, and they were embraced by the entire Stutchbury family. Ros not only had a passion for music, unmatched by any of Hedwig's other close friends, but as a cellist herself who moved so intimately in musical circles, she understood profoundly what life as a performer entailed. She was the first woman cellist to play at Glyndebourne, and when Iso was at Gayles, they would often play sonatas together – a sure sign of Ros's ability, since Iso would play only with very accomplished instrumentalists. Anna once related how he would step back and ask Hedwig to accompany their friends or acquaintances who were less talented. Hedwig did not mind; always ready to encourage others, she would play enthusiastically with anyone at the drop of a hat. Not only was Ros a good cellist, she had an extraordinarily good cello that after her death went on being used at Glyndebourne. It took on a remarkable form of specialness in 2009 when, during a performance of Rusalka, the lead soprano lost her footing during a dramatic love scene and fell backwards into the orchestra pit a couple of metres below. The audience and cast froze in instant horror. But the soprano's life, or at least her back, was saved – by no less than Ros's cello, which had broken her fall. The cello, inevitably, was badly damaged but could be repaired.

Ros had an easy manner about her, and Hedwig fell in love with her house, Gayles, which lay between gentle hills and was close to the South Downs. It turned out that the Stutchburys not only owned Gayles, but also some of the Seven Sisters between Cuckmere Haven and Birling's Gap, where swimming later proved to be a regular pastime. Although not right on the sea, the Channel was visible from the front windows of the house – on the horizon, a blue or grey triangle, depending on the weather. Hedwig and Iso were given a room at the front with a large balcony and 'at night that bit of water, when lit up by a moon, glistened magically in the distance while aromatic shrubs from down below sent up their perfumes to our delighted nostrils!' The magic continued through the days they were there, days filled with music when even, exceptionally, Hedwig played as well. Deep friendship with Ros, and the pleasures of Gayles, were to remain constants in Hedwig's life. It was by no means one-sided:

Gayles, Friston, West Sussex.
Photograph reproduced with the kind permission of the Gayles archive.

Ros spoke of Hedwig and Iso as two of her and her family's "most special friends who remained faithful to them all through good and ill and were utterly generous, almost to a fault."[29]

There was much in Ros's background to provide a fertile base for a deep relationship. Her family had musical strands stretching back to the mid-1800s. Her aunt had been a violinist who had attracted the attention of Paganini and later Joachim, and celebrities such as Ellen Terry and Clara Schumann had joined in music-making at her soirées. Ros similarly had an enormous circle of friends, musicians and others. She introduced Hedwig and Iso to many of them, including Frances Dakyns, who in turn was very friendly with the violinist Adolf Busch and the other members of his string quartet. All had left Germany in the early 1930s, and were frequent visitors to Gayles. It must have been at about this time that Frances and Ros were advising the businessman John Christie on his idea of setting up the Glyndebourne Opera. I lighted on this information at about the same time as I discovered that David Hare had recently finished a play called *The Moderate Soprano*, then on in the West End. It was about Christie's ambitious plan for a new opera house where his wife, the eponymous 'moderate soprano' Audrey Mildmay, could shine, and the ups and downs of getting the project off the ground. I had to see the play, of course, and felt almost as though I knew these characters who featured in Hedwig's Diary. I noted one exchange in particular:

John (Christie): He [Adolf Busch] got to stay the night with my friend Ros. She put him up. Do you know Rosamond?
Busch (Fritz, who had been summarily dismissed from his conductor role at the Dresden Opera): No.
John: Everyone knows Rosamond.
Busch: Not in Dresden.
John: Good woman, Rosamond. Plucky. She happened to mention she had a friend who was starting an opera house, and would he be interested? He said not personally, he played the fiddle, but he did have a brother [Fritz], who conducted.[30]

And so Fritz Busch, brother of Adolf, who in turn Hedwig and Iso knew well, came to be the music director and conductor of the Glyndebourne Opera. I was intrigued to know what had brought David Hare to mention Rosamond in this context and wrote to ask him, wondering if he would be able to proffer extra information about her. Not so. But he did say she had been:

> "a crucial figure in the bizarre chain of coincidence whereby Glyndebourne was founded. Fritz Busch's brother stayed with her overnight and that – we believe – is how John Christie first even heard the word 'Busch'. You may say Christie was extraordinarily lucky to bump into three refugees from Nazism almost by accident, but then visionaries have a way of being lucky."

Indeed. As were Hedwig and Iso in getting to know Ros.

Frances Dakyns was constantly on the go, helping here and there, and Hedwig warmed to this small and very energetic woman with short hair, half open spaniel-like warm eyes, a smiling mouth and a way of darting from one subject to another, which she illustrated through impulsive hand gestures. She was an eccentric figure who had driven a Red Cross ambulance during the First World War, and who now lived a rather Bohemian life, dressing up only when she had to, such as for Glyndebourne first nights. When not engaged in her pig breeding, Frances fairly spun through the musical scene, counting Joseph Joachim, Donald Tovey and Ralph Vaughan Williams among her acquaintances. She managed Pablo Casals' stays in London, and helped Arturo Toscanini when he was in London, driving him round in her ancient Rolls Royce. She was a force locally too, in the Haslemere, Hindhead and Headley Music Club, to which she attracted performers such as Myra Hess, the Busch Quartet, and Elizabeth Schumann, and to which she invited Iso more than once.

There was no doubt: Hedwig and Iso had fallen on their feet. After a few moves to various boarding houses in London, they finally found a flat in Lancaster Drive near Swiss Cottage. It was, of course, a complete contrast with the splendours of many of the homes they were invited to, invitations that as a rule were combined with a private recital by Iso. But the differences did not bother either of them in the slightest. Hedwig had lived the grand life in Heidelberg. Now she was content with their simple life and paid little attention to material things. Once the Home Office and Ministry of Labour had in 1935 lifted the restriction on their earning, she and Iso were able to live fairly comfortably even though they had no regular employment; concert engagements, radio broadcasts and private pupils, together with Hedwig's modest cash injections from her grandmother's legacy in Germany, saw them through.

Hedwig was fascinated by London street life: the calls of the milkman with his horse and cart, the coalman who almost yodelled his messages, the markets and the straw hats and blue aprons of the fishmongers, the displays of fruit and vegetables in the shops ('so much more 'poetic' than barrels of sauerkraut or pickled herrings!'). She spent hours walking with Anna in her pram, peering into shop windows, and marching across Hampstead Heath, sometimes accompanied by Iso, munching apple after apple – almost a daily need for him.

I gleaned more about Hedwig's initial impressions from a clutch of Hedwig's letters to her German schoolfriend Lilo, which spanned a period of eleven years from 1927 and were wrapped inside rather crumpled, worn, faded and fragile tissue paper – itself now nearly 40 years old. On the outside Hedwig had written:

> 'Re-read in 1981. Mostly Hedwig letters returned to me by a very nice German schoolfriend-girl. Very interesting. (My studies – concerts – Berlin etc. Iso, wedding, going to England, births of A and M. Ros etc.) Lively and decently written, and clear'.

This correspondence tells how she found London shatteringly big and fascinating. Everything pleased her and Iso, she said. They had no regrets about coming to England, but nonetheless hoped fervently that it would prove in the long run to have been the right thing to do. They were still a long way from Iso being known as a pianist; contacts were the passport to success.

Full of familiarity and warmth, Hedwig was anxious to share her pleasures and disappointment with this long-standing friend of hers who provided one of the few links back to Germany. And she still supported Lilo's book-binding business as best she could, sending her special musical scores, such as presents for Iso, to give them a distinctive and personal touch:

'We are thrilled with the bound volumes you just sent – exactly my taste. What a present! And of course, leather and gold lettering is far from what we would order. But let me convert my protestations into an order for binding two other books of music. I would like the Bach bound in black, with a dark green linen spine. And Volume II of the Busoni will complement the first book that you did for me for Christmas... in the same brown with a brown linen spine... Such music is our capital!'

Hedwig's pride in Iso shines in many of her letters to Lilo: what he was playing, when, and where, and when it might just be possible for Lilo to pick up a live transmission on the radio. She bubbled over in describing how Anna was developing, and showing some musical tendencies. She described the marvellous hospitality offered to them by Ros Stutchbury at Gayles. And time and again she stated how she and Iso liked England, and how very pleased they were to have come. She commiserated with Lilo's circumstances as she recalled her and Iso's early days in London when things were not materially rosy and they had to live in one room with Anna, gathering a few sticks of old furniture together, and the uphill efforts she in particular had had to make in helping Iso to make his mark. And she did not fail to say occasionally how she wished she could play more.

The entire tenor of Hedwig's correspondence to Lilo is of deep trust and affection. The letters are both chatty and soul-searching, written quickly and spontaneously, though Hedwig was sharply aware of the need to write only in general terms because of political developments and a fear of writing anything that could compromise Lilo: Lilo's brother had been sent to a concentration camp in 1933.

She wrote at length about her new status as a wife and mother, however, both states for which she was ill-prepared and bereft of any guiding help. On the one hand, Hedwig's approach to being a wife was the traditional German way, and she found herself swamped with washing nappies, cleaning, shopping, cooking, mending socks, and taking Anna out on walks. She had to navigate her way through all this pretty much alone, though once settled in London there were occasional gentle pieces of advice from Ros and a few others:

"Darling Hedwig – in England we put on the nappies when they are quite dry!' (Yes – but I felt I had not got a big enough store. So Ros produced more!)'.

On the other, she was firmly committed to making life run as smoothly for Iso as she possibly could and took on the roles of concert facilitator and secretary. That was in no way straightforward. They had few connections and routes into the musical world in England, and there was also the question of language. Conversations at home were still in German, and although Hedwig's school English was proving good enough to get them through social occasions, the writing of more formal letters was another matter. How should she address Henry Wood, the 'father' and conductor of the Promenade concerts in the Royal Albert Hall: 'Dear Sir Wood', or 'Dear Sir Henry', or 'Dear Sir Henry Wood'? It was baffling and exhausting, and at times Hedwig had to resort to asking some of her new English friends, especially Ros. On top was the business of typing whatever they had composed – a task that neither of them had undertaken before. Any mistakes meant starting again. It was a slow and painstaking job.

At the same time, Hedwig was not about to relinquish her own ambitions as a performing pianist. Those, she was clear, were merely on the back burner. She was in the sort of relationship that at that time went far outside the norm. Yet she must have had an unshakeable conviction that in the long term, she would find a way of following her own musical ambitions. Helpfully, Iso staunchly supported that view. Although he was the star of the Elinson duo, he knew from the time they met that Hedwig was already on track for a career as a pianist and he admired her playing and respected her needs.

Another daughter, Marga, was born when Anna was three. There is something inordinately touching about children when they sleep, their complete trustfulness, and Hedwig felt moved to write this rather special entry in the Diary:

'(Failing a sonnet-writer's gifts I have to do so in feeble, stumbling, sentences!) Marga in a pale, transparent, pink, flowery nightie – she lies pale and sweet – with the fragrance of Botticelli's Primavera; her little mouth energetically shut, her tiny nostrils of lovely proportions, the closed eyes quiet, serene; her thin arms slightly raised with a little tiny baby-smell (milky!) just inside her elbow-hollows! A little deep-grunting noise comes from her, akin to snoring of the most *ppp*[a] kind! One sees a peaceful, intelligent face… Against this, Anna lies in bed with the gracefulness of a Murillo-child. Her fuller, dark hair forms the perfect background for her pinkish-rose complexion and her black lashes stand out in the semi-dark of the little room. She raises only one arm upwards, gently curved, and there is no sound, except her regular, quiet breathing. (And occasionally there is a suspicion of a drop of moisture on her cheeks from her mouth, when her beloved (!) thumb has 'had a good time' and I, ever so gently, take it out)… I wish their future husbands could see them now! I say this not only as a mother but as an objective, aesthetically-minded onlooker. It is near perfection – to behold sleeping children like these (while the guns abroad roar and kill the 'begetters' of the little ones)…'

Despite having two young girls, Hedwig managed a bit of teaching. When they visited friends who had two pianos and Iso grasped the chance to practise one of his concertos – Rachmaninov, Brahms, Tchaikovsky and Mozart – Hedwig took on the orchestral parts. It was a challenge: Iso

---

a   In music, pianississimo, meaning a passage is to be played extremely softly.

was demanding, and Hedwig had to master difficult music having had very little time to practise. The radical change from having lived entirely absorbed in a musical and artistic world niggled at times, but she knuckled under and got on with the job. Iso's successes were more than enough compensation for her.

Trips to Gayles provided a wonderful diversion. The Elinson family was now such a regular feature that Ros and her husband Mervyn offered them the flat above the newly built garage as their 'holiday home'. This might sound rather unappealing. As I saw when I went to Gayles to meet Ros's granddaughter, however, it was quite the opposite. The flat had been designed by Edward Maufe, Mervyn's brother-in-law and the architect of Guildford cathedral – with a particular aspect to the specification from Ros and Mervyn: the sitting room should be able to accommodate a grand piano and have excellent acoustics. The other rooms were also of a good size and it was well equipped and close to the main house, which meant that much time could be spent with Ros (and her piano) while giving Hedwig, Iso and the children their own base in the country. The building was near the stables and had magnificent views over the Downs and fields. Paradise! After a year or two, the family was spending big chunks of time at Gayles. With a firm foot in the area, Anna and Marga were christened together in the tiny Saxon church in Friston, just down the road from Gayles – the vicar having popped out to collect christening water from the pond across the lane – with most of the Stutchbury family present and Anna dressed up in a borrowed Brussels lace dress that made her look more like a bridesmaid.

Ros introduced Hedwig and Iso to one of their neighbours, Oswald Birley – the painter and a member of the Royal Society of Portrait Painters – and his Irish wife Rhoda, 'a strange and great beauty'. Their home, Charleston Manor, was different again from Gayles. Quintessentially English, it was a 12th-century manor house surrounded by formal and informal gardens, with a stable block they used as an exhibition gallery and a tithe barn for performances of the Charleston Festival, which Rhoda founded. It was in the barn that the Birleys hosted a Russian ballet to which they invited Hedwig and Iso. Despite the accompanying caviar and vodka, Iso could not resist trying the Steinway in the lounge, and while he was playing some Chopin, in crept a woman to listen: Hope Kilby. She immediately struck up conversation and invited Hedwig and Iso to Bournemouth to meet her mother and two sisters, Ruth and Avice. Lifelong friendships with Hope and Avice were spawned, with more openings to breathe in some sea air and enjoy walks through the countryside, and for Hedwig and Iso to give occasional concerts in Bournemouth and round about.

Charleston. Today the name is inseparably linked to the Bloomsbury Group, and to Vanessa Bell and Duncan Grant in particular. At the time Hedwig and Iso were going down frequently to see Ros, there was not yet any aura around Charleston. But Vanessa and Duncan, and from time to time Vanessa's husband Clive, had established themselves and been working there for some 20 years. Charleston is but a good stone's throw away from Gayles. Although there is no mention in the Diary, it is hard not to imagine that Hedwig and Iso encountered Vanessa and Duncan, who would have been obvious friends for Ros. Also, the then Bishop of Chichester, Bishop Bell, who was the prime mover behind the restoration of murals in churches in Sussex, had offered Grant a commission in 1941 to revive the murals in the local church of St Michael's and All Angels in Berwick, which he undertook with Vanessa and her son Quentin Bell. The project must have been talked about by local people like Ros, and surely Hedwig visited it on one of her visits to Gayles, given the remarkable nature of these murals. Later, it was Bishop Bell who would open up recital opportunities for Hedwig and Iso.

One of the – relatively few – pieces of the underlying jigsaw picture to my portrait of Hedwig that turned up near the end of my writing was the joint letter from Iso and Hedwig to Gretel, written around October 1936. It is in German, and has a comment from Hedwig at the top: 'After we made it up!' Clearly this was a reference to the reconciliation between Fritz and Gretel, and Iso and Hedwig, initiated by Gretel. Iso writes first, in his Sunday-best script, by thanking Gretel for a picture of Chopin – "a symbol of peace after such a long time" – and saying that if she still remembers him, he believes she did not form an impression of him as an aggressive person. All he and Hedwig wanted was a set of normal family relationships. There was no bitterness on their side; the reasons behind the separation could not persist forever. He was even convinced that he would one day again perform in Germany; he wanted only "to bring immortal music to audiences". Hedwig contented herself for now with expansive descriptions of Anna and Marga, and a reassurance that their marriage was good and that they were well on their way to establishing themselves in England, step by step.

As a result, Gretel came over to visit the family and meet her granddaughters, bringing news from Germany – though Hedwig writes nothing about how extensive that news was or whether they discussed their personal past and the political situation. While any embarrassments were navigated sufficiently for all to feel there had been a reconciliation, Hedwig and Iso had gathered enough from news bulletins to have a fairly clear picture about the state of affairs in Germany. By the late 1930s, Teddy Crankshaw, one of the good friends of the Elinsons and a journalist who had lived in Vienna and written extensively about music and musicians, feared the worst from Hitler. Iso continued to follow developments closely through radio bulletins and a daily read of The Times. More top-class soloists and conductors appeared in London from Germany and elsewhere, no doubt heightening the competitive pressure Iso felt as he so keenly sought concert opportunities. But most people in the wider Elinson circle were sanguine, talking about how good the German autobahns were and gossiping more about Edward VIII's potential and then actual abdication. The apprehension Hedwig and Iso felt must at times have seemed exaggerated and unreal.

In the middle of this, in 1937, the concert agent Harold Holt advised Iso to try his luck in New York. Easy to say, far more difficult to realise. With huge generosity, Ros and Mervyn stepped in and covered the costs of the trip, which was to include a recital at Carnegie Hall. After a fair amount of preparation and armed with some letters of introduction, Iso set off on a passenger liner, dispatching odd cables to Hedwig along the way. His expectations were high: experience from his tours in Sweden made him expect that the planned concerts, recitals, and private performances would trigger immediate bookings for others, and he was well aware of the successes of other Russian musicians in the US – Horowitz, again, to name but one. Iso was almost desperate for success – not only 'for the glory of music', but also for Hedwig's sake, to help with their income, and to boost his reputation in England. The signs were good: he made many friends, audiences welcomed him and the press was fairly enthusiastic. But as for future engagements, nothing. He hung on for longer than planned, seeking out American agents. It did not help, and he returned somewhat crestfallen and bewildered, able only to assure Hedwig that he had done his best and his Chopin *Winterwind* and Étude in thirds 'had been as they should be'. Maybe next year would be better. As things turned out, the War meant that it would be 25 years before he was to return. In the intervening time, he looked every so often across the Atlantic, wondering if he might have reached greater heights had he and Hedwig gone there rather than London.

Hedwig was her usual supportive and stalwart self, diverted to a certain extent by the demands of their two small daughters. But it was different for Iso. He fretted, commenting at one time during a tour in Scotland that "maybe we do not belong here, Bautz",[a] and he was affronted by the triteness of many of the remarks people made when they came backstage after a performance. This is how Iso wrote about it to Hedwig in 1937 (interestingly, in English and by now with considerable fluency):

> "It is clear to me that our main difficulty is that we are not right for England, and England is not right for us. My musicianship is not for audiences here (with a few exceptions) and I have no feeling for them. Maybe we haven't yet found the right place? In Berlin … the contact was much closer and I could play as I wished. I did not need to question whether people would understand because I knew and felt that they would fully appreciate the feelings in Chopin's Études, or Schubert's sonatas, or Bach's fugues – and even Moussorgsky or Scriabin."

a   Short for Bautzel, Hedwig's nickname.

In another letter:

"It is true: we have good friends and acquaintances here, we enjoy complete freedom – politically and otherwise such as our work permits – and yet we are so strange and distant from the various circles in which we move. It's not a question of individuals, but the entire attitudes and ways of interacting – 'great fun', 'enjoyed', 'lovely', 'thank you so much', 'it is so nice of you' – and so on. These are simply not us. And in the eyes of others, we must seem 'funny' or 'nice', or even 'peculiar'!

"Even as far as music is concerned, people here have a quite different attitude to those everywhere else in the world. For example, what would be regarded elsewhere as 'demonic' is here described as 'noisy' or 'funny' or 'without self-restraint'… Music here is regarded as 'artificial'.

"But we must live in reality and since at the moment there is simply no other option, we have to make the best of a bad job… When I come home tomorrow, we can think through what we might do. I have already prepared a list of nine points. I am not pessimistic, firstly because I am convinced we will reach our end goal, and secondly, because I believe that everything has its own meaning (which in our case is the question of survival). I know that I have always had, and have, an enormous feeling for you, and always will have. It can never be different. But since I am against 'pathetique', I will write no more of that…"

A few years earlier, he had written:

"…I know that I give true art. Our duty therefore is to use every means we can to convey my art to those who love music."

Looking back on their first five or six years in England, however, Hedwig counted her blessings. She found many: England had provided a haven for her and Iso, with countless kindnesses, a cultural environment in which they felt at home, and a natural environment that she had taken to and now loved. Together, she and Iso had managed to establish a base, were raising two children, and now had a large circle of people they could count on, some of whom had become dear friends. The complete unknown was now familiar in many regards, from the quotidian through to their lives as artists.

Money was still tight though. In order to save, they decided to let two of the rooms in their four-room flat in London, and arranged for Anna to spend some months with the Linders who had taken them under their wing from the very beginning and for Marga to go and stay with Ros Stutchbury at Gayles. In one of her letters to her friend Lilo, Hedwig seems not to have been unduly perturbed at this. She wanted more time to practise, and thought it would be good for the girls to become less dependent on her.

Becoming part of their society nonetheless took time and effort. To their advantage was their standing as celebrities, even if not major ones; Hedwig had the background to contribute to any conversation in their new circle of acquaintances; and Iso was constantly ready to perform. A lack of sophisticated English or familiarity with English norms appeared hardly to matter. However, German was still by far their preferred language, and Hedwig and Iso each had to come to terms with their status as émigrés. Hisham Matar, in his poignant account of his own exile, says it is a state of permanent guilt and soul-searching: should one have stayed, standing together with those who were opposing the threatening forces, or even simply sharing whatever they were going through? Does it not mean that one is forever estranged, living day to day with a constant sense of wanting to belong, yet unable fully to do so?[31] On top of such feelings there was for Hedwig and Iso now the steady drying up of communication with family and friends in Germany and Russia. At this time, they – like everyone else – could not know how national and international politics were going to crash through their personal histories and lives, but there was now fevered talk about war, war between the country in which they were settling down and the country Iso had grown up and honed his pianism in, and the country that was Hedwig's family and cultural base and which had taken such a repulsive direction. What added strains might have arisen in this Russian-German marriage? Anna is clear about part of the answer: whatever external arrows might have come their way, the commonality of exile was a bond whose strength went far beyond any other. I think that also probably applies equally to any internal ripples, or even storms. Hedwig had shared with Iso the decision to leave a great deal behind. For both of them, that decision had been in the knowledge that major upheaval in Germany had started. They were going to circumvent that together by going elsewhere, and would somehow get through. Yet they had had no way of knowing that where they would go would be best for them. Their decision had been based on a threadbare set of recommendations, a miscellany of anecdotes and bits of knowledge, and feelings about what might be right (or not) about another country. What they could know was that getting it wrong would mean wasted time and energies, and have implications for their children and for their careers.

NINE

WAR AND WELCOMES IN SUSSEX

1939

The build-up to the Second World War is well-known. Hitler occupied Prague and Czechoslovakia in March 1939 and invaded Poland on 1st September 1939. Two days later, the uncertainty and any residual hopes that things would sort themselves out was removed: the UK declared war on Germany. A fissure resulted between lives lived up till then and from then on.

The start of the War must have been as bizarre for Hedwig and Iso as for most of the population, yet with an added anguish because it was war against Germany. Self-evidently, something had changed: drills were arranged and gas masks issued, though there was no immediate discernible danger for them. But suddenly their worries were no longer limited to the question of how to further Iso's career. Their refuge, having fled Berlin, was threatened. With the real threat of bombardment, they were keen to get the children out of London. But how to do it? The lease on their flat had to be paid, and although Iso toyed with the idea of doing a Bach cycle in New York, Hedwig was sceptical about such an endeavour. Even if successful, it was hardly going to solve all their worries. They spoke to their closest friends about their predicament. As a result, more remarkably generous offers: their ever loyal benefactors Enid and Leslie Linder offered to take on the rent of the flat for a year (the princely sum of £80), and friends Helen and Max Page invited them to come and spend some time in their house in Selling in Kent. Helen was a lover of all the arts, and had probably met Hedwig and Iso through other artists in London. Enormously relieved, the Elinsons found tenants, abandoned most of their belongings in the Lancaster Drive flat, and set off on a new adventure.

The Pages lived in a substantial Georgian house surrounded by large fields. The Elinsons were about to get involved in something entirely unexpected and new: hop picking! Hedwig wrote with gusto about the start:

'We found this a wonderful and new experience – at least for a number of hours a day! They gave us 1½ pence an hour (!). The 'tally' man came and saw how much one had gathered; the beery smell of the hop plants made one a little dizzy. The 'hoppers' were Dickensian types – huge women (some from Ireland) with big bellies and many children, thin and pretty girls, slender, cheeky youths – all helped. They lived in gypsy fashion, in huts, for weeks on end and many days one heard a gruesome story – how a youth had lost all his savings in a fire in his hut, or the woman whose 'hubby' ran off with a beauty of 16! – and all the children, noses running, scampered around, almost naked, and got toffee-apples from the salesman. Iso became the 'pet' of 2 large women, Covent Garden stall holders, who regarded hop picking as a cheap holiday. When it rained one of them produced a gargantuan fancy umbrella and urged Iso to get underneath with her – she felt there was something special about this outlandish young man with the fine white hands; he had to be protected! (She looked like a clucking hen, babbling over him.)'

A feature of the hop picking season was tea and a dance for the pickers, organised by Helen at her house. After a reel, Iso played Liszt's *Hungarian*

Rhapsodies – surely as novel to the pickers as Iso was to hopping – and Hedwig improvised on some folkish pieces. 'Happy we all were on that afternoon. Next day concentrated hopping!' The evenings, though, alone with Helen and maybe a few guests, were devoted to Iso's performances of the major classical and romantic works. There was something of a common bond between Hedwig and Helen, each frustrated by the demands of a home and family and each trying to pursue a serious career – in Helen's case as a painter. With the outbreak of war, Helen had decided she needed to offer concrete help and took in not only the Elinsons but several others too, including an old Welsh schoolmaster who was a protégé of hers. It was not easy: the boiler broke, there were problems with the domestic helps, and feeding everyone was a struggle. She faced the prospect of her husband Max, a surgeon, leaving for France where fierce fighting was expected. But Helen did her level best, trying also to help with getting concerts for Iso. She even suggested approaching the Faversham Cinema, a seemingly incongruous idea. But Iso was not too proud and went along with it, all togged up in his best suit, and proposed pieces like the Chopin Études. Not surprisingly, the manager declined: it was hardly the sort of music that would appeal to his non-highbrow audiences. So, to earn a little extra money, Hedwig turned her hand to making little knick-knacks which she sold in a local shop.

For Hedwig, the world had turned upside down and was spinning. The precarious existence she and Iso had managed to establish looked increasingly imperilled. On top of that, there was her family in Germany. She had no communication with them. 'What does Maertel do?', she wrote in her Diary. The international news was shocking and it was hardly possible for Hedwig not to be preoccupied with the War as she read of many suicides and mass arrests in Germany. She wrote about the SS *Athenia* being sunk off Ireland and the heavy artillery fighting on the Siegfried Line along the western border of Germany within a week of war being declared. She and Iso were glued to the radio, and Hedwig listened to Hitler's two-and-a-half-hour-long tirade against Roosevelt and his peace plan. The first air-raid alarms went off, Marga cried bitterly inside her baby gas mask and clutched her battered teddy, and RAF planes set off, flashing above their heads, to drop 6 million propaganda leaflets over Germany. Germany warned the world it would bomb civilians in Poland. By mid-September the Red Army was on the move against Poland, and another British ship, HMS *Courageous*, was torpedoed and sunk with more than 500 crew. Before the month was out, Warsaw had fallen, Ribbentrop had gone to Moscow for a second time ("Why?" people asked), the U-boat blockade was strengthened, and more and more leaflets were dropped over Germany. Activities intensified and got closer. Planes began to be shot down over the Firth of Forth and the North Sea, and warnings of air attacks were issued in Kent. A first attempt on Hitler's life, in Munich in early November, had failed and not long after, Russia attacked Finland, bombing Helsinki. Events piled up alarmingly; it was difficult to grasp the emerging situation. Hedwig sat as often as possible under the big chestnut tree on the lawn outside the Pages' house, musing on the autumn while Iso and Anna were hopping:

'...early morning white mists, and later in the day a crystal-clear sky, a light rosy sheen over all the shrubs and trees, that nearly-autumn feeling with a slight melancholy tinge. Millions of golden or red leaves blew to the ground...'

Maybe now she was even more aware of what was around her – the beauty of the house and the garden, and the surrounding countryside. She wheeled Marga around the edges of fields, stopping to read Julius Caesar or other English classics, which she adored, finding them a 'gigantic' enrichment to her literary appreciation. She discovered a book on English architecture and mentioned it to Helen, who in response took her and Iso to see Canterbury and its cathedral, and they celebrated the experience in the evening by listening to Iso playing the Goldberg Variations.

In this surreal state, the family started to bed themselves down in Kent, seeing this as a 'lucky interlude' and fully realising how good they had it. They moved all their belongings from the flat and put them into a barn, and their 'dear old Steinway' from Germany was given space in a back room of the house. Iso registered the family with the Kent authorities. They were not yet naturalised and Iso was stateless, having only a Nansen passport. The agent Harold Holt warned Iso to expect concert life gradually to die down now. Hedwig worried interminably. Iso could hardly take any old job; he was entirely bound up with music. But the friends who had stood by them since they had come to England continued to do what they could, engaging Iso for private recitals. Lady Swaythling contacted a music critic to try to interest him in Iso and she arranged with Myra Hess that Iso should take part in her series of daily recitals at the National Gallery – a remarkable institution Hess initiated as her 'contribution to national service' which she kept going throughout the War. The Royal Academy set up 'emergency concerts' and the Wigmore Manager informed Iso that it would now be much cheaper to hire the Hall.

Hedwig found it almost impossible to believe that the distinguished old ladies who had been so supportive of Wigmore concerts such as Iso's cycles would continue through the War. Yet they had to carry on. In constant hope, she and Iso continued their letter writing to conductors, concert organisers, and the BBC, Hedwig trying to improve her English by reading Carlyle on Goethe, dictionary in hand – surely the first and only time Carlyle has been used in that way. Iso insisted that they compose letters together – a difficulty for Hedwig, who took on the lion's share of the exercise. Iso's lack of concern about polishing his English still irritated her from time to time. He focused on reading only The Times leaders, and Hedwig felt that they were still a long way from being able to engage in proper conversation. 'It is not all intuition, Iso. Some grammar surely counts!' But then she pulled herself up. English was a third foreign language for Iso: he had mastered German well, learned basic Spanish quickly (for his South American tour), and now was having to master English. Nonetheless she fretted, also about Iso's appearance. He gave no thought to what he should wear, while she was convinced that impressions counted and that it would help them if they tried as best as they could to fit in with the norms of those around them. All that mattered not a jot to Iso. He continued as the free spirit, almost other-worldly. Apart from music, what counted was being able to earn sufficiently to live their chosen way of life, and so Iso's other contribution was frequently to review their personal finances and to save wherever possible. When Ros Stutchbury said she would like to see him, he simply put on his tennis shoes, stuffed his pockets with apples, and walked the 32 miles to Gayles.

In time, Hedwig received an answer to her question about what Maertel was doing: somehow he managed to get a short note through to say he was working on a farm in Romania, and then, through contacts in Holland, that he had taken up a post in music in Breslau (now Wroclaw in Poland), which had been a considerable economic and cultural centre in the Weimar years. It was a small relief. Breslau was a city that could boast of earlier having had Max Bruch as a conductor of its orchestra, and of being the dedicatee of Brahms' *Akademische Festouvertüre* when he received an honorary doctorate. Nonetheless, Hedwig continued to be deeply troubled, indeed sickened, by the developments in Germany and by Molotov's speeches accusing England and France of 'crimes' as the aggressors. She was convinced that few people would see through the Nazi propaganda. Might she meet this or that person after the War who would by then still not have realised the horrors of Nazi Germany, she wondered? She must too have agonised about where her parents stood in all this. Was she frightened to think about the implications of her father having taken such a senior position in a state institution? None of this did she explore in her Diary, and by this time there is no trace of correspondence with her old schoolfriend Lilo. Nor did she detail how she herself felt about being a German émigrée (she would now have been described formally as a 'friendly enemy alien' – a linguistic masterstroke in the absurd). Possibly, given the long post hoc nature of the Diary, this is simply because she felt it more important to record events. At least they had the comfort of knowing some others in a similar situation, and people in the intimate circles within which they moved were understanding and deeply appreciative of the musical gems she and Iso offered.

Generous as she was, Helen Page could not offer the family a long-term harbour. Teddy Crankshaw came to the rescue, writing warmly to invite Hedwig and Iso to go and stay with his family in Sandhurst in Kent. It was quite an offer; he proposed they go for one to two years. Despite her fears of moving and having to find her way in yet another home and family set-up, Hedwig packed up so they could be with the Crankshaws by Christmas. There was some sadness. Through her walks with Marga, taking Anna to the local school and Sunday school, and having to register with the police, Hedwig had become a familiar figure in Selling and she had warmed to quite a number of the locals. She bade them goodbye, including the tally man from the hop picking. 'How utterly nice they all had been to us foreigners.' As a final thank you to Helen, Hedwig and Iso gave her a farewell concert of Chopin's F minor concerto, Hedwig taking the orchestral part on a second piano.

They set off the next morning. The bus journey from Selling to Sandhurst, where the Crankshaws lived, was an ordeal. Buses were not heated and it was freezing cold – 'a brute of a winter' – the coldest since 1893. Although only thirty miles, the journey took several hours. Anna was ill, and Marga not yet old enough to be happy to sit still for long. Upping sticks is unsettling at the best of times, which these were not. They had not even seen where they were about to reside, but sensed it would be somewhere quite different from the Georgian abode of the Pages with its large adjoining area of hop land. Indeed, the Crankshaws' house was on a hill close to the 14th-century church, and older and smaller with white painted clapboards and a creaky staircase going up through the middle.

The family started to settle in. Iso managed to get some engagements: with the help of the Kilbys, a small series in Bournemouth; offers from the BBC; and a number of private recitals, including for Sir Thomas Bazley, one of Iso's new pupils. Long-standing friends, the Bülow-Jakobsens in Copenhagen, suggested a large private recital. This last one presented some difficulties. Getting a visa was not straightforward, possibly hampered by Iso still being stateless and having only a Nansen passport (it was to be 1947 before he received a passport from the British authorities), flying was too expensive, and going by boat now was risky because there were no convoys. In the end he got his visa and took his chances by boat. Hedwig worried about all their friends and family in Germany, and their musical contacts in Scandinavia, and continued to be struck by the absurd concurrence of war on the one hand, and the hundreds of menial tasks to do with the family and household that demanded her constant attention on the other. Unlike Iso, she did not find it easy constantly to accept the generous offers of hospitality and support that came their way. His view was that since all these benefactors were music lovers, he could give them inexhaustible inspiration and comfort by playing for them. Hers was more nuanced – possibly because she was taking a back seat musically – and she kept thinking that dependence in this way was hardly appropriate for a professor's daughter.

1940

Anyone who has had the opportunity to read Hedwig's Diary and to have met her must surely notice the similarities with the way she traversed a conversation. She raced from one interesting subject to another, assuming the person she was addressing would already have fully digested what she had just said and be ready for something new, despite the number of words and intermediate interjections that provided the added seasoning to whatever was on her mind. The way she described this period in her life in her Diary had a particularly powerful impact on me, conveying with immediacy the big political and war developments and at the same time the War intrusions on daily life and the major unforeseen impacts it had on the family. The transitions from one year to another and even between one week and the next anchored personal and large-scale changes and were significant in charting the course of events and Hedwig's reactions to them. I decided to use them as punctuation marks.

By spring 1940, the general view in Germany was that Hitler would soon invade England. Sea battles raged, and Iso hoped the invasion of Norway might prove to be an end. Hedwig read the book by the exiled left-wing Expressionist playwright Ernst Toller, *I Was a German*. Like Joseph Roth and Stefan Zweig, Toller fled to Belgium in 1933 and then to London, where he had been a neighbour and acquaintance of Hedwig and Iso's. Like them, he left London when war broke out

– though in his case for New York, where he committed suicide in 1939. Toller had felt excluded from the mainstream for most of his life because of being a Jew and he had joined up for service in the First World War to try to demonstrate his nationalism. But his experiences, and the failure of the Bavarian revolution to move to a more Soviet social organisation, led him to become an ardent pacifist with a vision of a classless society based on brotherhood in which art and politics meld together. Hedwig's choice of Toller's book at this time maybe gives an insight into her openness and interest in trying to understand the background to what was going on in Germany, because Toller was a radical political activist of the sort who, in earlier times, Hedwig would most likely have distanced herself from. She did not concentrate on politics though: from somewhere, she picked up a book on Buddhism; she rather liked GB Shaw's thoughts on marriage, and adolescents and their parents; Rousseau's *Confessions* she thought full of conceit – 'Are there any French geniuses who don't suffer from this complaint?!' Years later she would doubtless have answered this question in the positive, as she came so ardently to embrace Debussy's music.

Out of the blue, Iso received a letter from a stranger – in what Hedwig considered to be 'rather an excellent 'academic' handwriting – a little like a gifted bishop'. It said:

"Dear Mr Elinson,

I heard your radio playing of the Bach Preludes and Fugues last night, and admired it very much! I am an old woman of 72 who studied the piano all her life, but I should so much like to conquer all the 48 before I die. Will you help me? Could you come to my cottage to give me some lessons? When you happen to be in London… the train leaves at…

Yours sincerely,

Beatrice Bateson"

This was quite an antidote to the news about Narvik, up in the far north of Norway, which had fallen, and to the dazzling nightly experience of search lights probing their Kent skies when German planes were flying over. Hedwig kept thinking how the morning would bring the gentle and optimistic sight of daffodils while across the country some horrified parents would be hearing the dreaded call of the postman with a telegram informing them of their son's death. Yet, set against such spectres, here was an old woman anxious to study one of the major canons of classical piano. Iso quickly set about arranging the first lesson, and Beatrice came to his Bach recital in St Martin-in-the-Fields. His impression: "A woman who looks rather like the old Goethe. A real personality, who lives in a sweet old baker's cottage, full of art treasures."

Meanwhile, Hedwig and the family started yet again to build the framework of their daily lives. Anna started at the local school. The vicar's wife paid a courtesy visit and after enquiring about Iso's "Russian religion", concluded: "Well, it's all the same." So much for distinct religions! Hedwig, as ever, revelled in the spring flowers and the new countryside; they put her in mind of Mörike's poems. Iso secured engagements at various venues, including solo recitals and a concerto with the BBC, and another series of recitals in Bournemouth. For these, the family took the opportunity to go and stay with the Kilbys and to help with arranging the concerts and selling tickets. The night before the first concert, they were told that the hall where Iso was to perform was needed to station 200 French soldiers. Mrs Kilby immediately thought about the piano – hers – and Avice and Hedwig rushed over with dust sheets before desperately searching for another hall for the concert. Successful, the concert went ahead – listened to also by the French troops. It was fitting that Iso concentrated on Chopin works. The second recital, too, was a 'fine success'. Even Iso's new pupil Beatrice Bateson travelled to hear it and the subsequent concerts.

But the backdrop to all this was a frightening ramping up of war actions. Germany by now was in possession of three-quarters of Norway and had invaded Holland, Luxembourg, and Belgium. Members of the Dutch royal family arrived in the UK just before Holland capitulated. Around Brussels and along a 200-mile front, there were big battles until the Belgian King agreed a peace treaty with Hitler at the end of May. It must have felt very strange to Hedwig, for these were all countries that neighboured Germany, part of her familiar past, countries whose cultures were dear to her. From her 'adopted' country, Churchill oversaw the Dunkirk operation. Italy entered the War on the same day as Marga's fourth birthday. There were daily air-raid warnings in East Kent, where pilots were seen abandoning their planes. Yorkshire was bombed. With the Germans only 40 miles away, Paris too was suffering, and there were battles on the Somme, at Soissons, and Rouen. By 14th June, the Nazis occupied Paris and the majority of the people in the city fled, where possible in vehicles of some sort or another with mattresses and household items strapped to them; others resorted to carts, or simply set off on foot. The newspapers, Hedwig recorded, called it 'the darkest hour England has ever seen'. Maybe she wondered too whether she, Iso, and the girls would ever have to flee in a similar way. Certainties were luxuries now.

Hedwig now noted that most Italians in Britain slipped away or were rounded up, and, with an exclamation mark, that Group C aliens were being interned. This is a strange comment that does not fit with official records: Group C were regarded as no security risk as most were refugees and Jewish. Hedwig makes no mention of having been called before any tribunal to assess her status (their naturalisation papers had still not come through) but she was used to having to register with local police – first in Faversham, then in Sandhurst, and while they were staying with the Kilbys, in Poole – and she said there were many police restrictions. Tensions were growing. The Daily Mail led a campaign to have all aliens in Britain interned and those in work were fearful of losing their jobs. Hedwig heard that Richard Glas, her teacher in Kiel, had been interned on the Isle of Man. She cannot have known, however – few did at the time – that this was not such an uncomfortable situation; stories abound of the intellectual core of the camps – journalists, philosophers, musicians and musicologists, composers, economists, lawyers, artists, scientists, and members of the medical profession drawing on their talents to set up lectures, all sorts of discussion groups, and to perform chamber works.[32] But overall, the initial welcoming spirit in the country for German émigrés dissipated.

Hedwig, for whatever reason, was spared this – maybe because of Iso? Nonetheless, the developments inevitably caused tensions for both of them, exacerbated by their having to converse in English with all their friends and contacts, and heightened even further by their decision now only to speak English at home.

Then came a blow: in the interests of reducing the risk of helping the enemy, Germans were no longer to be allowed to live within ten miles of the coast. It was hard not to panic because the Crankshaws' Sandhurst home was now a prohibited area for Hedwig and Iso. Going back to London was clearly a non-starter. They racked their brains. Hedwig wrote to the stalwart Enid Lindner: was there any place she could think of where the family could live? Before she had had any reply, Beatrice Bateson, quite off her own bat, got in touch with Iso and invited the family to come to live with her in her cottage, provided they could get the necessary permissions. A truly magnanimous offer, even though Beatrice might in time have had to take in other refugees. For her, no one could have been better suited than the Elinsons.

As Hedwig packed up all the family bags yet again, she had little idea of what she was going into. She had at most encountered Mrs Bateson at Iso's concerts. But it was not an offer they could possibly turn down. Nothing else was in sight and Hedwig and Iso were in no position to pay the going rent for a house or flat for the family. While Iso was in London dealing with the residence permits, he used the time for recitals at St Martin's, staying with Lady Swaythling, who again was doing what she could to promote him. Finally, after some furious letter-writing by Iso and the intervention of a Sussex MP, the family was granted permission to reside in West Chiltington. By late June, all the necessary arrangements were in place, and the family travelled down to Beatrice Bateson's Mill House.

Mill House was full to overflowing with character and immediately felt just right. Beatrice's music room, once the bakery, housed her grand piano. Like the living room, it looked out onto the elongated garden which was filled with aromatic herbs and colourful flowers and housed a greenhouse that Beatrice tended several times a day. As she walked in, Hedwig was staggered – her word – by the treasures in front of her: William Blake's '*Satan exulting over Eve*' hanging above the sofa (it is now in the Tate Gallery), and his illustrations for Dante's *The Divine Comedy* and *The Book of Job* (though Hedwig preferred his poems); drawings by Tiepolo; a beautiful landscape by John Cotman, an English marine and landscape painter and leading member of the Norwich school; an etching by Rembrandt of his mother; prints of woodcuts by Hokusai and coloured prints by Hiroshige; 'and the drawers and ship's captain's chest stuffed with lovely embroideries and exotic costumes', all collected by Beatrice's husband William, a Cambridge professor who had pioneered the term 'genetics' to describe heredity and who championed Mendel's theories. Hedwig was ecstatic. Maybe it produced a small echo in her mind of places she had stayed in in Germany.

All this might convey the sense of a large country mansion, and indeed that was what I had expected after reading the Diary. Not at all. When I went down to West Chiltington to see where the Elinsons had lived throughout the War, what struck me was how the family and Beatrice, and Dorothy the housekeeper, must have got on top of one another. The rooms are cosy and modest rather than grand and imposing, and given its central staircase, there is no way of moving around without jostling against others in the house. It is rather remarkable that the constructed living together of strangers worked out so well. Partly that must have been down to Beatrice's enormous good will, the musical gifts that Iso and Hedwig offered, and, for all of them, the inescapable awareness of war and encroaching danger. Quite quickly, daily routines were established once Hedwig had unpacked the nine cases that arrived from Kent, though I wondered how they fitted everything in, since the attic, where they were mainly quartered, was not large. Anna and Marga soon learnt about Beatrice's Victorian rules, and everyone got used to simple and economical meals that, to Hedwig's delight, were usually improved by a generous addition of fresh garden herbs. Hedwig and Beatrice would walk together through the surrounding countryside, enjoy the lilac regalia pelargoniums in the garden, and pick sweet peas and fruit. Hedwig loved too being able to walk on her own – 'my greatest rest' – while the

Mill House, West Chiltington.
Photograph reproduced with kind permission of Chris, Elaine and Harri Hunt

children were having their post-lunch nap. To her reading list she now added Blake, Shelley, and Butler's *Way of All Flesh*, Gilchrist's *Rossetti*, and Albert Schweitzer's *From My Life*, inspired probably by having heard personal anecdotes about him from Marga Deneke. Iso secreted himself away in the music room to practise while rooms were tidied and dusted. Beatrice took the bus to the shops and was diligent in working on her preludes and fugues every day. From time to time, Hedwig played too. She was touched by Beatrice's comments lamenting that she could not play more: 'It's so unjust, Hedwig! You are so gifted.'

This then was their new base – at least for the initial duration of their permit. And although all the signs were that the War would last a long time, Hedwig and Iso thought too about their longer-term future. Hedwig wanted to settle down before too long, in their own place. Iso thought about writing to his pianist acquaintance from Berlin, Rudolf Serkin, who was now in the USA, and to his contact in Palestine. Might there be an opening in Canada? he pondered. Adrian Boult wrote to say that once their naturalisation papers came through, there might be a teaching post somewhere. But the processes leading to naturalisation had been put on hold. A range of options, therefore? Not really. Their own experience of the last seven years had well shown them how long it takes to build up even a small reputation, let alone to use that both to satisfy artistic needs and to provide an adequate living for the family. The best possibility, if at the moment unrealistic and out of their hands, was indeed the teaching positions mentioned by Adrian Boult.

It was on reaching this point in the story, as I read the Diary for the first time, that I came across an entry that literally produced an immediate sense of panic, for Hedwig wrote – after only a month with Beatrice Bateson: 'Today I 'undid' the Blake out of its glass'. How *could* she have dared to do such a thing? I asked myself. How on earth would Beatrice Bateson react to such a heinous act? Was there – underneath all I had come to know about Hedwig and contrary to my understanding of her – something I had not perceived or experienced, some trace of disrespect? I need not have worried. It was the War making itself felt very directly: a bomb had exploded in a field very near Mill House and had caused all the windows to rattle frighteningly. They were worried that any similar incident could cause debris to splinter the glass and damage the painting. 'So 'Satan exulting over Eve' now lies flat in a folder!' No bomb came, but soon afterwards, while having tea with Beatrice Bateson and Jelly d'Aranyi, they all heard an air fight followed by machine gun fire from just behind the mill; a parachute floated down towards the Downs.

This was a time of many mass raids across the country, with a record 78 enemy planes shot down one day in mid-August, and night raids over London aimed at hospitals, schools and museums as well as strategic targets. The East End suffered most and survivors had to seek new accommodation. There were huge fires on both sides of the Thames. Even nearby Eastbourne was hit. Near Mill House, the sight and sound of anti-aircraft guns became more frequent. 'We all sleep much less now but much more than Londoners.' Churchill reported 90,000 men wounded or missing, and warned of an invasion, but thought Britain's air position was cause for 'great pride and hope', given that Germany had lost over a thousand planes in the three months up to September 1940. News of some of their friends came through: Janet Brooke, who helped to arrange concerts for Iso in her London flat and had started on the task of helping them with naturalisation, had had her flat bombed; Henry Moore was working all day at a munitions factory.

Hedwig now read Irmgard Litten's book.[33] Litten's son Hans had been tortured by the Nazis because he had represented some of their opponents in court and had subpoenaed Hitler to appear as a witness in 1931. Hans was a steely and incisive barrister and was courageous enough to cross-examine Hitler sharply to reveal the direct link between Hitler and the campaign of using violence against Nazi enemies. The book was published in 1940 and included an epilogue urging America to confront the threat of Nazi Germany. Juxtaposed in Hedwig's diary with the mention of this book is almost a cri de coeur: 'I think of my father and what they all might be doing.' Recently I saw a stage adaptation of Litten's book at the Chichester Festival Theatre.[34] It struck me powerfully – the strength found by son and mother individually to call out wrongnesses – but ultimately they were crushed, with nothing left except a small legacy to today's historians and theatregoers.

All this could not but have an impact on the Elinson family. Stresses developed as Iso continued to hunt openings for concerts, but the lull in engagements over the summer got him down and he became moody. Hedwig felt she was getting on his nerves, and he threatened to go and live in London – though she dismissed it as probably reflecting his way of getting out of having to go to a dentist. She struggled with constant tiredness and had the occasional weep.

Iso did continue to secure concerts, however, from St Martin-in-the-Fields to the local Chanctonbury Music Club. A glowing review said Iso was among the greatest Liszt players in Europe, an echo of Glazunov's early judgement in St Petersburg. The BBC in Bristol and Harold Holt invited him to play the Chopin Études in a live broadcast in the near future. He joined Adila Fachiri, grand-niece of Joachim and sister of

Jelly d'Aranyi, in a charity concert, and his seventh London recital of Chopin works was due. Most pleasing to Hedwig, though, were some unexpected openings for her too: through Beatrice, she and Iso got to know Roy Armstrong, a powerful figure in the Workers Educational Association, who thought there was a local appetite for *both* of them to explain music to audiences as well as to perform. As part of these, a Mrs Hanbury-Aggs invited them to give a series of 20 lecture recitals at her home, Little Thakeham. 'This seems wonderful and I look forward to work with Iso so much!' It helped their overall togetherness: 'Iso is now particularly nice to me since we started our lecture recitals.' And at long last, Hedwig started to feel that she was really doing something other than just being a wife and mother – and helping Beatrice in the house. She was indescribably grateful to Beatrice for sharing her home and treasures with them so completely, but she still struggled with always being the recipient of good will and generosity when their only way of paying back kindnesses was through music. It was largely Hedwig who filled the lecture part of recitals. Iso regarded it as enough that he played. The fact that she was German and still spoke with a distinctive German accent seemed not to arouse any antagonism at all; audiences warmed to her, rather. Indeed, she said: 'according to reports, how different was the position of German-born people in the First World War', though as we now know and as Daniel Snowman relates,[35] it was far from an experience shared by all émigrés. It was surely Hedwig's innate ability to connect with people, her deftness in establishing links between seemingly disparate phenomena, her humour, and the immediate sense she gave to people of her love of music and her desire to share it, that won over audiences and acquaintances. For Anna, however, exposed to other circles and children, there was not an undiluted embrace. She felt excluded at school – in part because of her German mother.

In their West Chiltington world, things were looking up for Hedwig and Iso in other ways too. Most important was that a new Bateson piano arrived in time for Hedwig's birthday, celebrated with home performances of works for two pianos. Beatrice was happy to accommodate their desire to make her music room look more professional and Hedwig took on her first private pupil. 'After all,' she said, 'this was and is my job.' Growing numbers of people were coming to their lecture recitals, and word about them was getting around. Beatrice was enjoying having the family with her and set about embroidering a piano cover for them with all the Bach 48 fugue themes on it. It was hardly surprising that Hedwig, for one, hoped that their long-term future could be in England.

The summer of 1940 moved into autumn. Outside their immediate Mill House world, bombing continued in the Sussex countryside and raids on London were relentless; Greece had effectively entered the War; many English merchant ships were lost plying the US-UK routes; just a few minutes too late, the RAF had bombed a Munich beer hall where Hitler had been celebrating the anniversary of his 1923 putsch; and Molotov went to Berlin for German-Soviet Axis talks. Hedwig wondered what on earth might happen next and thought it significant enough to mention in her Diary that Chamberlain had died.

It was at the end of November that Iso left for Bristol to do his broadcast of the Chopin Études. Hedwig and the girls, and no doubt Beatrice, sat in front of the radio at Mill House to listen. Iso started playing. What they did not hear was that after the first few pieces, someone entered the studio and whispered to Iso that the house opposite had just been bombed. Iso continued. Ten minutes later the messenger was back to say the furniture stores were on fire. But Iso was not going to let this opportunity be spoilt, nor disappoint his listeners. He finished the broadcast – with poetry and passion, as Hedwig put it – and only then did he join the BBC staff in the cellar, where he was given the most admiring of receptions. This was the first blitz on Bristol, aimed at destroying the Bristol Aeroplane Works. Everyone waited for the all-clear. That didn't come for six hours, well into the night, when Iso staggered back to his hotel. Except… Wine Street and his hotel had been wiped out in the raid. Gone were his favourite jumper and night things. What he really cared about, though, was his large valuable Mikuli[a] volume of Chopin – crammed with all his markings, in Russian;

---

a   Karol Mikuli was a student of Chopin's and made detailed notes of his lessons as well as editing Chopin's piano music. He was therefore regarded by many – and by Iso too – as the primary authority on Chopin. *Wikipedia, 19.01.2020.*

fortuitously, he had taken that with him to the BBC. Unhesitatingly Iso decided the most sensible thing to do was to make for the station, and clutched his beloved Mikuli as he struggled through the streets of Bristol, trying to find his way along unknown and unrecognisable streets and, where he could, avoiding the areas that were burning. It was not possible to bypass them completely, though, and on his way he lent a hand with the rescue operations, grabbing a hosepipe to help to put out the fires. After that he calmly boarded a train that would take him back to Sussex. When she heard the story, Hedwig could hardly believe it. 'The playing was serene and controlled; even the girls had listened attentively.'

1941

This surreal way of life continued in 1941 with war impacts near and far. Severe rationing was introduced – only two ounces of butter and cheese a week and no biscuits or chocolates. At Mill House, the pattern of day-to-day household life was interspersed with practising, lecture recitals, private pupils and concerts. Iso broadcast more Chopin, prompting people who had heard it to stop Hedwig in the street. Harold Holt wrote: "I've never heard such fine Chopin, Iso." And the series of lecture recitals hosted by the Aggs at Little Thakeham was well underway. As I went about visiting some of the houses that had been homes for the Elinsons, I tried to go to see Little Thakeham too, but could not get hold of the current owners. From pictures, though, it is a magnificent large Grade I-listed Arts and Crafts house that nestles on the edge of the South Downs. Designed by Sir Edward Lutyens, it was modelled on Elizabethan country houses, and he considered it to be "the best of the bunch" of all his houses. Sadly it is not open to the public. It looks wonderfully inviting, built in gentle honey-coloured Cotswold stone with striking top-to-bottom stone-mullioned windows in a large central hall and a musicians' gallery on the first floor. Anna described Little Thakeham as a child's paradise because of its countless rooms and endless staircases and corridors, its rocking horse,

A lecture-recital venue: Little Thakeham, West Sussex.
Reproduced with kind permission of ©Peter Wright Photographer

and the extensive gardens that so lent themselves to games needing secret places. The Aggs' grand piano fitted perfectly into the dramatic space of the hall. What better setting for intimate music-making? Hedwig and Iso devoted at least one lecture recital to the Bach *Goldberg Variations* ('How well one has to know them, to love them fully,' Hedwig commented). On occasion, they had the offer of two pianos that they used to play concertos, sometimes performing two or three in just one recital. Concerts here ended as elsewhere, with a cup of tea and a bun.

Despite all that was going on, Hedwig still somehow managed to carve out time for reading, turning now to Tolstoy's *War and Peace*, which she loved ('but not his appendix'). Maybe she was drawn to it in part because of the story about Iso's father having met Tolstoy in a railway carriage. And maybe it seemed particularly topical for her now when she was forced to think about war: how this one had come about, and about people's roles in it. Fritz? Maertel? There is nothing more that can be said about them at this point.

Such routines as they had were about to be shattered. Beatrice Bateson had a stroke, affecting all of her left side and subsequently – probably as the result of another stroke – her right. Hedwig and Iso's local lecture recitals, for the first time, did not include Beatrice in the front row wearing a large hat and fur collar and 'surveying the scene like an ancient proud eagle'. It was not long before Hedwig was repaying Beatrice's generosity in a way none of them could have foreseen: by looking after her, which included feeding her, reading to her, dealing with incontinence and changing her bedding, sometimes getting her out of bed and turning her (which required strength because she was very large), and comforting her when she became disorientated. The housekeeper Dorothy helped as well, and a nurse who came in regularly. But most of the burden lay on Hedwig's shoulders. From the way she wrote about it, Hedwig had no qualms or reservations. It was indeed a development that she had not, could not have, anticipated but she took it on wholeheartedly and sympathetically. One sad and irresolvable problem did crop up, however: Beatrice's urgent wish that Iso and Hedwig play for her. There was no way. The staircase was far too narrow; not even an upright could be got up it.

Looking ahead, the situation begged the question of what would happen to them if Beatrice did not pull through, an increasingly likely prospect. When Lady Barlow, granddaughter of Charles Darwin and a great friend of Beatrice and executor of her will, came to stay for a few days, Hedwig must have shared her worries. They were short-lived. Beatrice arranged that Hedwig could sign cheques for necessary expenditure. Not only that, she made provision for the family to stay on at Mill House for the duration of the War, together with Dorothy and Giggle the gardener (whose name was pronounced Jiggle), both of whom would be paid for. 'A noble deed', wrote Hedwig. She and Iso must have made their way into Beatrice's heart.

Beatrice deteriorated over the next weeks and Hedwig's life was more or less completely taken over with caring for her. Hedwig felt she needed to write detailed letters to Beatrice's son Gregory in the USA, whose wife – the anthropologist Margaret Mead – had visited Mill House just a few months previously. It was Mead, as it happens, who exactly at this time was putting forward pivotal ideas about how the American 'democratic character structure' could be a model for German re-education and global citizenship, an idea that took hold during the US Occupation with its emphasis on the role of literature, film and the media in transforming the German psyche.[36] Hedwig also contacted Hermia, Beatrice's sister, who came to visit. The War still felt very close. When she walked Hermia back to her lodgings, the sky was lit up by German flaming onions,[a] and Canadian and Polish military vehicles from the stations around West Chiltington sped by them on the small road.

As the weeks went by, the demands of looking after Beatrice became too much. Hedwig and Dorothy were utterly exhausted and felt they could cope no longer. Hedwig took the decision – for there was no one else to do so – that Beatrice go to a nursing home. She now wrote daily reports to Hermia and slept fully clothed so that she was ready to do whatever was needed at any time. When the ambulance finally came, Beatrice was desperately unhappy and wept. Hedwig felt dreadful. But she also felt

---

a   A German revolving-barrel anti-aircraft gun.

relief at losing the burden of being the person primarily responsible for Beatrice. From then on, the family visited her every day.

It was high time, after these intense months, to return to the business of correspondence and arranging recitals and concerts. Anna and Marga went to stay with Octavia Adler at her house, Kings and Princes, just down the road, where they enjoyed petting the horses in the stable and chatting as best as was possible with the toothless gardener, a figure of some enjoyment for the girls. Hedwig concentrated on practising the Brahms *Variations on a Theme by Haydn* for two pianos between the basic household chores. The sudden quietness, without the girls, was almost disturbing, fractured only at odd times when Hedwig's frustration with Iso bubbled over for some reason or other; then she shouted. The period of respite was short-lived, however. Beatrice insisted she go home after only three weeks in the nursing home. Iso took refuge and slept in the music room, which was about as far away as he could get; he had to prepare new programmes of all the Bach 48 Preludes and Fugues, as well as the 32 Beethoven sonatas. The turbulence affected him a lot but he at least got away for his concerts. Hedwig, on the other hand, felt she was being pulled from all sides: Iso, the girls, Beatrice and all that was entailed in caring for her, managing the house and garden and Dorothy and Giggle, her own practising, and the lecture recitals. Gregory did not write very often and Hedwig was pretty much alone in shouldering all the responsibilities. Not surprisingly, sleep proved elusive.

Hedwig wrote about Beatrice's dying which was now, ten days after coming home, in the late stages, and then about her death. It is a poignant description and tells us a great deal about Hedwig and her empathetic nature:

'April 2nd, Good Friday: Here I sit in her bedroom reading and looking at her who is dying. She looks young and peaceful, her pulse still throbbing. The kind Irish nurse has gone to Mass, and Iso took Anna and Marga to church! His idea. He means so well. Yet I find it not easy to take his moods when his great sensitivity is stirred. For five days dear Beatrice has been sinking; a hundred times did she beg for water and focussed only vaguely. This morning at 6 am the nurse called me; she thought death had come. Her fighting stage now – throwing off bedclothes – before Iso – was tragic and upsetting. Hermia sits in the room, looking even more ill. I sit in this cosy room and the slow dying has no sting for me: coming into the world is so often a struggle, for a baby or a mother! (What I hang on to most in life are the marvellous works of Art which one has to leave behind: Bach and Goya and Rembrandt and Renoir's child-portraits and the early Italians – and Debussy and Bach, Hugo Wolf and Mozart and the marble reliefs in Greece and Italy and Verona, the grey-green olives of Italy – and a black cat seen against a bright-green English lawn! Oh how lovely.) Hermia forces her thoughts to practical matters – she has to. But we are so young!

'The Nazis made their onslaught on Belgrade, Yugoslavia. Thessaloniki and then Greece has fallen to them. The war theatre is much bigger, and now includes Hungary. The lovely moon-nights are made for swarms of planes and the noise of the Coastal Command is terrifying (only 7–9 miles away). "Blood and tears" says Churchill. Again, I miss the children though their departure quietened my nerves. While observing Mrs. B, I am sewing two gay little aprons for them. I do so much hope they will not witness a big War. I read E Forster's Howard's End; it is thought-provoking.

'Iso's birthday (he is 36!) falls on Easter 1941. Sunday today. A subdued occasion. Easter flowers out: daffodils, bright blue scillas, anemonis (so multi-coloured-gay) and most buds are nearly open – the finest state! … Her breath often stops; colour quite grey. Anna and Marga were in church with us; they behaved quietly though the bad singing of Psalm tunes mildly surprised them! The Montefiores[a] had a grievous blow: their little son (11)

a Earlier entry from Hedwig's diary: 'The family Sebag Montefiore showed much interest in Iso's music – and later, in the War, they became tenants of Rosamond at Gayles and we got nearer to Violet, her husband John and children (there were recitals for them or scholars when everybody roamed in the garden afterwards).'

died in Canada, the first casualty of evacuated children there. (He was with an uncle and got run over.)

'15 April: Dear Beatrice Bateson died on Easter Sunday at 9.55 in the evening; on Iso's birthday. For a full 4 days she was not conscious… only the left arm moved a very little to and fro… Now her (alas, so slender) body lies under the white linen. (I had helped the pious Irish nurse with the last "washing".) The change which takes place in a face after death is almost frightening… We all went to bed after midnight, I so grateful that Hermia was still there… We are all deeply thankful that this bitter fight is over… The next morning was spent with the men who talk about "velvet, in mauve" etc (cremation) and waiting until Dr Venables had filled in his forms. (He is very kind and slow.) Anna and Marga said a prayer but then went sent on their business at 'Kings and Princes' without any fuss. Soon they'll come here!

'Life goes on: the most utilitarian jobs have to be done! Cleaning rooms, sorting out (I shall try to do things in an orderly way, in future!). Today it is beautiful, and there is no lecture recital. Tulips are coming out, big ones, and little 'chic' stripey ones in white and light red. The son Bateson must have a really long letter, I feel (even if he does not think so!).

'April 16th: Goacher, the taxi, drove us to Brighton through all the ugly little back streets with (deaf!) Hermia telling us again many funny stories of their childhood. So to the ugly modern chapel where cremations occur… Iso tried to make the big harmonium sound as if it were noble. He played a Chorale and the C major Bach, Book I and the C# minor Prelude and Fugue (the great one, with three themes and five parts). Hermia, old Mrs Daykins and we were the only ones present when the simple coffin disappeared behind a curtain.

'That night the air activity was terrible. I took Hermia to her lovely hostess in a neighbouring village: so much traffic of troops – tanks – and she in the middle of the lane, again! The sky gold-red with fireworks (of a kind) and with goldlit 'onions'… Hermia noticed them and squeezed my arm like in a grip of iron. (She chooses now to tell me about Darwin!) German Radio claims they are in Belgrade (a horrible war).

'Next day Anna and Marga come back (I clean like mad). Gregory sent us a warm telegram (good). Our Fittleworth concerts start soon.

'We are now living at the Mill House – without our very loud hostess Beatrice Bateson. A strange feeling, at first. To look after her good things [Art] – the valuables, and keep them well – is an honourable job. Also to be trusted like this is unique.

'The garden blazes with hundreds of yellow daffodils. Anna and Marga hop in the garden, Giggle is so nice to them. Iso is not too well. These past months affected him much.'

What an extraordinary situation for Hedwig: to have been taken in by someone who up to that point had known only Iso's piano playing and had a couple of lessons with him; then made from the outset to feel totally welcome and to be part of the community in a village they had never heard of; within a short time to have nursed their benefactor throughout her last months in the most intimate way, and in the most devoted manner conceivable; and now to be able to continue living in her house, with much provided for, for the duration of the War and charged with taking care of the art treasures, and the house and garden.

It is one thing to have financial benefactors. Of a quite different order is someone who opens themselves, their home and their life to help you. In this, Beatrice stood apart from all who held out their hands to Hedwig and Iso.

TEN

MORE WAR, MORE CONCERTS, AND YET
ANOTHER BEGINNING

The War was in its second year. Sussex was proving a haven for the Elinsons, as it had for a number of artists before them who found the countryside, cheap rents, and good railway links to London an appealing combination. Small communities of artists began to grow, notably including the artist Ivon Hitchens, the composers John Ireland and Arnold Bax, and the poet Hillaire Belloc. Whether or not that had been a factor leading Beatrice Bateson and her husband William to choose West Chiltington, the area certainly provided a congenial environment for the itinerant Elinsons, even if they did not have many dealings with most of the other artists. The focus for Iso had to be London and wherever else he could perform, and for Hedwig – who was still occupied mainly with looking after the girls – there was the pull and comfort of Gayles not too far away. Nonetheless, the Workers Educational Association lecture recitals and the relationships with Roy and Sheila Armstrong became central. There were many visits to Highover, the family home that Roy had built himself over a number of years. As they looked out at the spectacular views over the South Downs, Iso (but never Hedwig) would play for everyone on the grand piano. Then they would head out into the rather wild garden, pottering languidly round the small lake that Roy had constructed and

16 May 1941

Messing about on the water: the Elinson family (left-hand punt) at
Roy and Sheila Armstrong's
Photograph reproduced with kind permission of Jean and Ian Macwhirter

taking picnics in Roy's various self-made punts and boats up and down the
stream. Lyn Birtles, the housekeeper and Roy's secretary, was always there
too. She sparked with Hedwig. It was to be a lifelong friendship – later
pursued through prodigiously long and frequent letters. Even though she
was a communist and not always very tolerant of others' ideas, and with
no great love for music, she and Hedwig shared a love of literature and the
arts, and she had a robustly independent attitude to life. Talented, albeit
with no formal training, Lyn was confident enough and had the chutzpah
to give lectures and write knowledgeable articles on art.

There was a hearty appetite for Hedwig and Iso's lecture-recitals,
which must have provided a welcome escape from the news of the War.
People other than the Aggs also loved opening their homes for audiences
to come and listen. Just a few miles away from Mill House, in the beautiful
Georgian Fittleworth House, lived the Du Cane sisters with their brother,
'the old Mr Du Cane'. It was an eccentric family, and an eccentric set-up,
as I discovered from the current owners. Old Mr Du Cane had suffered
from shell shock in the First World War and was allocated rooms at the
side of the house, whereas the 'senior' sister (probably the one who had

Fittleworth House.
Photograph courtesy of Mark Saunders.

been a Lady's Maid to the Queen) resided in the main part of the house on the first floor; the other sister had her rooms in the attic. It was just the sort of setting that tickled Hedwig:

'Recital in graceful Fittleworth House. The Du Cane sisters now appear regularly in our life. 100 people. The silver gleams still, in spite of the War. They keep their hats on. They ought to be exhibited: half birds on them, at least the feathers! Iso and Mr Sala[a] played Brahms and Beethoven sonatas to a well-dressed, understated south of England public. They don't make much noise. Old Mr Du Cane in knickerbockers, Mrs Aggs from Little Thakeham, wagging like a type of bird, the musical Dr Venables who had looked after Beatrice.'

---

a   Antoni Sala, a Spanish cellist. Whether he too lived locally, and whether Iso had met him previously, I do not know. While in his teens, Sala had been appointed cellist to the Court at Madrid. He was considered one of the great players of this time and played with John Ireland and Gerald Moore.

These events are still vivid in Anna's memories – not the concerts themselves, but rather outside the splendid concert room playing on the lawn under its magnificent sprawling cedar, while:

'...we 'dealt' with Brahms Paganini Variations and Schumann. Among our listeners is the man who designed the 8-cornered threepenny pieces, and Martin Armstrong the writer, and his clever American wife... Tea at the Du Canes: impeccable house and style – like in an old English comedy of manners but without little obscenities! Home-made jam scones, old silver, maids with caps (still). Yet they do value and must open their house in all weathers. Every week each sister sits there in a different hat: real compositions with ribbons or feathers. One of them followed an English composer to Russia once!'

Fittleworth and Little Thakeham were recital places. But Gayles was very much a place for friendship, like Highover. Things were about to change dramatically for Ros, however. On one occasion when Iso and Hedwig were visiting, they looked out of the window of the garage flat. Something was clearly amiss: 'a sudden darkening of the sky', wrote Hedwig. Mervyn had suffered a heart attack, probably brought on by a bee sting. His death, and the War, spelled the end of happy music-making at Gayles. Ros was no longer flush with money, and the threat of invasion and Gayles' location on the cliffs led the RAF to requisition the house, outbuildings, and land in order to construct an emergency airfield. Ros's brother-in-law, Edward Maufe, lent her a primitive cottage. Ros was forced to adapt her lifestyle accordingly. At least she was still close enough for Iso, Hedwig and the girls to visit.

While Hedwig and Iso were not as close to Frances Dakyns as Ros, that friendship grew too. Frances came to some of their recitals and invited them over to her Elizabethan cottage. What struck Hedwig about that was not its age so much as Frances' indulgence of having swallows *in* the upper bedroom, the smell of sour milk throughout the house, and the masses of programmes and cuttings scattered across the grand piano. Frances would read letters from Adolf Busch and Rudolf Serkin to them, and share the latest on her dealings with John Christie in getting the Glyndebourne Opera off the ground.

On 22nd June, Hedwig was overcome by the news that Hitler had invaded Russia:

'All further news by the German High Command must be accepted with suspicion, we feel. It said: They occupied Minsk and destroyed 400 Russian planes (against 141 of their own). A front of 1500 miles.'

Iso himself was moved to write in one of the Boots diaries:

'I always knew that pacts, and agreements, or eternal friendship which Hitler concludes have only one meaning: Damnation. He enslaved many nations, but Russia will destroy this dirty Satan, murderer of hundreds of thousands of human souls, nay, millions. Through Russia's resistance, Great Britain and the USA will gain time, Nazism will be over in 3 years. My broadcast is the last 3 Beethoven sonatas...'

'So it was for Iso,' wrote Hedwig. 'He was as though lit-up when he said this!' Each of them was preoccupied, thinking about their families back in Germany and Russia.

Through Mrs Aggs at Little Thakeham, the next venue for lecture-recitals was the Deanery in Chichester, and Hedwig was clearly pleased by the way in which the Dean spoke also of her when he announced the season ('my Mama would like that!'). The concerts took place in a large room. As more people arrived, the Dean's not-so-young wife gave up her chair and sat on the carpet. Hedwig could not believe it: 'This could not happen in Germany! Complete informality reigns, the huge carpet full of dust.' Audiences there were soon up to around a hundred people, including airmen. Although it was a struggle to get to Chichester from West Chiltington – several buses – and to get themselves looking decent, Hedwig was pleased to be earning.

Altogether they now had five lecture recitals a week, and as soon as one series at Fittleworth House ended, the Du Canes asked for another. Hedwig was being asked to take on more private pupils. It all meant less time for concentrated reading, taking advantage of the Bateson library, 'but after War and Peace I do not mind. I admire it very very much...'

Iso's reputation was growing. Earlier in the year Harold Holt had arranged for him to play the Chopin F minor concerto at the Queen's Hall, London's principal concert venue. Intense bombing had forced the Hall to close in September, but now Iso was offered the opportunity to appear with the London Philharmonic Orchestra at the Royal Albert Hall. There were recitals with Jelly d'Aranyi and more broadcasts. In addition to the lecture recitals, Hedwig was managing steadily to build up her solo concerts – even if they were still few in number compared to Iso's and in much less prestigious venues. The composer Arnold Bax, who lived nearby and who Hedwig and Iso would often meet on the station platform on their way up to London, dedicated his *Burlesque* to Iso and gave him a "special" composition: *In a Vodka Shop*, from his Russian Suite. And Arnold Haskell, the ballet critic – who, with Ninette de Valois, was influential in founding the Royal Ballet School – and the writer Martin Armstrong each dedicated books to Iso (though quite what led to these two latter dedications is unclear to me). With all the concerts, ongoing financial support from the Linders and various little windfalls, Hedwig and Iso were now able to savour their achievement of putting aside £1000. It felt like a major milestone, given that they had arrived in England ten years previously with next to nothing.

On the domestic front, Lyn Birtles and their Bournemouth friends Ruth and Avice Kilby came often to visit, each helping by looking after the girls from time to time so as to enable Hedwig to take on a little more. Managing the rations was difficult: 'one sometimes longs for an egg, or some fish... but real complaints would be so silly and bad'. Apart from looking after the girls and the house, she still needed to manage much of Iso's non-performing life. That extended from writing letters to accompanying him to the hairdresser, deciding what sort of clothes would be suitable for whatever function and going with him to buy them, and packing for him when he went away for concerts, which was increasingly the case. In a sense she felt alone. Her friends could not fully understand what it was like to be married to someone driven to perform and fixated on a career, as Iso was. But Hedwig was sensitive, never pushing him.

> 'I am not the elegant worldly-wise artist's wife, full of burning ambitions. No! Others can not understand the tension which living so near such a gifted man means... we have 'only' music, and so far good health, good children and very good friends to fall back on. It is much.'

Towards the end of the year Hedwig started to feel decidedly unwell. She would have to consult a doctor. What, she asked herself, if she were pregnant? An Opus 3 would be so unsuitable and make enormous inroads on her precious time and energy, to say nothing of the additional costs, and the fact that it would take her away from the joint lecture recitals. Iso was uncomfortable talking about the possibility. As usual, he wanted to concentrate only on his music. And after all, his mother had had ten children! Hedwig was left to worry on her own.

On the war front, developments were physically distant: there had been no planes over their part of Sussex for many months of the year. The big set-back in December was the Japanese attack on Pearl Harbour. But of more direct interest to Hedwig and Iso, the Russians had recaptured many villages and towns, and the German army was even in retreat in some places. There was fierce fighting near Moscow, the Russians had raided Berlin, and the British had relieved the Axis siege of Tobruk that had started in April. In response, Hitler appointed himself Commander-in-Chief of the German Army. The destruction in so many places caused Hedwig to say she wanted now to read 'serene' literature, rather than Dostoyevsky's *The Idiot*, which, after getting through the first couple of hundred pages, had upset her; Iso on the other hand continued to consider it as the greatest of all books.

We have lingered in 1941, and I considered whether to abridge Hedwig's account of the following years of the War. It is, in some ways, more of the same: Anna's and Marga's growing up, concerts, friends, thoughts about money and the future interspersed with notes about battles, numbers of people killed, and big political moves. And yet I felt I couldn't give a full enough picture of Hedwig without recounting these next 3–4 years in some detail. After all, she and Iso were exposed to the horrors, with the added distress of knowing on the one hand that Hedwig's home country was the despicable aggressor, and on the other, that Russia was in turmoil and torment. At least there had been a reassuring message through the Red Cross in Geneva: 25 words from Gretel saying all were alive, Maertel was still making music, and they liked having Iso and Hedwig's news. About Iso's family, however, there was only silence. It is inconceivable that all these events did not have a profound effect on Hedwig – witness her noting of so many of the staging posts in the War. And no doubt she was selective in deciding what to mention, most likely reflecting those things that made the greatest impact on her, so they too contribute to the story. I decided to continue year by year.

————

1942

The year started wholly unexpectedly. In the first week, Hedwig had a sudden miscarriage. Her reflections on what an Op. 3 might mean had been well founded:

'After a deadly tiring Chichester lecture, Roy took us home in his very old car. It started with a pain at 10.45pm and went on all night (and we were very amateurish about it as we resolved to keep it from the old maidish Dorothy). Iso tried his best, running around. When I nearly fainted 3 times, he offered me a glass of cold water. I thought that magnificent of him. I telephoned our elderly doctor near midnight. He said: "I'll call tomorrow." He came at 1pm and confirmed a miscarriage in the third month. Iso tackled the Thakeham lecture alone. I thanked him again profusely for the cold water! I know he does not like medical things… The nice village nurse attended me. Three days in bed. I direct the children what to do and how. Anna very goodhearted and clever in this situation (she is older). Marga naturally does not understand and refuses even biscuits with her tea. Lyn and Octavia spoil me (women are very kind). Dorothy's face is often as red as Falstaff's! (nerves). Iso, the dear, with his white unblemished lovely hands, fries potatoes and onions for supper and declares it to be "excellent!" Yes! (He sleeps all right at night!) Many lectures to do.'

The three days stretched into a week, and given the immediacy of the miscarriage, Hedwig used it to read and spend some time thinking about the 'soul'. The Roman Catholic belief about when a human life begins seemed to her arbitrary, and she noted that in the letters Bartók wrote in his early twenties, he had been excited about the soul – after which he abandoned Catholicism. She asked herself from what point in the development of a human being it should be regarded as having a 'soul'. Although she and Iso had had the girls christened – the conventional practice at the time – Hedwig was not an ardent follower of any faith, and she wrote of 'a tense atmosphere!' when she accompanied an amateur singer at Storrington Abbey during Warship Week through verses about colours and the Bible's association of black with sin, white with innocence, and gold with heaven.

Back on her feet, the lecture recitals continued: 39 of them focused on Bach's 48 Preludes and Fugues, and the 32 piano sonatas of Beethoven. Chichester was top of Hedwig's list in terms of enjoyment, because the audiences included young people. 'In the so-called 'genteel' houses, the older people are glad to listen and don't want to discuss things so much. They need prodding.' There was a considerable overhead in giving the lectures: not only all the preparation, which fell largely to Hedwig, but also reading essays afterwards, which grew to be tedious. There were one or two unexpected side entertainments though: Jomo Kenyatta came to many of their recitals – always with his silver-knobbed walking stick – encouraged to attend, no doubt, by Roy Armstrong, who took him in for many of the War years; and initially unbeknown to Hedwig and Iso, the infamous Acid Bath Murderer John Craig, apparently himself a proficient pianist, came more than once. The amounts they earned were pitiful:

sixpence for each lecture (about the equivalent of a cup of coffee today) – but they provided some reasonably reliable income for their beginnings in West Chiltington. By the summer of 1942, though, Hedwig and Iso decided that after 75 lecture recitals at the Aggs, enough was enough. (Later, Hedwig counted up how many they had given throughout the War: over 700.) Hedwig continued to teach about seven private pupils each week and became so well-known for her lessons that she had to turn some people down. Teaching had become, and remained forever, a major component of her career and one in which she had innumerable successes. Key factors in that were not least the inventive ways she found to encourage her pupils – even those who were not first-rate – and, no doubt, her fascination with people and her effervescent personality.

Although they were tucked well away from London, Hedwig and Iso still kept reasonably close ties with the capital through Iso's concerts. He regularly performed at the Royal Albert Hall and St Martin-in-the-Fields, and continued with broadcasts. To ease the burden on him, Hedwig took on lecture recitals in Brighton on her own. They kept up with close friends such as Ros Stutchbury, and Roy Armstrong and Lyn Birtles, and had a fair number of visitors – as ever, interesting and often illustrious people. One who only makes a single appearance in Hedwig's Diary was 'dear, ancient Maud[a] Joachim: shrivelled, shrewd, and so correct! – now like a lovable tortoise.' Maud lived in nearby Steyning but had been a major player in the suffragette movement and imprisoned several times, including in Royal Holloway, where she spent time in solitary confinement. She had been a staunch supporter of Sylvia Pankhurst's activities, working with her on her anti-fascist Ethiopian campaign. Sylvia's weekly journal, The Ethiopian News, launched in 1935, aimed to give greater prominence to Emperor Haile Selassie's efforts to persuade the League of Nations to prevent colonisation. Not understanding the background, Iso was baffled that on each visit Maud would present him with an Ethiopian newspaper – presumably the News. Hedwig did not write any more than

a   Hedwig wrote of 'Joe' Joachim – possibly a nickname? – but from the description she was undoubtedly referring to Maud Joachim. Maud was the niece of Joseph Joachim, the famous violinist and close friend of Johannes Brahms.

that, though it seems inconceivable that the three of them did not talk about politics. This is entirely congruent with what Anna related: that she has no recollection of either of her parents talking about politics. In fact, when I first asked about Hedwig's political leanings, Anna said she couldn't really say. Since both had fled from repressive regimes, she thought they probably tended (slightly) towards the centre right, but that their lives were almost totally bound up in music. I found that hard to follow. Hedwig was intent on knowing what was going on and ready to form opinions and judgements in all sorts of matters. On something so central, surely she had well-formed views? Yet for the life of me, I have no recollection of Hedwig having talked much about politics during our evenings together. Well...

The particular day that Hedwig chose to mention a visit by Maud was the day of Gretel's birthday – noted with a single sentence, book-ended by noting a battle in the Channel with significant numbers of bombers, Japanese gains, and Hitler's deploying huge numbers of men in his Spring Offensive. By mid-1942, Rommel had taken Tobruk and the Nazis had advanced into Egypt – a source of worry for Hedwig because the third Kilby daughter, Avice, was in Cairo. But of greater impact were the reports that Russia had lost Sebastopol and that the Nazis were moving towards the river Don and Rostov. Then, a report in The Telegraph in July that 72,000 Jews had been killed by the Nazis in Minsk, leaving no doubt – had there been any left by this time – of the Nazis' hideous agenda. By August, Germany had amassed a million men at Stalingrad at the start of what was to be the largest confrontation of the War; nearly two million military were killed, wounded, or captured six months later. Closer to home, although there had been no raids over London for a year, the telephone in Mill House rang at 3.15 one night: a local raid was expected. We are given an almost laughable picture, despite the underlying gravity. Together with Dorothy, Hedwig and Iso formed what she described as their own fire-fighting party. There they stood in the garden 'under the heavenly firmament', in the middle of the night and only partly dressed, and with nothing more than a stirrup pump in hand. But they were left only to wonder at the stars. Nothing happened.

At other times:

'...the radio news which Iso turns on always when he is at home is a great strain – yes, a personal one too – on Iso and me. Sometimes I may 'burn my mouth' (a proverb) just a little by saying something which induces Iso to lecture me almost severely. (To this he is of course fully entitled!) 'Our' two countries are enmeshed in a most bloody war. It is very much if people living closely near one another can always be kind to each other! (I don't see how the physical side in marriage should help so much – on the contrary...).'

As they sat huddled next to the radio now and at critical stages in the War, what must they have said to each other? Did they ever think that invasion might be possible? Unlike we, who have hindsight, they could not at any point do more than conjecture about the turns the War might take, and how they might yet be even more closely affected.

Some consolation, or escape, continued to come through reading. This year's batch included Stendhal's *Chartreuse de Parma* – which she loved and hoped the girls would read some day, Charles Lamb, Shakespeare (a constant companion, and probably in English), Goethe's *Wilhelm Meister* ('difficult'), and a number of Russian works including Chekhov's short stories and letters.

Reflecting on their own small world, Hedwig continued to feel some disquiet about what she considered to be the discrepancy between recognition of Iso's talents and those of other pianists. This was, she felt, one of the drawbacks of living in West Sussex rather than in London, where they would have been continually mixing with other artists and influential people. She had always had a deep love for the countryside, though, and was aware of the better air and conditions that Anna and Marga were growing up in. 'I am so grateful for our present activities (and blessings!) and most friends are very kind.' Iso's approach to bettering the situation and getting his name recognised was to do as many concerts as possible, even to the extent of hiring halls himself. Hedwig was ambivalent. Her analysis of the situation was:

'These 'good cause' concerts (that is: small expenses paid!) cut both ways. They are also of real disadvantage to Iso! My eyes recently caught Louis Kentner's[a] name on placards. He plays at least twice a week in London (in a 'real' Hall). For the sake of the artistic principle more than petty selfishness I feel Iso must do bigger things in London soon! Otherwise with 'safe' lecture recitals, a good fire, a nice garden and vegetables and good air, after the War we might become artistically 'squashed' by all the foreign musicians who will flock to London again. This sentence proved to be true as I had occasion to observe when Iso – in the coming years – tired himself by detailed and often small work. To hear him hundreds of times for 6d in the WEA 'frame' will make it hard for his real admirers to rally to normal peace-time concerts and their normal prices! I heard that V. Horowitz made £750 per New York recital after his sensational German successes in the 1920s. This is extreme. I mean only something sensible. It seemed to me, early on, that in England, a certain 'legend' is important to be created round the artist; perhaps this applies to other countries as well. (Iso thought mainly of music and used the word 'great' hundreds of times – far oftener than I – who does not measure art always in 'depth'!) Iso's idealistic views to make Bach's 48 better known seemed admirable to me; yet Harold Samuel[b] (dead now) was greatly backed in just this task by great success in the USA (sold-out halls – yes, for Bach!). He was also connected with the British Music Academies, pupils etc. And Iso is still a freelance! He now wants to turn out 'best' Chopin and we shall have to lose money on it (?!) So many orchestral undertakings are springing up. It is such a pity. No Proms contact, no real man to do 'business' for him! Too 'haphazard' connections with a few conductors.'

In other words, although together Hedwig and Iso were making some small inroads for Iso – largely through contacts and countless letters, the

---

a   Kentner was a Hungarian pianist, famous for his performances of Liszt.
b   English pianist who concentrated on works by JS Bach.

composition of which they still poured over before laboriously typing them up – their proper agents, Harold Holt, and Ibbs and Tillett, were not getting him into the status venues.

———

1943

The year started well, in contrast to Hedwig's miscarriage start to 1942. This was primarily because news on the War front was better, with Stalingrad and Leningrad almost recovered. Hedwig heard it on the German news, where the announcement was accompanied by a background of mournful music. Progress was made towards regaining Kharkov, Kursk, and Rostov, and even in Britain the 25th anniversary of the Red Army was celebrated.

> 'The papers show appalling photographs of old Russian women, digging in frozen streets for their own frozen dead among German bodies… It's estimated that Hitler lost quarter of a million men in these 'setbacks'.'

Also pleasing, even if comparatively trivial, was the mild winter in southern England. Hedwig noted that crocuses were out by the end of January, and daffodils by mid-March. More significant were new opportunities opening up on the musical front. For one thing, Iso was approached by the Council for the Encouragement of Music and the Arts, a body set up to provide wartime entertainment that gave money to ballet, opera and drama companies, and music institutions to perform in military camps and to civilians. Its chairman was John Maynard Keynes from 1941 until his death in 1946, when it was awarded a Royal Charter and renamed the Arts Council. Iso must have been one of its first artists, with a request for about ten concerts in and around Manchester. These he combined with concerts at the Edinburgh National Gallery and in Glasgow – all successes. 'New towns like Torquay clamour for Iso.' A group of his loyal admirers – neighbour and friend Octavia, the Du Canes, the three Kilby sisters (looking like film stars, commented Hedwig), and the Crankshaws – went up to hear Iso perform again in the Royal Albert

Hall with Adrian Boult. And with Hedwig's agreement, Iso decided to try out his idea of three London recitals, for which they would hire the Aeolian Hall.[a] The first recital was to be all Chopin, followed by all Beethoven, and then a mixed programme. Hedwig felt there should have been more like this, and that Iso was wasting his talents in spending any time on the old ladies of Brighton. So she and Iso continued to plug away with the letters to conductors and music societies.

The first Aeolian Hall concert in April was:

'Gratifying. The day before Iso had given a romantic performance of Chopin's F minor concerto on the air. And now his Funeral March Sonata, B minor Scherzo – tigerish attack!, G minor Ballade, Nocturne in F, entrancing Mazurkas and six Études which were received with loud noise by the well-mixed public. I sat there, not too nervous, as Iso is always master of the musical situation. Iso so enchanted and looked extra nice in neighbour AH Wood's striped trouser suit! Iso had stayed the night before at the Kilbys' flat and was spoilt with an egg for breakfast! We met so many old friends, and the Crankshaws (Teddy freshly returned from Russia), and Ros and her ancient lovely mama, Mrs Wycliffe. I am overjoyed for Iso. So many bravos. He is in his element. He still does some lectures and in good humour, though it seems a bit wasteful to play the immortal Chopin Study in Thirds to people who might prefer John Peel or Noel Coward tunes!'

The following two London recitals were no less successful, and ticket sales so good that Hedwig had no need to worry that they might make a loss on the venture.

'I admired Iso's artistry from the bottom of my pianistic being. At the end thunderous applause. Iso has acquired much better

---

a   Used also by the BBC for recording and broadcasting concerts towards the end of the War.

platform manners, repeatedly thanking for the applause. He looked young and happy.'

As he had hoped, these spawned other engagements, not least two concertos at the Proms later in the summer: Brahms No. 2 and the Chopin F minor. And in the meantime, another Royal Albert Hall concert with a Rachmaninov concerto, since the agent Harold Holt thought it a 'good plan' to have a live Russian for this work, Rachmaninov having died in the March of 1943. Afterwards Holt said: 'I will push you.' What a fillip. Iso seemed at long last to be making his name. No wonder Hedwig wrote that 'it looks like some crescendo'.

Now the girls were older, Hedwig was finding a bit more time to play, especially in the evenings when Iso was away, and she was loving her solo lecture recitals. It wasn't enough, though: when there was talk of Iso maybe doing some recordings, Hedwig wrote 'my great wish is that even I may record in England'. Sadly, that never came about, but the flame inside her to perform was still burning strongly. That was not the only flame: Hedwig was all too well aware of all the support she and Iso received. She desperately wanted, one day, to be able to help musicians who were just starting their careers, and struggling.

Avice Kilby came to stay for a few days before leaving again for Egypt, bringing generous presents for all: savings certificates for Anna and Marga, eight (no less) silk ties for Iso, and a silk blouse for Hedwig. They had grown very close, and Hedwig was anxious about this adventure Avice was going to undertake, including the six-week journey out there. There were countless other visitors, some good friends and then other newer acquaintances who Hedwig felt needed to be invited for lunch or dinner. Quite how did she manage it, given the severe rationing? 'The War tells now. We eat very simply, particularly vegetables, potatoes and bread (one egg per week per head is little).' There were times when Hedwig felt tired out and entertaining was simply too much. But she was acutely aware of the help people were giving them, and of the necessity to embrace new contacts.

Despite the activities and her weariness, Hedwig somehow still found time to read. She mentions the correspondence of Joachim, Brahms, and Schumann, and of Mozart, Chopin, and Beethoven; Goethe's *Die Wahlverwandtschaften*[a] and Faust. She managed a few outings to the theatre, usually with Iso, to see Congreve's *Love of Love*, a production of *War and Peace* in 32 scenes, *A Month in the Country*, *Love's Labour's Lost*, Shaw's *Heartbreak House*, and *Uncle Vanya*, as well as ballet and some films, including Chaplin's *The Great Dictator*, which they were enthralled by. Her wider cultural cravings were being satisfied.

On 12th June, Hedwig put a heavy box around one Diary entry: 'War news so much better!' The British were in control in North Africa and on two Italian islands before they invaded mainland Italy and bombed the Ruhr. Mussolini resigned at the end of July and most of Sicily was controlled by the British. Hedwig was elated:

'Fascism has crumbled overnight. Big demonstrations against it everywhere! Streets renamed; Palermo citizens greeting the British and American troops enthusiastically. It is fantastic and shows the short life of man-made, wicked institutions.'

Ah – if only it were that such movements could be put down permanently and Hedwig's trusting judgement held…

The Albert Hall sold out for Iso's Chopin Prom under Sir Adrian Boult. Lady Swaythling invited Iso to stay with her the night before, promising him an egg for breakfast. "It will help!" she said. And so it did. The concert was a huge success, with no less than five calls for Iso to return to the platform to receive the applause. Hedwig, Anna, and Marga joined Lady Swaythling in her box before her reception in Iso's honour. The good publicity from the Proms led to engagements pouring in, some through Holt, some through Ibbs: Scotland, Huddersfield, clubs and schools, and a great many more recitals for the Council for the Encouragement of Music and the Arts , which thankfully now offered fees for expenses. Decca also invited Iso for some recording

---

a   'Selected Affinities'.

tests. 'We are grateful for the turn in Iso's artistic fortunes. He is so busy: 13 recitals in 14 days.' All in all, the financial position was much rosier, made even more so by a letter from Margaret Mead to say that should there be any illness or other problem, the estate could easily bear more expenses on their behalf. 'How very tactful, generous, and kind.'

'Beginning of autumn – Fragonard's colours all around! – that pinkish London light.' There were constant big raids on Berlin. 'I think of my father. Where might he be?' She knew he was most likely still in Berlin, but had no recent information about him. At least she did not have to worry too much about her mother who was permanently tucked away in the countryside for most of the War. Any news came very sporadically, through the Red Cross. Still there was cause for their friend and neighbour Octavia to appear with a bottle of red wine in early September to celebrate the unconditional surrender of Italy, though small battles here and there continued for some time. At the end of the year, Churchill, Stalin, and Roosevelt met in Tehran, the first conference of the 'Big Three' Allies, and the Commission for War Crimes started its work in Kharkov knowing that the Nazis had used special lorries as mobile death chambers – the first time German personnel had been tried for such crimes by the Allies; they were found guilty and executed. War was speeding up and hopes rising that it would end in the next year or so.

For Hedwig and Iso, the end of 1943 provided an unexpected climax. Iso had given a concert in Manchester, which the head of the Royal Manchester College of Music, Robert Forbes, attended. That was sufficient for Forbes: he immediately offered Iso the post of Professor of Piano at the College. The official letter arrived on Christmas Day, asking him to start on 11th January. Iso and Hedwig were over the moon. Since the College had been founded by Sir Charles Hallé, and maintained strong links with the Hallé Orchestra, it meant not only an official position for Iso and the way out of being a freelancer, but it also opened up possibilities of closer ties to the Hallé and music societies in the North. This was 'surely our last Christmas in Sussex', wrote Hedwig. 'Surely' proved not to be the case.

1944 TO WAR'S END

It was out of the starting blocks early in January for Iso, up to Manchester where he met his first students – ten of them. One, a young man of 22, he pronounced to be a 'near genius'. This was Joseph Clough. Hedwig was elated. She had always rated Iso's teaching abilities highly, having herself learnt a lot from him, and she hoped that he would have many good students. Not giving up on her own aspirations, she wanted the same for herself too. As ever, she used the evenings when Iso was away to practise. 'This is my 'chance', for which I had to wait. How could I bear it for so long?' she asks. The response to her rhetorical question was crystal clear in a separate Diary entry: 'Only by understanding Iso's vast musical superiority!' After only a couple of months in Manchester, Iso had gained a few private pupils, and he seemed strong and in good spirits, also playing again at the Albert Hall, this time under Sir Malcolm Sargent.

It was time for Hedwig to venture north – her first exposure to this very different part of the country. Not straight to Manchester, but first to Glasgow, where Iso was due to play the Mozart C minor concerto in the impressive St Andrew's Hall.[a] Iso travelled ahead. When she arrived at Glasgow Station, Hedwig's first problem was the language: it was impossible to understand what people were saying! The city she found grey and cold. 'Everyone wears fur coats (often cheap-looking, like a dog's fur!).' Edinburgh was a little better, but still cold. 'No relief of light or white as in the South or in Germany.' From there to Manchester, where they stayed at Iso's usual hotel, the Norton, which invariably provoked some negative remark or other. Hedwig's curt judgement: 'unspeakably dingy'. The inside of the College she found little better, and the thought flashed through her mind: 'What have we come to?' But she quickly put that to one side; the reports she heard from three or four students at the College were of how

---

a   The Hall burnt down in 1962 and although rebuilt later, the concert hall was not restored to anything like its previous size and form.

good a teacher Iso was. It was that that really mattered to her. Yet again, she marvelled at how far they had managed to come:

> 'Out of a beginning with not much except his wonderful hands, great natural gifts, his sense of humour – and, may I add: a good and willing wife, even if poor and cut off, without real connections to the British musical powers – comes this development. He brought the four of us into safety (materially and mentally), if nothing unforeseen 'bad' happens.'

Prophetic words.

By now Iso had met Sir Henry Wood, and he and Hedwig wrote to offer their congratulations on his 75th birthday. He replied the next day, mentioning that he too had 'helped' with Iso's Manchester appointment. How kind, they thought. And of extra significance, therefore, that Iso was invited again to be part of the Proms, the special 50th season. In preparation, Hedwig and Iso practised the third Beethoven concerto at home and performed it for friends. Alongside that, she was building up her own repertoire, revisiting some pieces she had studied years before and adding new ones – all around Bach, Beethoven, Mozart, Schumann, Schubert, and Chopin – and a new request for a solo recital came in from Crawley.

As she often did, Hedwig reviewed their current situation in the summer of 1944. She was very satisfied: already they had 51 talks lined up for the autumn and spring; Iso's pupil Joseph Clough was highly praised by the press; and as for Iso himself, 'everywhere the press is now delighted with him'.

From Mill House they had seen many sorties of bombers leaving at night for Germany, prior to an invasion. (Might this be the end for her family?) The Allies had entered Rome. And then, on 6th June, D-Day landings on the Normandy beaches. They heard countless planes in the early hours and spent the day hanging on to every radio bulletin, listening to descriptions by eyewitness reporters. Iso, she wrote, was near frenzy. On 20th July, Claus von Stauffenberg and other conspirators attempted to assassinate Hitler in the plot named Operation Valkyrie, aiming to remove the Nazis from power and make peace with the Allies as soon as possible. It failed, and Hitler continued to say that victory was certain. Unusually, Hedwig's reporting of Valkyrie is not completely correct, because she thought Graf von Moltke was a co-conspirator. In fact he was not, and had opposed any attempt to kill Hitler. Rather, as a lawyer, he was concerned with developing a post-Hitler moral and democratic framework for Germany. Von Moltke was put in front of a Volksgericht[a] and executed in January 1945.

In August, Hedwig was relieved to be able to write that Paris had been liberated and US forces were retaking much of the country. Brussels and Antwerp were soon freed, and the Allies were in Dutch territory and even in a small part of Germany. Progress was less marked in the east: there were weeks of heavy fighting in Warsaw, and civilians were suffering badly. All cinemas, shops, and schools were closed, and conservatoire concerts were halted in Germany. There were prayer services everywhere in Britain in September to mark the fifth year of the start of the War. Iso wanted the family to attend. 'He is often very highly emotionally stirred.' As a diversion, he gave the fourth 'proper' recital at Fittleworth House, playing Beethoven's *Hammerklavier* sonata. 'A glorious intellectual deed, to play it like that!' Between concert events, the family would go and bathe in the River Arun at Stopham Bridge, an ironstone bridge dating from 1422 – 'that is, Iso cannot really swim! – he paddles!'

Throughout the War, Iso had had no idea what had happened to his family. He and Hedwig arranged to send the odd package and regular small amounts of money to his parents. In 1941–2 he had tried to glean news of them through their close friend Teddy Crankshaw, who went on war service at the British Military Mission in Moscow. But to no avail: Teddy's probings led him to an old and distinguished woman composer who knew Iso's parents. When he asked about them, she broke down, sobbing bitterly, but revealing nothing about the circumstances. Maybe they were still alive; maybe they weren't. Later, however, a parcel of thick country clothes that Hedwig and Iso had sent was returned, and later they were faced with the return of their latest £3 and the bald reply: 'Addressees dead'. That was all...

---

a   People's Court.

Iso was now left without knowing whether his parents had died of old age or how they had suffered under the Revolution and Stalin as he had no contact with any of his siblings or anyone else in Russia. The news cannot have been anything but a blow, even though it had been Iso's own decision to leave Russia and remain in Germany beyond his four-week permit. He had always hoped for an easing of the Communist situation but since he did not speak of his feelings about Russia, we cannot know whether, or how much, he still felt a pull towards his homeland and family. It is hard to imagine he did not. Iso almost led two lives that were totally separated: one in Russia, and one in Germany and the UK. Hedwig and the girls lived only with the second. Hedwig at least had the slight consolation of having written – years before – a long letter 'from the heart' to Iso's parents, telling them of her joy at having 'found' Iso. She kept a copy of that letter. It is in German and tells movingly of how she met 'for the first time, a musician sent by God' who had changed her completely and whom she loved deeply. His father's reply – in Russian – was a 'fine classical letter', which talked about Iso in his childhood and his musical gifts. It meant so much to her that Hedwig had it translated after Iso's death and kept it with her 'small treasures'. But Iso's daughters heard almost nothing about their Russian family; half Russian, yet Iso offered them no introduction to the language, the history, the culture, or the politics of Russia. And there was little by way of religion; Iso maintained only that his mother did not bring him up in the Jewish faith. There was never any opportunity to visit Russia together either: Iso feared that he could be detained, having left illegally. For similar reasons, neither Anna nor Marga ever went. 'How my mother urged him to write down his recollections,' Anna said, 'but he would not take the trouble; I think English was not his favourite medium for expressing himself.' Nor did he consider doing so in German – even though he remained fairly fluent. I could not help but regret that.

The autumn season of regular concerts for Iso got underway, starting with three with Barbirolli in Manchester. Hedwig went up for one of them and she and Iso stayed with the College Principal, Robert Forbes, and his family. They were delightfully welcoming. Forbes was a splendid sight-reader, spontaneously joining Iso in a Mozart concerto in his living room, just for fun. Hedwig also played a little. Forbes then made yet another wholly unexpected offer: why didn't Hedwig join the College staff and take over some of Iso's students when he was away? They needed not a second to think about it. The answer was an immediate 'yes'. How they celebrated! For the next few weeks, Iso moved up to the Norton. It was at least cheap, and maybe for that reason remarkably successful in attracting musicians. Despite its scruffiness, Hedwig even met Clifford Curzon there at a later date.

Hedwig was now able to practise more and more, and gave the odd solo recital. Audiences were not of the polished London venue types, nor of the Wigmore connoisseurs. Instead, she won the heart of a fruit grower in Crawley, for example, who, after her performance of Schumann's *Carnaval*, presented her with a collection of rare apples, rare flowers and a poem written by him. That was just as good as a large floral bouquet for Hedwig. Nonetheless, when the offer of a public recital in Manchester came along, she was excited.

War news was generally good, but as yet without conclusion. At the end of January 1945, Hedwig wrote:

'The RAF batters railroads etc in my former land! The misery is difficult to imagine. Yes, Hitler says in his 12 year foundation speech: God saved him from the bomb last June as He loves him and Germany. (Naïve – the old stories that this was forced on him 'by the Jews, Kremlin etc'.) I wonder what my mother and Maertel and Ilsabe are doing and so much hope that Maertel need not fight in the newly-formed 'Volkssturm'.[a] I have to live by such contrasts: grim news of death and cutting people to pieces, alternating with my playing of great Mozart!'

By now, all they could wish for was an end to the War. The Allies moved steadily into the German Rhine and Ruhr regions, and into Darmstadt

---

a   A nationwide militia established by Hitler in the last desperate months of the War. All men were required to sign up.

and Heidelberg. The V2s stopped. But there were still fierce fights in Berlin. She was in no doubt that it would be the three million civilians who would be most affected. Then: 'the most awful shock to civilisation was the discovery of the horror camps of Belsen and Buchenwald. I kept articles by an eyewitness in case someone ever argued about Hitler's 'greatness.''

Finally, on May 1ˢᵗ, Hitler was found dead in his bunker in Berlin. The Russians hoisted their flag on the Reichstag, with the German radio announcing Hitler's death as that of a hero against the Bolsheviks. Admiral Dönitz said he would carry on the fight. It did not last long. A week later came the day of unconditional surrender.

'It is terrifying news, but as we all had 14 days' mental preparation for it, we can take it more easily... wonderful May Day with the scent of lilies-of-the-valley floating in the air. (Thanksgiving services all over!) A big simple tea at Octavia's; the young son's wife expects a baby tomorrow! All in red-blue-white (except us). Huge local fireworks in the evening! M asks 'will they be on every evening?'. The neighbour's cottage floodlit, including their blossom trees (apples!). It does look fairy-like (and ghost-like as well). The flimmering trees throw their shadows on the whitewashed cottage wall. (I shall never forget this.) Some joyful loud bangs from Worthing! (We think of bombs – too conditioned to it.)

'Second day of Victory celebrations brought huge crowds hailing Churchill, the King and Queen (who appeared many times on their balcony) 'mafficking'ᵃin Piccadilly (!), many church services. I played the piano – among many items our beloved Chorale (Ich tret' vor Deinen Thron, o Gott) which, Iso said, he wanted played at his death. All thinking people stress the difficulty of getting accustomed to the new state. ... The bombers now bring prisoners back to England and again drop 1000s of tons of food for the Dutch, instead of bombs. Russia too has had her victory, a day later than England. In Czechoslovakia they still fight

---

a Public and extravagant celebration, written by Hedwig as 'mefficking'.

on in a few places, against Germans who do not obey Doenitz's orders. There will be no more fighting in the Bavarian Alps. All the Goebbels family are said to have poisoned themselves in a bunker in Berlin, very near Hitler.

'Iso went to Manchester for 2 days.'

While the end of the War allowed Hedwig to breathe out, however, some changes to the family situation were necessary, and some unforeseeable events lay ahead.

ELEVEN
FEET-FINDING POST-WAR

Much of the world was on the move after the War: people returning; people seizing on the opportunity of the new. In 1943, Hedwig and Iso had found themselves with out-of-the-blue offers of teaching positions that had been tentatively mentioned by Adrian Boult years before. Associated with them was sought-after recognition and the chance to savour independence for the first time. Small wonder they had grabbed them.

Now Hedwig and Iso were faced with the realisation that, with Beatrice's will contingent on the continuation of the War, their living situation would need to change. Hedwig wrote to Margaret Mead at the end of 1945, having written to Gregory Bateson a few days after the Japanese surrender:

'After being here for the main part of the War, we feel you might like to make definite plans about Mill House and we frankly feel somewhat embarrassed still to enjoy unbounded hospitality. If you give us any idea by what time or month you might like to settle the affairs of the Mill House, we would naturally get most active to find a future home. The housing problem in England is acute and it takes time.'

(I note, in passing, the assurance with which Hedwig was by now writing in English.) Duly, a date was agreed, and Hedwig and Iso decided that, on balance, it would make most sense to go and live in Manchester.

Another move. With it, the optimism that accompanies the prospect of the imagined new: the equivalent of verdant pastures, shining sun (always the accompaniment to such imaginings), the leaving behind of unwanted events, the relief at bidding farewell to embarrassments that might have occurred. And at the same time, the obverse: anxiety about the unknown and unknowable, the absence of certainty, the dread of potentially lost friendships, and the discomfort of dealing with all the sheer physical arrangements, giving up the old abode and finding a base for the life ahead. All those elements of light and shade accompanied Hedwig and Iso as they now set about this next move – about their tenth since leaving Berlin twelve years previously – together with the background nag of how it would be trying to further enhance Iso's reputation once away from London, the where-it-all-happens in music in England, then as now.

Nonetheless, the starting point was not bad. Financially, after years of counting every penny, they were increasingly on a stable footing, achieved through hard graft and the years of support from their benefactors: the Linders, Beatrice and Gregory Bateson, Ros Stutchbury, the Pages, the Crankshaws, Lady Swaythling. Hedwig, as we know, found it more difficult to accept their unconditional generosity than did Iso. Her desire for independence in every regard bubbled on, rather than below, the surface. Although immensely grateful for the lifeline thrown to them by Beatrice, they had had to live with the constant responsibility of her 'treasures' while looking after the property, and the housekeeper and gardener as well. Manchester offered freedom and an end to Iso's constant commuting from south to north; but still, those doubts about friendships, the decision to move to the provinces, and the prospect of leaving the deeply appealing Sussex countryside were bound to be difficult.

Hedwig continues her Diary after marking clearly the break at the end of the year 1945, promising to 'summarise' the next five years and to give fewer dates and record 'more about what I really remember, emotionally and intellectually'. From here on, much of the Diary is about the day-to-day. There is a great deal of predictability about it, and as with most people, there were chunks of time in which little of import happened. Of course there were the excitements about concerts here or there, for both Hedwig and Iso; Anna and Marga were more or less grown up and forging their own lives; there were waxing and waning friendships – as much to do with distance as anything else; and trips to France, Italy, and Greece, each, in its way, of special interest for Hedwig. But as she moved into her forties, much of Hedwig's life had become established and the musical career she had hoped for was not looking entirely out of the question. From now on, years flowed into years, and Hedwig only noted as and when there was a major political event such as Suez, Algeria, the Cuban crisis, and the Russian invasion of Prague, or new scientific findings and developments – the moon landing, for example.

Central to this part of the story is someone who had stepped onto the Elinson scene a few years earlier through a contact of Iso's in Manchester: Dr CEB[a] Rickards, known by all as Tex – oddly, it might seem, as he was the resident obstetric surgeon at the St Mary's Hospitals in Manchester. But Tex was also the music critic for one of the Manchester newspapers, and an enthusiastic amateur singer, pianist, and playwright. He had been much impressed by Iso at an early recital in Manchester and had introduced himself afterwards. More contacts followed and the friendship between Tex and the Elinsons quickly became close.

The end of the War coincided, then, with the big move from sunny, kindly and generally 'lento' Sussex, with its whitewashed cottages and rolling countryside, to the harshness associated with the 'agitato' of Manchester's high activity and its dirt. It was difficult for Hedwig – she so responsive to her external environment. The girls were not enthusiastic. Apart from leaving the environment and people they had grown accustomed to, the immediate consequence for them was having to accept that there was now no prospect of having ponies and riding. They too did not like the all-enveloping urban surroundings, unrelieved by any greenery. With all the logistical difficulties of trying to find a house

---

a   Charles Edward Bernard.

so far away, Hedwig – for it largely fell to her – had enlisted Tex's help. Tex had done his best and found them a semi-detached Victorian house that was cheap and yet – the major consideration for this family – large enough to house the pianos, of which there were soon to be no fewer than five. It was one of hundreds like it in Whalley Range – hardly the upmarket end of Manchester, and at best to be described as respectably suburban. It was about the furthest extreme from their picturesque and highly individual home and village in West Chiltington. Hedwig loathed the place, with its pile of rocks in the front garden looking like some funereal bed and the grime-covered evergreen shrubs, its fancy fussy glass entrance, its internal doors – each of which was covered with thick brown oil paint and sporting a sign, 'F.S.', that made Hedwig think of her father, Fritz Stein. She could see that after years of being uninhabited and used only by the Fire Service (hence the 'F.S.' signs), the house would need considerable amounts of cash to do it up. Iso, however – focused, as ever, solely on music – could not see the problem and thought the infestation of rose bay willow herb was nice – there were always compensations, he said. It caused little fights with Hedwig. But they were both now earning and each, thankfully, had a strong sense of humour. 'Much Bach and the incomparable mazurkas by Chopin make one less mindful of purely conventional dislikes.' That carried them through. And by the time they had furnished the house with some treasures from Mill House, which Lady Barlow had insisted they take – the Georgian table on which they had written so many letters to agents and concert organisers, old chairs 'on which Darwin had sat!' and now brightened up with Romanian hangings, the old black church wardrobe from Vienna that Gretel had sent as part of the reconciliation, and the German Steinway – it felt more like their place. They 'lit candles in winter, cooked simple stews and drank cider, and had quite a stimulating life', though they would forever struggle with the dirt and polluted air that they felt was clogging up their entire insides, and the sheer ugliness of their environment.

For Hedwig, there was in addition the relief of avenues to re-establish her relationships with Fritz and Gretel. Her short visit to Germany in 1946 opened the door for them to visit England once the family was ensconced in Manchester, and Hedwig quickly set about making plans. Fritz and Gretel had not seen each other for some years, and given the ongoing turbulence in post-War Berlin, they decided that Gretel should stay on at the farm on the Baltic coast until she could meet Fritz in England. The father of one of Iso's private pupils, Barbara Stones, offered to help to organise the flights from Germany, which in those early days were still difficult because of the airspace over individual sectors, requiring Fritz and Gretel to fly separately. He suggested the reunion be at their family home in Derbyshire, over Christmas 1946. In the way of such momentous events, when they came face to face there was not any high drama to stick in everyone's minds but rather Fritz's first remark to Gretel: 'Goodness. You have become fat!' Whereas Fritz had had ever more meagre supplies of food in Berlin, Gretel had at least had potatoes and bread in plenty from the farm.

After Christmas, the Steins went to stay with Hedwig and the family for six months. Iso and Hedwig's concert and teaching lives continued apace, with Hedwig devoting hours of practice on the old Bateson piano in their bedroom to prepare for her upcoming Wigmore Hall recital, and Fritz spending hour after hour in the Henry Watson Music Library while Gretel pottered around at home and occasionally walked around the patch of miserable scrubland close to the house. The new political situation, and the relaxation of the internal tensions, meant this was just the first of many family visits between England and Germany. Whatever Fritz might have thought of Iso – and maybe more to the point, whatever Iso might have thought of Fritz in 1933 – by the end of the next decade, the relationship seemed now to be on a smooth footing. Anna recalls them having a warm friendship, no doubt greatly underpinned by the overwhelming love each had of similar sorts of music.

Hedwig could not help but be alert to the differences between Manchester now and what she witnessed on her trips to Germany:

'Building houses seemed slow in Manchester! Evening after evening I went for my walk past those dull, dull houses with their bronzed dog in the window, or blue curtains (a funny sameness here!). And so 1899! … Still, kind people in many of them. Their visual outlook on life has little to do with snob values or how much or little money one has… The English were visual in earlier times! But air was what I wanted – even bad air – after deciphering such beasts as Chopin's B minor sonata or Beethoven's Op. 110'.

Tex was a regular visitor to the house. Being an established consultant, he was in a very different financial league from Hedwig and Iso, and had bought a Georgian townhouse in St John Street for his practice. It was surely the only doctor's waiting room ever to have boasted a Steinway grand, and was to become a huge asset to Hedwig and Iso over many years, both for practising and small concerts. When Tex invited them to the opera and then to a drinks get-together for his friends, as he often did, it was at his practice, and Iso would play to all, as he always did. Impromptu concerts were a feature of Iso's visits anywhere where there was a piano.

It is a sign of the way Tex was one of their inner circle that he gave one of the main speeches when Marga married in 1958. He started not with the bride but with the family, and the whole took on the flavour of a paean to Hedwig and Iso:

"When I first met the Elinsons fourteen years ago the impact they made on me was roughly similar to that of a hydrogen bomb, but on a somewhat larger scale. I was flabbergasted, amazed, bowled over, and then very gradually, very gropingly, very uncertainly, over a period of many months, I had to admit to myself that they were really true. Indeed, I just had to come to terms with the historical fact that so much brilliance and joie de vivre were actually concentrated in one little human quartet.

"I followed them. I followed them from Manchester to West Chiltington… five times, I think, in the first year. I lazed through an enchanted summer of Chopin and sun. An unusual musicologist who lived with a mill at the bottom of the garden and had a wife whose eyelashes turned downwards instead of up and got stuck together when she blinked. Arnold Bax came to tea.

Hedwig gave him a tumblerful of gin. She said it was English, was called liquor, and would do him good. It seemed to. I followed them to the Wigmore, to the Albert Hall, to the Stutchburys'. They followed me to Manchester, bought a house which had been previously inhabited by a posse of air-raid wardens and they never took the fire-bucket instructions off the doors. I fell in love with them. … I have never had friends like the Elinsons. Of all the people I have met, they are the best. There is nothing of the journeyman about them. They fly high. They breathe the bright sunlit air of their own stratosphere. They are aristocrats in that they never compromise with the shoddy or the second-rate. Their courage in adversity is known but most precious about them is their warmth, their loyalty, their tenderness and their kindness…"

Tex became a mainstay for Hedwig and Iso. He had a similar allure to some of their acquaintances in the south of England: deeply interested in the arts, and an interesting person, he moved in rather elevated circles and had the style and confidence that goes with that. And he was as generous in his affection and caring as Ros. It is impossible not to be swept away by some of his letters to Hedwig and Iso:

"My incomparable Iso and Hedwig –
What can I say to thank you for so much freshness – so much warmth – so much gaiety – so much happiness?"

And after they had been together to see Arthur Miller's *View from the Bridge*:

"Dearest Iso and Hedwig,
How can I thank you for all your dear kindnesses – for everything that makes a weekend with you a lightening of the heart?
It is a real joy to be with you again – to discuss the world – to fling observations into the sparkling whirlpool!…
Salaams…! Obeisances!… Salute!"

Putting aside Tex's rather florid expressions, this was clearly a permanent and empathetic relationship.

One friendship led to another. Within a fairly short space of time, they got to know Mary Walsh, the matron of a nursing home who also took in unmarried young pregnant girls, for whom Mary did her best to find employment. Iso particularly must have been pleased when two people approached him after a recital at the University, probably as the result of an introduction by Tex: Sara Doggert and her husband John became staunch friends. Not only was Sara Russian, but she too, as a child, had fled with her family from the impacts of the Revolution and after settling in Berlin, had fled again, this time from the Nazis. Hélène Foucher was a different cup of tea. French and one of Tex's distant relatives, she was inordinately elegant and stylish – features that did not greatly endear her to the Elinsons. Private pupils were another reservoir of new friends, together with all the College colleagues and pupils, like John Ogdon, Barbara Stones, and David Wilde. Hedwig herself also had some pupils who were growing stars, most notably Peter Maxwell Davies, with whom a close relationship grew. 'We always laughed much together, he and I.'

By the late 1940s and early '50s, Hedwig and Iso were able to be fairly confident about their future. Both were established at the Royal Manchester College of Music. Iso had in addition gained another part-time position as professor at the Guildhall School of Music in London. Between 1944 and 1946 he had appeared twelve times with the Hallé orchestra and seven with the London Symphony Orchestra in London, and played with the Liverpool Philharmonic, the Birmingham City Orchestra, and The Scottish Orchestra; he had given two Beethoven sonata cycles in York and Manchester; he had played every season at the Proms; and he had broadcast several times through the BBC. He also had his annual trip to Scandinavia and the occasional other trip abroad – including to Berlin to perform Beethoven's Piano Concerto No. 5 with the Berliner Philharmoniker, and to Hamburg for broadcasts with the North German Radio. For her part, Hedwig was giving more recitals and some concerts as a soloist; was accompanying Martin Milner, who later became the leader of the Hallé; had also broadcast through the Manchester

BBC – Book II of the Debussy Preludes, which Iso considered 'First class playing, my darling'; and she had more than enough private pupils. Moreover, Hedwig had been 'noticed': the Manchester Evening News published a profile of her. As ever, none of this was handed to them on a plate. Exercise books filled with draft letters to conductors and music agents bear testimony to that.

That was not all. There were also countless small recitals up and down the country, neither of them being too proud for any of the invitations that landed through the letter box. Hedwig played at the Denbigh Hospital for mental health patients, who loved the Schubert impromptus. And Iso accompanied the famous soprano Eva Turner in a concert in Maidstone Prison, where the audience included murderers, wearing special armbands.

'The jovial chaplain introduced the performers: 'Look boys – Miss Turner will now sing arias about matters you know only too well – death, jealousy, revenge, and love. Everyone roared with laughter. Iso followed with the Appassionata sonata. The prisoners were rapt throughout. We had tea afterwards, sitting with the Governors. It included slices of bread and margarine, biscuits, and a little watercress sandwich. I thought it all very, very English!'

Over many years after the War, they gave concerts for all manner of good causes: the Royal United Kingdom Beneficent Association for impoverished old and infirm people, the Hirsch Jewish House in London, the East London Juveniles, Catholic and other schools, the Manchester Rabbis, the Spiritualist Society, and the Council for the Encouragement of Music and the Arts, and they even continued to play for some of their fans in their old Sussex haunts like Fittleworth House.

But as ever, there was a drive in Iso to perform in prestigious venues and to perform cycles: the Beethoven sonatas, the Bach 48, and collections of Chopin works, such as the Études. Hedwig put any physical complaints of his down to nerves and the pressure of work, and in her wisdom, she wondered whether there really was any market in England for these concentrated presentations of works by a single composer. Nor was Iso open to composers outside those he had known and studied from childhood, other than odd exceptions – Rubbra and Bax, each with personal connections, for example. As a result, he got into a no-win situation by arranging 'cycle' concerts, sometimes putting them on himself and not infrequently losing money on them as other pianists were now doing similar programmes. But Iso put it down to not being better known and this in turn made him feel he needed to give even more concerts, augmented by lecture recitals in universities like Sheffield and Nottingham. It was a recipe for stress, overwork and tension, and led to his conviction that he was becoming too provincially based and hence away from the eyes of the critics.

Astoundingly, Hedwig did not sink under the weight of her role as mother, as 'carer' and 'secretary' for Iso (Hedwig continued more or less as his factotum – still always having to chivvy him into going to the doctor or the dentist, and into buying clothes), and as the person who ultimately made sure the household ticked – while all the time trying to build up her own career. She never gave up racking her brain to try to come up with ideas to interest the big names in music in Iso, who himself simply could not fathom why he was not having the sparkling success he thought he deserved. It provoked discord at times, Iso accusing Hedwig of always having been against his Bach cycles and against the lecture recitals, though each had to accept the latter had been life-saving when they had first come to England. Hedwig thought part of the problem was that they could now hardly build up a 'legend' around Iso because people could hear him so often in small towns at low ticket prices. "He just doesn't make anything of himself," said one commentator after a successful Berlin concert. Before any of the Wigmore or Festival Hall concerts, Iso would take piles of advertising leaflets and scribble on each short messages in biro to people he knew or was acquainted with, or even those who had simply expressed some love of Beethoven or Bach or Chopin: "Hope you can come," he wrote. It was far from any guarantee of a full and enthusiastic house, let alone a paying one. Hedwig was sure all this was a waste of time and would not impress people. Nonetheless, she sought constantly to keep Iso buoyed up and on an even keel.

This problematic situation did not diminish. And so, after some years in Manchester, they took another major decision: to go back to London. They, or rather Hedwig, again set about trying to find a house – no easy task from Manchester, with no car. It took some time and meanwhile their lives followed twin tracks in Manchester and in London – more complex than it had been when only Iso had travelled back and forth from West Chiltington. Now, Hedwig had her teaching base in Manchester – including standing in for Iso when he was travelling – and much of her recital work. How easy, or otherwise, would it prove to be when she was trying to manage their household in London and yet be engaged musically in Manchester, assuming the College would agree? Marga was still living at home, and Anna had decided on St Martin's College of Art in London. Iso was little troubled. As Hedwig ruefully noted: 'About me we were silent for a while!'

In 1953 the family moved to Platts Lane in Hampstead, this time at least into a house that Hedwig liked. One uncertainty was removed when the new Principal at the Royal Manchester College of Music, Frederic Cox, agreed that she, as well as Iso, could continue her teaching there. 'I felt I left Manchester without a heartache but was very pleased I was going to be able to return every 2 weeks for college teaching.' Somehow she managed to keep the other parts of her Manchester life going – musically as well as with Tex and probably one or two other friends as well – while slowly building contacts in London, and picking up some of their old friendships – with Ros Stutchbury and one of her sons Oliver, the Kilbys, and the Armstrongs. Other friends dropped in when they happened to be in London. Sigurd Raschèr, the saxophonist, visited Hedwig once when Iso was on tour, 'as of old, dressed in sports clothes and Basque cap'. They talked and talked, and Hedwig might have been a little comforted to hear how, despite living in New York and receiving overt praise from Toscanini after a Town Hall concert in Manhattan, Sigurd still found it extraordinarily difficult to make his mark with the New York concert circle. Maybe after all, it was not so remarkable that Iso had not had a major success there.

Hedwig reflected on the past years. Her life had indeed been continuously enriched through their ever-widening circle of musical and artistic friends. But while the girls were at home, juggling everything that had to be done was a daily challenge, as was the squeezing in of practising and playing. When external circumstances had allowed, or when Iso was away, she played late into the night. But day-to-day duties had had to come first, setting up a tension inside her that she released on occasion, but most of the time managed to wrap up inside herself.

'Looking back, I wonder how I bore it to play so seldom. I suppose my German instinct to put a far greater husband first helped me. …I never suffered from quietness or boredom, nor from Anna and Marga (though they naturally had their own critical outlook – 'too much music'). I never felt hen-pecked, but Iso did have a way of wanting me to be available just the moment he thought a letter should be written. He never said: 'May we do it now?' Or, 'Would you take my pupils please?' Rather, it was: 'This Monday you take my students at College' – transmitted as a note scribbled in the Boots diary.'

The girls grew up and started to forge their way in the world. Marga decided on a career in music, starting out on the path of singing, while Anna pursued dress design. The Elinson family was no different from most others; while there were periods of harmony, on occasion there were also tensions between each of the girls, and with Hedwig too. Marga might complain that they did not have many of the creature comforts of her peers – no good radio, or watches even. She would criticise Hedwig's approach to their family finances, or say she was muddleheaded, blame her in hindsight for not having made sure she and Anna had had the correct white socks at school, and for the embarrassment that came with the revelation in gymnastics and sports that they were wearing mended knickers. Anna quite often seemed angry for no reasons obvious to Hedwig. She said she had not always felt secure, that Hedwig would suddenly make a nasty remark. To herself, or at least in this confessional entry in the Diary, Hedwig accepted the criticisms: 'Naturally I did say too much about dust, cleaning, being tired. This was too much for all. It became a nervous habit, the talking… In London I had very few real friends.' Then the self-defence and self-consolation: any family had its ups and downs, but at least the girls had not been pressed into earning money, and 'within our small means we had tried to let them do extra things like ballet and riding while we were in Sussex, and we had got them right away from the war horrors'. They had experienced a rich life, with each of their parents in the public eye. There had always been something interesting going on, and they had been introduced to countless interesting characters. And for the Elinsons, life was different from most other people's. They needed to be prepared for concert deficits. That was how it had always been and was likely to remain.

Externally, things began to change with time. While Iso had had quite a number of glowing reviews in their early days in England, as the competition from younger musicians and pianists hotted up and the press lauded van Cliburn, Cziffra, Menuhin's founding of the Bach Festival, and Rostal's annual summer school in Salzburg, some of the London critics were less enthusiastic about Iso's performances. Hedwig mused about whether he might have fared better with someone other than herself:

'Iso was so unworldly-wise that even his haircut was a bit of a problem. But a wife of the 200% worldliness of Diana Menuhin would not have suited him (nor he, her!). I thought of the wonderful press Germany gave Iso before we left, but then no work came because of Nazism.'

There were other blows: after the elation at the emergence – finally – of a first record, how the views of a young critic writing in the Gramophone must have stung: 'Iso Elinson's technique is not up to these Chopin Études.' When the second record appeared, the press were still not very impressed. Iso tried not to see it too negatively, though he even feared it might influence Hedwig's opinion. For her part, Hedwig worried only about the influence on Iso's morale, and on his agents. All this was coming at a bad time, when Iso was trying to organise a second trip to the USA. Hedwig bolstered him as much as she could, and was able to breathe a sigh of relief when the much better-known, older critic of the Gramophone reviewed his Chopin Preludes, issued a couple of years later. That was in a quite different vein.

Iso's health was another constant concern. Alongside all the ups and downs of a frenetic performing schedule, Hedwig kept trying hard to get Iso to go to a doctor. After years of tiredness and feeling ill, and ignoring the signs, Iso relented. Type II diabetes was the diagnosis, which came with dietary recommendations that Iso felt unable to follow when he was hosted and were difficult for him to manage when he was on tour.

During these years, Iso went through periods of considerable irascibility. Hedwig felt he blamed her for all manner of things and asked herself why she had to face so many 'Dostoyevsky moods'. In one Diary entry, in the context of a trip in 1956 with Anna and Tex to the Dolomites, shortly after Iso had joined them, she wrote:

> 'I see no possibility for us to cope successfully... I hid my tears for hours behind my black glasses... Never mind – one has to go on living until one is called away – it is as easy as this and nothing helps. He can never apologise for small hurts and this is the most difficult trait in him I detect. It puts me back – into a wild non-understanding.'

But the downs were followed by ups, and by the end of the trip, Hedwig was able to write that 'it was a very successful trip. Iso very kind'. It did not signal an ironed, smoothing-out of the wrinkles in their relationship, though; the irritations continued. There were little annoyances on the other side too: when Hedwig once spoke of her eventual death and how Iso should use gramophone records of chamber music (Mozart) to make things easy, Iso became angry. Hedwig put it down solely to his extreme tiredness. There were, of course, other explanations.

From the outset of their relationship, Hedwig had defined her goal 'of doing everything possible so that people hear Iso and understand music through him'. That was the heart of her marriage, together with Anna and Marga. Contemplating the past as she compiled the Diary, she wrote:

'I did not then [in 1940] believe in very long-term happiness between bodies – only 'sprinklings' of it! – in Schopenhauer's sense – when the 'personal' is neutralised by something that is so much bigger than what one can want for oneself – like a beautiful landscape, or a Mozart symphony, or colour in a bed of roses, or a black cat on green grass! Art, yes, forever! In every family there are frictions between the people, and they have to try not to mind. Friends help. … When I was 24, I burnt like a sack with straw, lit up by fire. Now the feeling had given way to the joys of Art, the children, books. And instead of tumult, there was the hope that Iso would some day be able to lead a decent, settled – even if simple – life.'

Hedwig always talked. A lot. And at a great pace. As for many of us, it was one of her ways of working through ideas and problems. Although she did not have an overly fiery temperament, she could get angry. She tried, forever, to come to terms with Iso's reluctance to talk about things other than music and his concerts, and the girls. He wrote charming, endearing little letters about small topics when he was away. Even after 33 years of marriage, Hedwig wrote of the 'kind of love letters' Iso sent from New York during his third visit there, and how they felt such understanding for one another. Yet, 'like Bartók, Iso always admired simple small things, like apples. He really disliked much analysing or small talk, or weighing up his professional situation'. And so to discuss religion, or how they might chart the course of their future life, or Iso's pre-Hedwig history, or even what he was doing about their tax returns and whether they should take out life insurance, or the making of a will, was well-nigh impossible. Hedwig wondered if it was something to do with his being Russian but rather surprisingly came to no conclusion. Surely Iso being Russian was hardly pertinent, I felt I must say to Hedwig; we all know ostriches.

One of her Diary entries brought a small smile to my face:

'He never discussed love or whether one wanted a child or anything like that... Perhaps the fact that we both did not like double beds is quite a point! To have an arm 'cooped up' or in too stiff a position is – surely – for pianists unthinkable! The whole 'flow' – from the brain through shoulders, arms, wrists to hands is such a lovely feeling…'

Hedwig made various resolutions that she thought might avoid Iso becoming piqued: she would not read in bed, she would not even attempt to discuss difficult topics late at night, she would not go on about things… Inevitably, she did not always find it possible to keep them. Her internal wranglings continued:

'I considered: should I make a major effort and concentrate only on non-playing? And doing secretarial work for Iso etc? I dismissed the idea. He married me, a musician, and wherever I went, my deeply-felt and considered (!) admiration for Iso's kind of musicianship became clear to those who liked to know. Being thoroughly 'dedicated' and gifted, Iso had by far the greater personality between us two. But I had the outgoing 'nature' (whatever faults that contains) and could be useful to him by not needing too many 'womanish' things and helping to make the propaganda for him, and continuing with my music which touched upon his in many ways. (So different from what pop 'artists' and world-designers and hairdressers consider now the thing! – collect cars, or nonsense, advertise yourself – as a super-personality…)

'Iso was always for appeasement. Yes – resilience is as important as kindness (or more so). Dostoyevsky turns of mood – Slav moods – are not easy to understand; sometimes one seemed to be expected to 'bully' (just a little)… I married into the unknown – (except for our passion for good music!) and my nature needed some things other than always Beethoven or Tchaikovsky concertos and letters to agents (and his admirers!).

'Iso was so sure that he was always kind and always so willing. I wished for one small spot, like the one on Siegfried's back. No analysing about himself before me, ever. 'Let others think what my faults are,' he said. I was brim full of his gifts; the sink and the shirt-washings were so different! We should read books together, I hoped, or at least discuss one particular book. Strindberg's 'Beichte eines Toren,'[a] a highly disturbing book.

'If I died tomorrow, Iso would no doubt think he loved me. Now I found he lived enclosed, as in a shell, and I had no clue about it! Concerts, concerts...

'I reflected on Iso's brusque ways and came to the conclusion he did not mean to be like that, apart from the rather outspoken ways Russians seem to cultivate (see Tolstoy in his family as a supreme example). He was often nervous: too many concerts, pupils and general duties. He always allowed me much freedom how to use my time: when to practise, to shop, when to buy a necessary item. He became very slim. He earned most conscientiously. If he did not like to defend me a little before the girls – well, papas love their girls. I tried, and felt very grateful for the many good things we had (after all, we had never been short of a meal since we had met). The sun was out and the garden and the dining room got cleaned up by me and the hedge cut too (quite a job this!).'

Even so, and though her musical qualities were different from Iso's, Hedwig was his equal in many ways. She fully understood his build-up to important concerts, she could empathise with his drive to reach more and more audiences – even if she sometimes differed in her view of how best to achieve that – and, cementing the empathy between them, she knew intimately the music he so loved and could herself play much of it. Yet while she was not under the constant pressure that comes from public performance, as was Iso, she had to find the stamina to cope with all the rest of life. For his part, Iso not only understood Hedwig's musical needs emotionally, but was fully behind her giving concerts whenever possible, even if it meant putting on some themselves when there was likely to be a

---

a   'The Confession of a Fool'.

financial deficit. That, he maintained, could be balanced by privates, and his provincial engagements.

Hedwig wrote fondly about the various endearments that came from Iso and from Anna and Marga throughout her life at least as much as the irritations and self-examination about what she might have done to make home life smoother. She was proud of every success the girls had, however small, and enjoyed times of closeness with Anna, when they might go out together for an espresso in Hampstead, and when she was able to tell Marga about herself and her feelings until Marga understood the tricky balancing act Hedwig was trying to perform.

One might think, from all we have gleaned about Hedwig (and Iso) so far, that they would be very ambitious for their daughters. Away from family life, they were each trying to make an ever-growing mark musically, and each, from their childhood years, had had no other goal than becoming a concert performer. Each had been noticed within distinct musical circles, to a greater – or, in Hedwig's case, lesser – extent. From Hedwig's Diary, however, my impression was not of overt ambition for her girls, or a desire that they follow similar paths. She certainly sought the specialness in each of the girls from when they were very young, and celebrated in the core of her being every indication that Anna and Marga were able to do some creative things that set them apart from others – Anna's artistic, and Marga's (somewhat unresolved) musical, talents. But that was it. Anna said there had not been any expectation they would be star performers.

> "Iso and Hedwig had a great deal to think about. They were big personalities and had a focus on their own lives and careers. They provided so much that most people would never experience. They and their friends were far more interesting than anyone else Marga and I encountered."

My sense is that the relationships between Hedwig and Anna and Marga remained throughout those of mother and daughter, right through their childhood and adulthood and without any metamorphosis into friendships. This probably came from from both sides. I suspect Anna and Marga did not seek any change, and Hedwig was happy enough to accept and respect whatever the girls wished, looking to help them in whatever ways she could. Her love and desire to protect them was uppermost; the relationships were based on their shared history and tacit acceptance of their relative roles. But she did not often, I think, seek openings to discuss with them her innermost feelings and her deepest thoughts about the books she read, the works of art she observed, the philosophies that she held dear.

And so the years concertinaed along with high and lower intensity periods – always teaching, some broadcasts and recordings, and concerts here, there and everywhere for Hedwig and Iso; Anna and Marga started to find their ways in the world, left home, married and had children. Hedwig had periods of considerable worry about Iso's health and the way he drove himself. There were some ripples in the relationship, and one decidedly turbulent wave that we shall come to shortly. There was the death of Fritz; their 25th wedding anniversary – celebrated only with a few days in Edale because neither wanted any fuss; and some high points, such as Iso's trip to New York in 1963, when the New York Times wrote after a concert in the Town Hall: "It has been a long time since Beethoven playing of this breadth has been heard…The dignity, grandeur and granitic strength of his playing… His interpretations were authoritative", and the view of the New York Herald Tribune was:

"Some of the finest Beethoven in New York for quite a while… His technique has the solidity of the Rock of Gibraltar but the strength, the singing tone, and the careful articulation in even the most rapid passages were all made subordinate to what Beethoven had to say… Beethoven's message was monumental."

Geographically, there were one or two changes: after five years in Hampstead, they decided it might be better after all to move their base back to Manchester, possibly triggered by Ros once again offering them the garage flat at Gayles so they could have one foot in the south and one in the north. Iso was away for protracted periods of time, and Hedwig found herself moving down to the coast on her own in early 1959. Yet there were compensations: alone a great deal, Hedwig was master of her time.

'I just played as much as I could, which had not happened for a long time. A joy! Often I played until midnight – no one was disturbed by it, least of all the cows and their calves in the stables.'

Place matters. It can immediately engender a good feeling or an uncomfortable one; excitement or dullness; calm or turbulence; inspiration or indifference. Each of those is manifested in how we behave and how we manage our lives. For Hedwig now, having suffered the muck and drabness of the north, the Sussex countryside and her old haunts felt thirst-quenchingly familiar and the peace resonated. She would walk along the little lanes and through the pine forest nearby, wander down to the village for a 'cuppa' (always the word she used) and look at the sloping green, bounded by its coloured, weather-boarded houses and the rolling hills beyond, remembering some of the old times she and the family had had there. She visited the local tiny Saxon church in Friston where Anna and Marga had been christened. 'I plucked a little blue flower outside the church door where an old notice said: 'Please shut this door otherwise birds come in!' Charming!' She listened to all sorts of programmes on the 'wireless' – an eclectic choice of music and documentaries. I had the sense of contentment in reading her Diary about this period, which lasted the best part of a year, when she and Iso could only snatch a few days together here and there and had to communicate mainly through postcards and loving letters. At the end of the year, Hedwig and Iso gave up Gayles, and took possession of a flat in Manchester in the same block that Tex lived in: Platt Lane. Altogether a different prospect than their previous house in Whalley Range.

Through all this, the bonds between Hedwig and Iso proved to be indestructible – as powerful as any strong electromagnetic force. The deepest love of music and the route into exile that they had chosen together saw to that. As I dwelt on their relationship, I recalled the first time I came across the concept of an ellipsoid, how I had enjoyed the shape and the underlying mathematics. It seemed to me a paradigm for a perfect partnership in which the two individuals constitute the foci, which, because of their relationship to each other, together determine the outer shape and the degrees of freedom of their respective movements. The realisation of the ellipsoid in the form of an egg lent to it an additional, and absolutely appropriate, metaphoric fecundity. The slow movement of the Bach double violin concerto still seems to me to illustrate this rather well musically. When I tried to see Hedwig and Iso's relationship in such terms, it fitted. They were inextricably linked and together decided on the envelope of their partnership, what it would contain and what it would spawn, and each tolerated, and had to tolerate, considerable movement of the other.

Tolerance. From time to time, different forces came into play that would challenge the relationship. In Berlin, Hedwig had fallen completely for the exotic Russian pianist. In England, over the years, a few other women and students were similarly taken. Hedwig was probably not surprised. She had said to herself from the word go that it was a possibility. Nonetheless, when instances came to light, they hurt. Sometimes she got angry. 'I found the silly, thankless letter of the fair-haired pupil of Iso's at College: "If you still like me when I live on my own, we could then be together but probably you won't do so then..." Hedwig challenged him. "I only touched her hair once when teaching her Liszt's *Sonnet de Petrarca* and asked: is it natural?" said Iso. Hedwig was upset. 'This was careless.' But she obviously did not feel threatened. When it came to one serious relationship, however, the hurt went very deep. She refrains from revealing everything in her Diary, but it was fairly easy for me to piece the clues together once Anna had given me the name: Hope Kilby. It was an affair that lasted some considerable time. Hope was the most sophisticated of the three Kilby sisters: fashionable and stylish, and in her own way somewhat exotic too; she had had a relationship with an Indian philosopher who was related to Tagore, and been married for some time to a very much older Irishman with whom she went to Hong Kong for some years – much disapproved of by her family. These were maybe some of the attractions for Iso. Although he and Hedwig did not overtly crave the trappings that sometimes go with culture in society, Anna thinks they were somehow fascinated by them and felt flattered when anyone from those circles paid them close attention. It was all too easy for Iso to start the liaison: Hedwig was used to him travelling extensively to play in concerts, and at the height of the affair, their base in Manchester was far away from Hope. For many months she thought Iso was staying with Anna in her Chelsea flat when he was away. One day, the oft-described situation arose: she found a note from Hope to Iso in one of his pockets. It was clear what was going on.

Hedwig swallowed hard, again confronted Iso, and was prepared to move on. How Iso reacted I do not know, but presumably he terminated the affair. There were some agonising times in the subsequent months before they could recover their equilibrium. But they did, and Hedwig continued to teach piano to Hope's children, and managed to maintain a warm enough friendship with Hope herself.

Life's concertina continued to play, until 1964.

TWELVE

IMPLOSION

1964. Precisely, the 6th May 1964.

'Iso left for Sheffield to give a private lesson and stay overnight. In the morning of 7 May he was due to teach his students at the Guildhall before the charity concert in the evening. He waved to me from Platt Lane as I stood at the window. It was 8 am. He even tried to telephone me at the station – a dear thought. I was out, shopping. (Oh God.) I did my usual college teaching and went to the Unnamed Society to see 'Romeo'… (Iso had said: 'Support them. They need it!…') This took place in a very shabby part of Manchester behind Piccadilly Station and it smelled badly of paint and untidiness. However, I was under Shakespeare's influence and hurried along a very lonely street – indeed I ran as this was a part of the city I did not know – absorbed and deeply impressed by the stark horror of Shakespeare's ending. A cup of tea at home and 11.10 in bed, I thought. Suddenly the telephone rang. It was Hope Kilby (!): "Hedwig, could you come at once to London?" "Why? – is Iso suddenly very ill?" (He had played – begun – the Beethoven – 2 sonatas – for that charity…) "No – he has died…"

'It is impossible to understand now how I could have sustained a certain amount of (necessary) activity after receiving this blow. Iso often said: "one does as one has to". So I even had to think like lightning when Hope asked: "Would you like me to be at the station when your train arrives in London at 5.15 am?" Not to offend her in the face of such a huge happening to all of us, I said: "Yes" and put down the receiver. The most pressurised thoughts, sensations flitted through my mind. I ran outside the door of my flat – like an animal – but there was no one around. (Tex – by a very odd coincidence – had travelled that very night in a train from London to Manchester, probably returning from one of his tragic electric treatments.[a]) I had to think of elementary, trivial things: money, a toothbrush, a few things for staying in London… it did not occur to me to telephone the girls: Marga's family had mumps; Anna's was always very disturbed. In any case, it was very, very late. I asked a 'stranger' – the tenant next door – if he could lend me £5 (I never kept much in the flat). Shortly afterwards, a young, pink-looking policeman came. Could he be of any help? I don't know who 'ordered' him – the hospital or the rich man in London? He got me into a taxi and I soon sat among very indifferently-mixed people in the train, my brain in a tumult. I could not just call it 'grief'; my main idea was what a loss to music – to us – but then I thought of poor Solomon[b] and how dreadful Iso would have felt if he were half paralysed… This was the only 'help' I had not to become despairing. I felt much would rest on my shoulders in future (I must have instinctively felt that Anna's and Marga's marriages were not what they had hoped for). After hours of complete awakeness I heard the dear birds sing! Hundreds of timid voices first – then louder… 3 am. This (more than any 'religious' assistance) helped me and I entered the London Hospital very early, fairly composed.

---

a   Tex had been treated for depression after the War.

b   Solomon Cutner, a British pianist known always as Solomon. His career was brought to a halt by a stroke which left his right arm paralysed.

'The 'meeting' with Hope was rapid and odd: She said she had not seen him – dead... (not allowed, as no relative, said the ambulance men) and that he had been found on the floor by the patron of the concert who thought the pause after the second Beethoven sonata (he had played the *Pathétique* and *Moonlight*) seemed a little long. 'Sudden heart attack' was the finding... I went to the Charing Cross Hospital (alone) and was put into a little waiting room (one with Victorian style tiles which even when one is 'normal' get one down). There were two copies of 'Woman's Own[a] on a little table and a kindly middle-aged nurse brought me a cup of tea with much sugar. She said I could have 'a last look at your husband' at 8.15.

'To escape from feelings of being caged in, I left and walked around the Charing Cross part of London. A Post Office was open early. I thought: What about Maertel and Ilsabe – who so understood and loved Iso. By an instinctive intuition I made it not the very quick telegram to Düsseldorf, but the second best. So Maertel knew of it only after one of his most important concerts.

'Back to hospital and a few moments with dear Iso. He looked like a Russian icon. He was completely sewn (not wrapped) in a material of seemingly Bulgarian type (some colours woven into it) and his lovely hands were quite invisible, something that would have upset him. Only his white forehead, grey hair and beard showed. A most solemn expression as of a really old man. I felt almost guiltily 'alive' and comparatively young, in spite of everything. In the case of a sudden death it is unavoidable that one asks: "What could I have done to prevent this?" Well, I asked myself this (and about Tex later) many, many times. Part was due to Iso's single-mindedness in his art not being complemented by what in English would be called reasonable behaviour, by his not trusting perfectly correct and

---

a   Weekly magazine.

nice doctors; other factors were his near dislike of having me do things for him and his odd 9 months after the H.K.[a] 'discovery' (he liked 'darkness' in many senses). Maybe he felt he would not live long and drove himself mercilessly, as for the New York trip and all those smaller engagements in England. It surely cannot have been because he felt we would starve? He always risked a lot with those cycles but knew somehow we would recover, through our work or something from my parents.

'Three years before this shattering date of 7 May 1964, Iso had said to me as he sat rather pathetically on a park bench: "I have done rather good things in life?" – meaning music (he never touched on moods). It was said in an odd way – hesitatingly and wondering. 'Of course' was my reply. Another time, when he had said "my heart aches", I had replied: 'you surely cannot have all these illnesses…?' As long ago as Sussex – 1942 or '43 – I had written in my diary 'Iso has (or says he has) severe pain in his legs' (he was then only about 36). Perhaps he had been ill much longer than one had thought, and the maybe often nasty London press had got to him… (Manchester's in contrast was always very good).

'The remaining hours of this tragic day were spent on my own dealing with practical things – nothing but sheer duty. I had to see a coroner. I had to collect his (pathetic) little case at Bond St Police Station which contained some money and the new evening dress for New York but not his new and quite nice dressing gown (I did not think to worry how this might have come about…). The coroner was a most sympathetic tall slender man and when I thanked him he said: 'My only girl died last year and I vowed to help people who are saddened.' By then I had heard he might want me to stay in London for a night so I asked at a little Italian hotel. They were full up (big sports events in London that Friday) but gave me a cup of black coffee (the only thing I had had that day

a   Hope Kilby.

and night) and were 'simpatico'. When I was crossing the street near St Pancras, an old Quaker lady in uniform said: 'you look very poorly'. I told her why. I do not remember whether I did stay that night in some other little hotel or whether I already went to Marga's at Hitchin, where they lived in that tiny property with a little narrow back garden; Iso's favourite flowers were out: lilies of the valley.

'I do remember a visit to a 'superior' Funeral Director, somewhere in the 'good' part of London. I had resolved to have the College give us all some music and have a cremation service in Manchester, not London. This meant the coffin would be flown to Manchester; a young man came as an attendant. The coroner's opinion was that there was nothing out of the ordinary and I could go and do what I wished. I must have telephoned Tex and Marga. I am not sure about Anna: I believe H.K. had telephoned them at an odd time to find out where I was (seeing 'Romeo'…). All I remember clearly now is my arrival at Marga and Julian's: they were all ill with mumps and someone had bloodshot eyes and there was dear little pussy and gorgeous May weather. And little Matthew looked at my case (and Iso's) and said: 'Yes, I remember Grandpa with this case'…! (It is still going and annoys me greatly. It topples over and knocks one's shins. We had bought it in the sale.)

'Marga gave me a few cigarettes and a tiny bottle of perfume. Very perceptive! (Oma Stein would have been offended.) They were all very warm. I rang the College Principal, Frederic Cox, who I always admired though I never got very close to him. I think I allowed some of my despair into that telephone call. He was very upset by the suddenness of Iso's death. But he said: 'don't worry; we shall have good music' – or something like that. (I explained that Iso's 'religion' did not fit into any particular mold (Iso never told me whether anyone prayed with him as a child, and only once did he say: 'No, Mama was not Jewish.' He remained almost stubbornly dark as regards this question, but he did like those few old Russian photos of his family which I kept very carefully in our album). Cox said: 'I shall say some words, if I may...' A great load was taken from me... Iso – death – and no music would be an impossibility, it seemed (or worse, one of those dutifully employed players on the organ... No).

'With hindsight one may wonder: 'How did I manage to get through the motions of organising things after a life of over 30 years together, and now ended? My philosophy is that we are in any case alone, whether we marry or not – and all the outward shows of infatuation mean very little to me. What remains of infatuation – alas – seems to have evaporated when it ends. A few good 'smells', visual delights, the (so called) 'joys of sex'... Shakespeare's sonnet about 'Lust in action' fits all those who have loved much and lost their heads in the process! We are alone when we are born and when we die. If a marriage includes some affection, akin to friendship of the finest type, I am satisfied. Ours included living through whole worlds of the arts, and deriving infinitely interesting experiences from people, especially through having gone to another country. Death forces one to think about life in the round: yes – even about disappointments. Iso's tendency to hide his feelings, even things right back in his childhood, was very difficult for me. While I realise I sometimes show my cards too openly, I think this makes me someone who is fitted to play for audiences even though I always knew my place! I never felt I would become a sort of Myra Hess had I not married Iso (which in a few trivial matters was like having a third child). Iso did not trade on his many eccentricities which made it harder for concert agents: there was no book on Russia, no film, no sketches, only very mixed photos, no small scandals, no TV appearances ever. But people like Cox knew to appreciate him, and others, especially in Germany too, and I and Anna and Marga... 'A musician's musician' wrote The Times in the obituary. The Telegraph (Michael Kennedy) mentioned me too, as 'his brilliant wife-pianist....'

'The funeral director meanwhile did his work – like a mole –
unseen. On Sunday 10 May I sat in the train to Manchester and
at Central Station Tex and Hélène Faucher met me – wordless…
Tex had prepared a meal for us all. He was smitten by the event.
The same night I awoke very, very early and sat down to begin my
writing of far more than 100 letters, telling people in my words
and handwriting what had happened, rather than having printed
notices. This was a mammoth task but it helped me to live through
these times, somehow worthily.

'In the meantime I knew Anna had had the feared miscarriage
– I believe the morning after Iso died… Another great sadness. So
it had to be a cremation ceremony without any relatives of mine. I
insisted on the chapel of Manchester's big cemetery where one is
given half an hour. I even steeled myself to get my hair done (our
profession meant we were never really outwardly Bohemian!). Miss
Ryan and Mary Walsh were at my sides, Tex and Hélène behind
me. The dear Doggerts were there, Ernst Grünfeld, and a number of
students and colleagues. Mary put a black lace veil over my fair hair
in the Roman Catholic fashion (I let her!) and the service began…
Mr Knowles played Bach on the organ and the soprano at the
College (Mrs Meguigon) sang very sweetly from Fauré's Requiem.
In the main I remember Cox's remarkably composed speech which
I have kept in a box of special letters. This came from depths –
new to me. I thanked him. Then the Doggerts, Tex, Hélène, and
Alan Worthington came to my flat where I, feverishly anxious and
restless, showed them the old Russian photos of Iso, including of
him as a wunderkind, and others such as of him and me in Berlin,
perhaps as if to hold on to something.

'More letters, written in the middle of the nights, then to sleep
again. No pills – ever in my life. One big slice of my life had been
cut. The reactions to Iso's death were as I had expected. Those who
understood what had been lost expressed themselves beautifully:
Anna, Marga, Ros, Lyn, Avice, Teddy Crankshaw, Sir Thomas

Bazley, Olly Adelmann, and Rita Redlich[a] (with whom Iso had spent a happy evening in Berlin after a recital only in February 1964). The press, too, were as I expected. Most touching was the man from Pye who did the last recordings in London: 'how amazingly patient Iso had been with us too!' (Yes, such things and Iso's almost shy behaviour shortened his life… he should have been asked by HMV or others more powerful than Pye.) Ibbs and Tillett sent a bill (and not a word!). The old Viennese agent in New York wrote beautifully and the Kipnises were deeply shocked – they sent me a recording of the New York interview with Iso.

'I went to College again and tried to behave as usual. Barbara Stones had appeared like a thin ghost on the afternoon of that sad cremation-day.

'Going to Lloyds Bank was necessary. Tex took me to Liverpool one evening to hear Max Davies' music in 'Musica Viva' – so much explanation about the programme and by Max himself. I disliked it. Death sharpens one's real artistic tastes. I played a little, taught much, or sat in the park, reading poetry. To be alone did not hurt; I had had this for half of our marriage of 31 years.

'Letters arrived en masse. David Wilde's perceptive newspaper article in the Worthing paper moved me profoundly. Tex was not 'easy' in the following weeks and he looked awful, blaming himself for believing Iso that the tummy pains were real, and giving him something for this, whereas it was surely the heart.'

With Iso's death came, in literal terms, the end of the marriage; but I do not think it ever ended. Even the first time I met Hedwig, she talked about Iso. He was part of her, as she had been of him. And the heights and depths they had together experienced through Iso's music-making, too, were with her forever.

---

a   Fritz's secretary.

THIRTEEN

ALONE

I cannot imagine what it is like to live on through the death of the person most close to you. Other than in extreme circumstances, there is no way of preparing for it, least of all of course any desire to do so. Yes, one might make a will, one might take out life insurance, as Iso did (for the paltry sum of £1000). One might, as Hedwig had done and thereby upset Iso, even suggest music for one's funeral. Nevertheless, these are all nothing more than sensible actions while one is bound up in the here and now of living and the unadulterated expectation of its continuance...

Hedwig wrote expressively about some of the events of the weeks and months after Iso's death. It felt to me as though she was reaching out to any reader to accompany her. I will let her do a lot of the talking therefore. They are words that became a part of her, because I remember, even after all those years, how she shared some of them with me as we sat together in the bay window in her flat over cups of coffee.

Within two months of Iso's death, Hedwig had written by hand to all the people who had expressed sorrow and consternation and sympathy. She had a list: the total number was 320 – an indication of the extent to which their circle of contacts and friends had grown. Tex was doing his best to divert her, with invitations to Verdi's *Otello*, and to *Rosenkavalier*, 'which I hated. Tex shouted his 'bravos'. Hedwig was never going to be a lover of Richard Strauss (and, I might add, she said she could live extremely well without Wagner – and even added as an afterthought later: 'I feel this very strongly'!). She ordered six photographs of Iso that the magazine Cheshire Life had arranged to be taken some months previously. She gave the odd recital, dealt with Iso's life insurance, noted that the College would award her a (very) small honorarium pension, saw four of her pupils pass their examinations for music teaching, and started to make arrangements for Iso's ashes to be buried in the family grave in Heidelberg. She gave a present to the College: one Reger letter (which she considered not to be important), one by Clara Schumann, and one photograph of Liszt. She gave Tex a short letter written by Benjamin Britten to Iso as a 'souvenir' for the purposes of 'showing good will' (though it annoyed her that he thanked her only three days later). Then, it was time to go to Germany:

'Ticket for flight to Frankfurt, but a short stop first at Marga's. Then once more to the London Funeral Director and taking the little metal box with ashes of Iso – with the greatest reverence – on to the aircraft. (If someone had to do it, it could only be me, I told myself. It was so very, very hard.) The plane encountered big thunderstorms and landed at Stuttgart, and another plane took me to Frankfurt... Yes, quite alone. By train to Heidelberg which was filled up with people. In the end I found a little room and put a few flowers from Marga's garden and 2 small photos of Anna and Marga on the metal box. I was overwhelmed by fatigue and even slept a short while (to see these fat beer-drinkers of South German type the night before was not easy...).

'An old official at the Stadt Verwaltungsamt[a] in Heidelberg knew our family grave! He had been a nurse for my grandfather Czerny for years! I – alone – by train to Düsseldorf. Warm reception by Maertel. They were very sad but I was touched by Mechthild's[b] vivid remembrances of Iso and his last visit to them

---

a   Register Office.
b   Maertel's elder daughter.

(February 1964). She even copied some of his mannerisms: how he held his head often, or stroked one eyebrow! The next day Maertel drove us all to Heidelberg, through vast crowds of cars on the roads which always gets him very angry. We came just in time for the 'Beisetzung'[a] of the urn into the grave. No priest. Just Ilsabe saying 'Our Father'. A day of sun and green trees... To Königstein and to Oma Stein,[b] where Fritz Benedik[c] produced a tape he had made: In memoriam Fritz Stein.

'...Reading of old love letters by Oma and Vater[d] (those of 1914–18 War less pleasing – too 'patriotic' for my taste). They had their private difficulties. When I was born Gretel Stein seemed to have hysterical fits of crying: their flat was noisy, so Vater pleaded with the old Czernys for a house in Jena to be built. He got it – but a nasty letter by Oma Czerny to him first! He even reminded them of their son Paul's nervous breakdown and suicide...'

In the surreal time between Iso's death and the interring of his ashes, that time of the impossibility of 'normal', let alone rational thought and action, Hedwig simply did what had been discussed, and arranged for the ashes to be placed in the Heidelberg family grave. It was necessary only to deal with the situation she felt, and not to bother the girls. Her Uncle Friedel had arranged and paid for the headstone, and found it important to refer to Iso as 'Born in Mogilev. Fellow of Guildhall', put like that only because Friedel wanted the mention of some sort of academic achievement. 'What a silliness', Hedwig later thought, as indeed was the fact that they had made such an arrangement at all. After all, what did she and Iso really have in common with the Czernys? They loved England and the way they had been able to live their lives here. She excused herself to Anna in her Diary: 'If you ever read the gravestone, don't worry. It has no deep meaning.'

---

a   Interment.
b   Gretel – Granny Stein.
c   Cousin of Hedwig's who had made the tape from a German Radio broadcast.
d   Granny and Father – an interesting way of describing Gretel and Fritz.

In September, Hedwig once again took stock of her life. It was busy, with College matters, practising every day, recitals, teaching her privates, visits from ex-students (which she said she mostly enjoyed), some entertainments like visits to the theatre, extending and receiving invitations to drinks and suppers, dealing with financial issues, and correspondence. All these activities now were an unchanging part of the pattern of her life, and she took the leap of arranging another Wigmore Hall recital for the following year. Her daily joy became walking through 'her' park, just across the road from her flat. She loved its Georgian house, which housed a costume museum, and walking round the lake and feeding ducks. In October, the Daily Telegraph and the Guardian gave first-rate write-ups of her Manchester Midday Recital, which included the Schubert *Moments Musicaux* and two encores. Looked at like this, her life was continuing along known tracks. But the rest was totally changed, and internally the reality was like a deep cut from the razor edge of a rock face. Once or twice in the past, when Iso was alive, she had consciously noted how they had been apart for great chunks of their married life because of his concert and broadcasting engagements. Now, she wrote, the absence was constant. 'My life goes on – somehow.' She decided to pick up Anna's request that she write about her life, and started. Writing was mainly a middle-of-the-night activity, possibly to ward off other thoughts. She found it difficult to sleep. 'So many thoughts in my head – they 'work' at night. Alas.'

Hedwig's life alone was to last nearly twenty years. If she ever came anywhere near forming another close relationship, she gave no indication of it in her Diary, or in hints to Anna. From all we know about her, it is not surprising. How could she possibly have entertained any other companion – for that is what Iso quickly became after those first heady years of enthrallment, exposure and risks – than Iso? And a lover would surely have never been an option for Hedwig. No, for her there were the old friendships: the Sussex faithfuls Ros and Lyn, close emotionally but physically far away and therefore not able to offer constant sustenance, and Tex, close and nearby, 'an oasis of good feelings and common interests', yet without the gamut of overlaps that Hedwig probably most sought at this time. And, over time, came the deepening of some newer friendships, such as with Sara and John Doggerts, and those completely unknown until late in her life, such as the Crawley Millings, friends of Tex's who took a neighbouring flat.

Bit by bit, Hedwig gives glimpses in the Diary of how it felt to be an integral and central part of Iso's life, of this person who could reach into and reveal the depths of music. Her love for his music-making never diminished, never ceased. She wrote, and kept writing, about how captivatingly he had played at various concerts and at home. Only in the latter years did a few doubts surface. She noticed the odd occasion when he did not play as she knew he could. His underlying less-than-robust health, perhaps? And then the recurring question after his death: had she done all she could? She kept returning to all the instances of health problems and Iso's obvious increasing fatigue, re-living her frustration at Iso's refusal to speak to anyone for many years, and commenting that no one had thought there might be a problem with his heart (was Tex not, after all, a doctor?). There had been just the right consultant in Rusholme Gardens, only a couple of doors away. Iso could so easily have spoken to him. But he had thought a doctor might talk to other people, word would get out that he was not well, and that would have serious consequences for his performing possibilities. Preposterous! Hedwig had torn her hair out, trying to explain that doctors were discreet. Iso would have none of it. Once diabetes had been diagnosed, any manifestation of failing health was put down to that, and to systemic overwork. In his view, nothing further needed to be done. And so the circle of self-criticism and self-justification went on.

Motherhood too, now in a preoccupying and problematic way; the years immediately after Iso's death were the most troubling. The space Hedwig had always given Anna and Marga meant that there were periods when one or the other or both of them would go silent – sometimes for weeks – and others when they shared intensely the minutiae of what was happening to them, particularly as each of their marriages faltered and then disintegrated, one distressing episode after the other. Both Marga and Anna seemingly looked to Hedwig for help in the form of solace, and sometimes for material support, as they had throughout their lives. Anna was not surrounded by close friends in whom she might have confided and who might have advised her: she had been spoilt by her parents' circles of friends – all far more interesting people than those she had come into contact with during her own adult life. Neither she nor Marga had moved into a glittering world with those at the top of their chosen occupations. In a sense they were imprisoned in that world in which they had grown up – the world of their parents – yet not of it, and were unable to find a way out.

What does a life consist of, a life in which the main raison d'etre, the central bond, has vanished? In asking the question, I quickly realise I am formulating it incorrectly and, especially in Hedwig's case, inappropriately. For it seems to me that there had been four raisons d'etre in Hedwig's adult life up to 1964: Iso, Anna (and her children), Marga (and her children) and, to a colossal extent, music and the arts. With Iso no longer alive, there was much to think and worry about as far as Anna and Marga and their crumbling marriages were concerned, and there was still, as compelling as ever, the last of these. Nearly a year after Iso's death, Hedwig wrote:

'Only recently did I manage not to think on awakening in the mornings: 'Yes, it happened. Iso is no longer alive'. ... The sleep intervenes and blots out – probably many people have this experience... As I 'feed' so much on each day's work experience of people and the Arts, I am better able to live by myself than many. Half of our 31 years of marriage I was alone... Philosophy – yes – to me much more helpful than religion.'

Those 31 years of marriage, when times together with Iso were so often interrupted, and sometimes for long periods, must indeed have helped Hedwig to manage her new circumstances to some degree. But the impact of being alone is not determined simply by the absence of someone else. Up till now, when Iso was away, Hedwig could think that he might ring in the morning or evening, that a postcard might be waiting on the hall mat when she returned from College, that she must take care to remember events and write letters, and to review the most striking things that had happened or that she had read or heard or seen so she could relate them on his return, and that she could share her concerns about the girls. That had been being alone. Aloneness during Iso's lifetime, accompanied by expectation and by anticipation. Now she knew that any time the telephone rang it would not be Iso, there would be no postcard waiting for her, no excitements, irritations, disappointments, or overwhelming joy after a successful concert tour. This was a new alone. And it was compounded: given the power of music and its indefinable way of awakening emotion, Hedwig had to absorb the absence of the music Iso created. That hole must have felt limitless.

Built up as it is from jottings and appointment diaries and memories, the Diary for this period does not contain any lengthy expositions of Hedwig's thoughts or ideas from the philosophers and novelists she has read, the other musicians she has heard, or the artists whose works she has looked at closely. Nor does she – or would it be more accurate to say 'can she'? – elaborate on what emotions various pieces of music that she played evoked in her. Yet it is these that constituted the inner core of her daily life after Iso's death, and I am saddened that she left me in the near-dark. I rack my brains to try to remember any detail of the conversations we had about such things during those evenings at her flat. They surely contained so very much more than her Diary conclusions on various topics and artists, such as about Toulouse-Lautrec: 'what a genius!' and Barenboim: 'a star!'. But my memory lets me down.

The day-to-day, month-to-month and even year-to-year activities of teaching, performing, and meeting friends and family were interrupted from time to time by excursions. Hedwig glowed as she recounted these. There was an invitation from their old supporter Lady Barlow, the great friend of Beatrice Bateson, to come for Easter to her huge house in Wendover, which was stuffed with books and where Hedwig played many of the Bach 48 Preludes and Fugues – favourites of her host. Conversation was just as she liked it: intense, inquisitive and fast-moving. And, with a young biologist also invited to dinner, it was mainly about the natural world. This was as it might have been with Beatrice Bateson's husband, Hedwig thought.

Reviving friendships from the Sussex days, she went to see the Kilbys from time to time. Invitations came from Ros, where Hedwig indulged in nostalgia, playing the old Bechstein again, taking the familiar route to the church in Friston and to the village, and swimming, and catching up with the now grown-up family she had lived so close to when they were small. Then more reminiscing with Roy and Lyn, who had married in 1974 after the death of Roy's wife Sheila. Here she could talk deeply with Lyn in between walks and picnics on the Downs, strolls through their extensive garden ('a paradise') and excursions to old haunts like West Chiltington, Petworth, Fittleworth, Chichester and Midhurst – places for Hedwig still redolent of the times when she and Iso had brought music to the local communities during the War. Over the years, she witnessed and celebrated with them the realisation of Roy's dream of his Weald and Downland Open Air Museum to preserve local historic buildings and traditions, rescuing and restoring houses and cottages, a watermill, a village school and a market hall, and marvelling at Lyn's hands-on contributions to wattling, 'which involves cow dung'. The museum still thrives today.

Then there were always the extras that some of her concerts offered. In January 1969, after a Manchester Midday Recital and a Bradford Midday Recital within two days of each other, Hedwig gave a charity concert at Wentworth Woodhouse near Sheffield, which she found extraordinarily exciting. I was so struck by her description in the Diary that I used the opportunity of a trip to the north to go to see it. Hedwig described it as huge, and that is certainly no misnomer. The largest private residence in the UK, its east front is the longest country house façade in Europe. It was originally owned by the Rockingham family (of earlier Prime Minister fame) and then left to the Earls Fitzwilliam. By the time Hedwig performed there, though, the house had been let to the West Riding County Council for use as a teacher training college. But the Council did not touch it, and the house, minus its furnishings, still exuded the now-faded splendour of its society times. Stubb's famous portrait of the racehorse Whistlejacket,

Wentworth Woodhouse.
Photographs reproduced with kind permission of Wentworth Woodhouse Preservation Trust

owned by the Marquis of Rockingham and now in the National Gallery, may still have hung in the eponymous room, and the Painted Drawing Room was still as it had been for centuries – subdued green silk on which floral designs were painted. The Wentworth Woodhouse Concert Society, of which Sir John and Lady Barbirolli were Vice-Presidents, held regular chamber concert seasons in the late 1960s with soloists of renown: the pianist Yaltah Menuhin, the bass Owen Brannigan and violinist Alfredo Campoli. I could just imagine Hedwig, dressed appropriately grandly, entering the Marble Saloon: a breathtaking square Georgian hall, with restrained pillars from floor to ceiling, interrupted only by the balustrade gallery running around it, and white marble statues adorning alcoves arranged around the hall. The long windows along the entire east wall look out over the park – with just a hint on the horizon of the industry that had made this all possible. The magnificent marble-patterned floor, with its mix of elegant leaves and geometric black and white squares, might well have been covered by temporary boarding at this time – an improvement from an acoustic perspective, though. Hedwig spent the weekend there in a state of excitement. 'Bedroom like the Wigmore Hall!' she wrote.

Rising to the occasion was something Hedwig did well – whatever the nature of the occasion was. This little anecdote exemplified one rather unusual occasion:

'Another 'Jewish House Recital' – blazing May weather… It became a little adventure of absorbing interest to me: I had forgotten my latchkey at home and afterwards just could not make anyone hear my knocking (I should have telephoned!). So, a swift resolve: I spent the night c/o the newly painted Waiting Room, Piccadilly Station! From 11.30 – 6 am – long, it seemed! But not depressing and not dangerous! I, in a long robe, evening cloak (!) – made-up (etc) with a huge chocolate box under the arm (my 'fee'!). I must have looked odd. (However the English are not easily surprised! Phlegm (?) and fairness mixed! (Am I right? I think so!)) I have to be careful and observe, in the streets, as if my life depended on it! (Although it is not really so in Manchester – they crouch along – many avoiding looking. Iso noted it – also the bending forward of youths – when hurrying.) Now in these terrible shoes one cannot walk properly! A single one weighs pounds! [*At which point Hedwig offers a rough sketch of a heeled shoe.*] A nice pink-faced policeman asked me what I was doing, and understood the situation. I had only 13/- shillings on me – even at that time it was not enough for a hotel. But the Waiting Room had its interesting aspects: from 3.15 am the big cleaning machine did its work on plastic floors, and all the women were most cheerful! At 6.15 I spent 5/- to have bacon and egg at station (yes!) together with some young workmen, then bus home. A totally sleepless night (Tex thought it very very odd!)'.

In contrast was the idyllic experience of going one Whitsuntide, with Tex, to the Millings' weekend cottage in North Wales. It was:

'…a fantastic converted shepherd's cottage on top of a mountain. This was so new to me – everything – that it made me love Michael and Gee, and all they did. A childless couple who sail and are potters – he, a brilliant physicist,[a] now very high up in Geneva. The drive, the climbing of hills by jeep, the tender sheep, the loneliness, the May environment, a cuckoo, far off. I drew the landscape from the top: winding brooks and so on. Gee had made the interior superb, and what a cook! We met local farmers (very Welsh!). A marvellous country. A beautiful last drive, high up, before we had to go back to dirty Manchester.'

This first trip was followed by a number of others, always with Tex, including one at New Year in 1970:

---

a   Michael Crowley-Milling is now best known for his contribution to the invention of computer touchscreens. His early work was in accelerator design and he became a directorate member of the CERN (European Organisation for Nuclear Research) in Geneva in 1980 after working in the Daresbury Laboratory in Cheshire.

'Great hampers and meal and excellent hospitality. Snow. I stood in my huge woollen dressing gown outside and just looked at the landscape (they were all amused). We all tired… after champagne we went to our beds before midnight. Later small walks and good talk and lunch at Portmeirion… Farmer next to cottage told us amazing Welsh stories – of frozen corpses, standing up, until Spring. Millings took a colour film of Tex and me in the snow (reminded me of Ilsabe's film of Iso throwing his hat up in the Taunus Mountains), and Tex put in some hard work for his London exams, propped up in bed, in heavy woollies… One of the best treats in years, all this.'

There was the occasional excursion further afield too. In Amsterdam, after lugging her heavy suitcase around the streets near the station, she opted for a cheap hotel. It proved to be a room-share, where she and the other occupant were woken in the night by an insistent knock at the door: a young man looking to find a prostitute. Hedwig tossed the occurrence off. Her goal was to visit the museums and to see the originals of many works she knew about, especially the paintings of Van Gogh and Rembrandt. Typically, over a Chinese lunch she chose to have a long talk with some hippies from the USA – 'they did not see me as an old spoilsport!'.

When I first read her Diary and about all that they had done together, I wondered whether maybe there had been a little more between Hedwig and Tex, at least in the early days. Anna produced a photograph taken of herself, Hedwig and Tex together on an outing. It could well support that view. No wonder, as Anna had told me, most women Tex had any dealings with were smitten by him. Nonetheless I concluded that while there was probably an attraction between Hedwig and Tex, it had gone no further.

And there were times, later, when Hedwig was seriously vexed with Tex. She was wildly critical of his seeming lack of appreciation of some of the classical wonders they saw on their trips that Hedwig was so moved by. Some of Tex's plays she found less than compelling, and in the end she made it clear to him how she felt. But what hurt her most of all was now, after Iso's death, Tex seemed to cool off in his admiration for Iso. Hedwig

Anna, Hedwig and Tex on holiday in Italy

gave him records when they came out, yet Tex took days to respond and was sometimes not even enthusiastic about them. It came to something of a bust-up over a dinner in 1965 that Tex arranged for the two of them and his relative Hélène Foucher. Hedwig was so hurt she wrote out in unusual detail some of the exchanges that had passed between them, when each clearly expressed some of the years-long bottled-up grievances. Petulance and self-justification came to the fore on both sides:

> "'Hedwig, you go on to 1890 or so and only like what you call 'great' and 'what is appreciated'". Oh – dear, that 'hit'! (especially, as I saw 'Threepenny' – Brecht, the pictures by Klee, Ernst Gross etc etc, plays by E. Toller etc when only a child... (when he [Tex] got 'stuck' in Wagner – or Noel Coward...). *Tex:* if Iso, instead of having made that slip (!) with Myra Hess (yes!) had been friends with her, that would have changed the position' etc... [Diplomacy and success are now quite out of proportion to the talent involved.]

... I [Hedwig]: 'I shall not come to Dorothy Taylor's Peter Pears party (in aid of) but I'll send money. She wrote not a word to me after Iso's death.' *Tex:* 'I can't take this. I cannot have you 'censor' my friends and relatives (Hélène?). ... I work so hard among slummy people (yes – Salford!) and I like to take the rest of my time 'easier'.' (That is, with Hélène and DT's luxurious style?!) (Well: 'I [Hedwig] read Proust, even Arthur Miller, the Durrells.' And so it went on. I felt I am not a stick in the mud, but open to anything if it has something – Opa Stein never did Bartók or Debussy! I did...)'

But afterwards, as on countless other occasions, Tex came back, apologetic and often with a large bunch of flowers, with the explanation that he was weighed down by financial problems. Money, it seems, was something he craved; he even ventured into what sounded like a hare-brained offshore tax-saving escapade in the Bahamas with a couple of people he had got to know. Any diminution in his wealth, or even an indication of the possibility of losses, got him down. All this must have seemed petty and unnecessary to Hedwig. Tex was patently sufficiently well-off to lead a comfortable life. However, their long history far outweighed the discordances and the unpleasant dinner. It was, after all, a friendship stemming from Hedwig and Iso's first times in Manchester, which had embraced all Hedwig's and Tex's relatives, to say nothing of the numerous trips and concerts they had experienced together, and their joint music-making when Tex might sing or he and Hedwig played works for four hands or two pianos. So in the years after Iso had died, Hedwig simply took note of Tex's monetary escapades while continuing to tread the familiar, appreciated and well-trodden grooves of their relationship. Living in the same block of flats, they would often invite each other to dinner, or go to the theatre or a concert together, and most of the time each was aware of what the other was doing, and where. When Tex was ill, or became depressed – something that happened from time to time, possibly exacerbated by his wartime experiences – Hedwig would go out of her way to help in whatever way possible. And after a couple of years had elapsed following Iso's death, Hedwig and Tex resumed their piano playing together on the two Steinways, most usually on Saturday mornings – Mozart's D major Sonata, Bach's *Art of Fugue* (in Reger's transcription), and even arrangements of works such as the Mozart Clarinet Quintet and the G minor String Quintet. These get-togethers they rather oddly described as 'lessons'. More important for Hedwig was that they:

> 'proved that our very long and precious friendship still had much life in it. I'd make coffee or a good lunch while Tex might come with an armful of flowers or some bottles of wine (of course we could not exchange money).'

In the late 1960s, Tex arranged for several of his plays to be performed in a week. At the end, Hedwig gave a speech to the audience:

> '…As a musician I feel that the creation of a short piece – such as an Intermezzo by Brahms or an Impromptu by Chopin – requires a very special gift, to leave out all ballast and make the essentials convincing. This Tex has done in 'Interview', a little gem of many modulations… Tex's inventive faculty is astonishing, although he himself is far from a typical north-country type… We feel there will be other plays to come: short ones and long ones, psychological studies and dramatic works…'

In April 1970, Tex sent Hedwig a sad and pathetic little scribbled letter. He was seriously ill and in a London Hospital. She wired 'warmest wishes' at once, followed by a proper letter and a little Eau de Cologne sent to the hospital – though in all likelihood, he never received it since he discharged himself and went to one of his brothers before journeying up to his family's hotel in Blackpool. Hedwig did not know. A subsequent note from Tex said x-rays had shown there might be a spot on one lung. Along with many other letters that he wrote a few days later from the hotel:

"...am hoping to get back to Manchester before too long. I loved your letter... Thanks for the Greetings Telegram. I do so hope we shall be doing the Art of Fugue[a] again before too long. My warmest and dearest affection."

The following day, there was a knock at Hedwig's door. There stood Tex's niece, Pauline, who also had a flat in the same block:

'Tex is dead... He went for a very short walk on the Promenade, climbed up some rocks, and dived into the water, having previously drunk a lot and taken off his jacket. A boy of 12 saw him... ('...it was far too cold to bathe') and ran to the nearest telephone box... It was too late. Two policemen managed to get hold of Tex who had tied his hands together. He was still conscious, but died after ambulancemen had tried to give him the kiss of life...

'I thought the world had a big crack – so much came wrong... Yet I had to tell friends – Doggerts, Dr Taylor, even Alan Worthington, and others. Terrible. Alan W said: 'He was doomed, for 15 years – I more or less expected it.' Nearly ten years ago Tex had written to Iso and me: "I would rather finish with a 'big bang' instead of having one of these terrible illnesses."'

Hedwig kept thinking about the circumstances. They seemed not to fit Tex's character. Blackpool was so near to his family and hotel... why choose that location? He disliked Blackpool intensely. He loved his large family and was someone who cared about proprieties. His mother had been staunchly Roman Catholic. We need to remember that it was less than ten years since suicide had been decriminalised and society had hardly accommodated itself to that. 'My head was in a turmoil... Only work and concentrating on my many musical and other duties would keep me going.'

---

a Against which Hedwig noted later: 'Bach died over it.'

A few days later, Hedwig had to go to the main branch of Lloyds Bank. Yellow placards in town carried the headline: 'Well-known North of England Specialist Takes Life'. Hedwig had agonised over Iso's illnesses that led to his death: could she in any way have done more and helped to avoid it? Now Tex. And with a suicide, similar questions well up with an equal force. Those questions were still active, haunting her as she wrote her Diary. Yet reassurances came from others close to Tex, saying he had always been a labile character, prone to depression, and that while his early death was tragic, somehow it was inevitable.

Long after, Michael Millings told Hedwig how once, when he had been visiting them in Wales, Tex had forgotten his 'special strong sleeping stuff', so Michael had driven many miles to a chemist to get it. Had he not done so, Tex would have been unable to sleep at all, he had said. Hedwig reflected:

'How tragic to be so dependent. Iso, Tex and I must have exchanged millions of words in nearly 30 years of friendship but what really ailed him so terribly one could not find out. Was it overdriving himself all his life? Possibly sexual maladjustments? His mother's too severe influence early on? We shall never know. He was immensely ambitious on many levels, and often hid behind seeming adoration of the most diverse types. Artist manqué? "Hedwig, I could never had been a first-class actor", for instance. The pull of 'worldly' matters was strong – how one looks, dresses, eats, is considered by colleagues, where one spends holidays, how to meet old age. Yes, all this went in parallel with his true kindness to hundreds, even thousands, of people. Is it fair to say he sometimes 'bought' admiration by over-generous gifts?'

Six years later, Hedwig wrote:

'A cruel blow. We all thought: could we have 'done' more not to let this happen? He had one niece in the house – and me and the Millings. If he was so lonely I could have seen him far more often – but we all never even just 'knocked' at doors but telephoned or left a written message (no 'barnstorming'. Even Iso felt like that). A very busy person – Tex often up in the night – out in his Rolls Royce years ago. Consultant in 2 hospitals... plus much other work. Fear of old age played a big part; fear of not enough to do – lifelong taking of sleeping pills... Migraine occasionally. And this March obviously the fear of lung cancer or suchlike big illness. (The x-rays did not show it?)

[*Inserted later by Hedwig:*] 'Alan Worthington thought he had that illness! Fear of getting poor too (!). That new business enterprise which worried him so much (though all was so 'correct'!). Those 2 very rich men influenced him...

'This is all in the light of hindsight – after 6 years – and sounds cold... What happened remains a part-mystery... Certainly his mother when young conditioned them all in a big way: they must get far, always do their duty; she believed in purity (etc) and saw no other religion but her (convert) RC... Had she not died and Iso was still alive might he not have done it?... His very valuable Paris golden watch and wrist chain was found lying in a bathroom in the hotel (and found by a guest!) – maybe he left it on purpose? (or was not quite aware...)

'All these letters seemed to make suicide not likely, but the tying of the wrists was unfortunately convincing. In the morning of that Sunday he had wanted to pour out – again – his worries before beloved Justin[a] (who was then madly busy) and had said: 'Dear boy – we discuss it tomorrow, or so.' Then Tex went for that fatal little walk. Hideous cold weather and big waves. I promised to play the organ two days later at the little RC Blackpool church. Marga came from Letchworth, deeply shocked – but she provided the wind for my playing... The night before we two spent c/o the hotel – all relatives there and I made music – ... C minor Nocturne by Chopin and they were brave. The priest mentioned the word 'sin' five or six times and there was no incense – not the

---

a One of Tex's brothers.

full occasion for a Catholic! But I played Bach… And Justin and I played the great Mozart G minor String Quintet! (Iso's, Tex's, and my great love.)'

Six months after Tex's burial, she visited the grave again. It was just before Christmas:

'…blue skies, and birdsong. All so sad… Simple and barren this very orderly grave. The name Tex is mentioned, and 'Pray for the soul of…'.'

This injunction Hedwig presumably disregarded since it meant nothing to her. A year later she returned again: this grave, 'so tidy and impersonal… (odd and sad feelings in me)'. There were at least a further two visits. I wonder why, what drew her there repeatedly? The need to reflect further on the odd and sad feelings, maybe? It is in any case an indication of the specialness of that long-standing friendship – turbulent as it might have been on occasion – and the countless times they had been together, all interwoven with music in some form.

Like the death of any central figure in one's life, Tex's, so sudden, must have left a vacuum that somehow Hedwig had to rebuild her life around. As always, it was music that she turned to.

Other punctuation marks in the general run of things came regularly in the form of Christmases, birthdays and anniversaries of deaths, and visits to graves: those of Iso – and thereby Fritz, and later Tex. Four years later she was back in Germany for another interment, this time for Gretel. Again, she went with Maertel from Düsseldorf, and as it was when she took Iso's ashes, traffic delays meant that they only just arrived in time. Once more, Hedwig faced that 'huge, odd grave'.

Are graves by their very nature disturbing, the only solid thing remaining after someone has died? Faced with a headstone of someone completely unknown, there is virtually nothing to tell you anything about the person: the odd biographical detail, a usually inexplicable epitaph, and hardly with exception, the 'dearly beloved of…'. From such paucity,

Hedwig in her later years

it is impossible not to have questions about the life, and the death. For someone known, it seems not unusual that various family members, friends and acquaintances find the service or the grave not quite fitting. Something jars with their own sense of who this person really was. So it was for Hedwig.

By late 1969, Hedwig noted: 'I am very, very sad. Both marriages 'burn'.' The first indications had been some time earlier, but the downward spiral of each was now clear. Marga's ended in 1970, followed by a new relationship a few years later. Anna divorced in 1974. For all these years Hedwig fretted, made numerous visits to each of the girls, advised them, left them space, and helped them financially through taking on more privates (which came to include me) and selling odd inherited treasures such as 28 letters from and to Max Reger, her grandmother's jewellery and various music documents. It was a constant worry. It meant there were no empty interstices in her life. She wrote time and again of being tired, of Sundays always being her worst days, alone. I myself well remember Sundays in Manchester – even without all the ordeals Hedwig was going through, her life with Iso now over. To me, it seemed the world hibernated into greyness and cold on Sundays, under an enveloping fog of gloom, enhanced by Manchester's ever-present grime. Activities were limited to Monday to Saturday, and the most that Sunday had to offer were the jumbo Sunday papers and church services. Any problem got bigger, any sadness gained new depths, and it felt as though joy at anything had to wait until Monday.

Through all these years, Hedwig kept her memories of Iso vividly alive, listening to his recordings, talking about him, and remembering their times together. Although there are not many, some of Iso's recordings are still available, including on YouTube. They are hardly enough to be able to get an all-round feel for his playing and interpretations, and how those changed over time, but they do at least bring closer the sense of what Hedwig lived with every day for more than 30 years, and what the absence might have meant. She re-read their old love letters from 1932 ('what a loving style I had!'), and Iso's postcards from his various trips. I do not know if she had read the entry about Iso in H-P Range's 1964 book (in German) presenting the most noteworthy pianists of the time, but it would surely have pleased her no end if she had: "a style of interpreting of past epochs… a true artist, always serving only the music, never himself… one of the most important interpreters in England." The old questions continued to pop up: had it been the right thing to do, to go to Manchester, or would Iso have had more opportunities if they had stayed in London? What could they have done to get him greater attention, in the concert hall and in recordings? And what more could she have done to avert Iso's early death? In 1974, she heard that one of their very first, most longstanding and faithful supporters, Leslie Linder, had died. She could not help herself, though: 'His will: £527,000; duty to pay £220,000; Iso had £20 for his last concert there.' Hedwig kept pushing all these questions and reflections to one side and got on with her life. That meant ever more exploration of 'her' composers – Bach, Chopin,

Schubert, and now Debussy – and the arts, teaching, and spending as much time as she could with her grandchildren. Until those questions pricked her again.

Enough was enough. By the end of 1976, she wrote: 'So I sailed into the New Year 1977. I am so busy. But in very good health…' With that, she finished her Diary.

FOURTEEN

CODA

From Schubert Impromptu No. 2 in E♭ major [a]

Having digested the Diary and all the other material, I am bound to look back at this entire process of writing about Hedwig and think about how I now view her. But first, I can dispense at least in part with an unknown that arose early: whether Marga's copy of the Diary exists. It does. It is with Matthew, one of Hedwig's grandsons, and although I have not yet read it, he revealed that the entire first part of Marga's copy, up to the day when War was declared, is in German. Anna's copy, however, is entirely in English. I can think of no explanation. From screenshots of the few pages that Matthew sent me, I could see that the transition is as abrupt as the

---

a   Schubert: *Impromptus and Moments Musicaux*. Henle Urtext. Copyright: G Henle Verlag e.K., Munich, Germany.

Declaration. The day before, Hedwig wrote (in German) that she had borrowed a copy of Dostoyevsky's letters and started reading Balzac's *La Peau de Chagrin*. The next entry is: 'Luton, Sept 3, Sunday. Here we are and it is War.' From then on, Hedwig and Iso ceased to speak German, even at home; they became as wholly English as they could. Yet they were not, of course. Hedwig certainly fitted in well, but I rather think she was always aware of her distinctness, her German and continental European roots. Although she gives no hint of having been aware of it, she was one of those émigrés who brought and showered others with inestimable riches, part of that surge of people who injected new energies and outlooks into musical life in England during and after the War. The soprano Janet Baker, in an interview for the Royal College of Music,[37] speaks of her endless gratitude to those émigrés who played a critical role in helping her at the start of her career and of the way they changed her life; more broadly, Daniel Snowman[38] has charted the enduring impacts of émigré artists on our cultural scene. These people were enormously grateful for the haven they found here. Yet for many of us, it was they who were the providers of gifts – Hedwig for me bringing to life a world that had been little more than an imagined frieze, and opening up the vista of a boundless life.

As I was dwelling on this coda, Anna came with more treasures from her trove: more packages of letters. There were some gems. Some were revelatory, others confirmatory or otherwise, and yet others with new information. One I found particularly striking. It was from Hedwig to Iso, written in April 1933 (on his birthday, as it happened), and it related the reaction of her parents to her and Iso's decision to marry and to leave Germany, and the news that she was pregnant. The letter was written (in German) very early in the morning after the 'discussion' of the previous evening. It was white hot. Hedwig was utterly clear about her position, and how it conflicted totally with that of her parents:

'...I am quite calm, as indeed I was during our long talk. This gave me absolute clarity: I and my parents are so different in our attitudes to life, to people, to our response to the arts, that we should – at least for some time, and who knows what will happen later – have nothing whatsoever to do with each other. For me this is utterly necessary, and at the same time liberating… It is clear: now they have surrendered themselves with body and soul to the currents of the new nationalism and intend to stand for their causes, we will stand for ours, our cause of goodness and therefore of humanity…'

Until now, I had remained on the fence about whether Hedwig was politically minded, or at least whether she paid much attention to it (Anna averred that neither Hedwig nor Iso concerned themselves with politics). Reading this letter however, and knowing how she acted, I found myself no longer straddling that fence, no longer able to think of Hedwig as apolitical, in some – or indeed, any – sense. I found her action brave. She, independently, rejected fully the nationalistic epidemic that was rampant throughout Germany and with which her parents were enamoured. They tried pulling levers to get her to change her mind. She would not have their agreement to her marriage; she would not receive any support other than the legacy from her grandmother. Her friends were understanding, yet none of them were contemplating any such move. Hedwig wavered not. She had her eyes wide open to what was going on, and rejected it. Over and above that was the fact of Iso's Jewish heritage. I conducted a small thought experiment: would she have acted in the same manner had she not been Iso's partner? I venture to say yes, I think she would have. She was 26 and had thought a great deal about the world as well as the role of music in it. For Fritz, the music he loved and had devoted his life to was that of the German masters and for him it was inextricably bound up with German-ness. I recalled his conviction that a nation that had produced Bach and Beethoven – and we could add, as far as Fritz was concerned, Max Reger – would not be defeated. None of that featured for Hedwig. It was only the music qua music and its central meaning in human lives that counted.

And so I surmise that while she did not talk much about political events, particularly as far as Nazism was concerned, she felt in no way removed from them and took positions. Indeed, before this 'new' letter appeared, it had seemed to me barely credible that in her interactions with her intimate friends, especially in the Sussex times, Hedwig did not speak at all about what the Nazis were doing. I imagine rather that people would have been curious, would have expected her to do so, and would presumably have questioned her about what it had been like in Berlin in the early 1930s. Understandably, she might not have found it worth recording in the Diary, reconstructed as it was long after the War, for by and large she did not record conversations. But the conviction expressed in this letter removes doubt as to the extent of Hedwig's political engagement and judgement. I also find it quite plausible that later, Hedwig became increasingly silent – one of those countless examples of people choosing not to speak about topics that have played a painful part in their lives. Dictators drive individual lives in dramatic ways and can bulldoze communities with no regard whatsoever for the impacts on individuals, who are no more than pawns and are fortunate if they can conceive options and have the courage to act on them. Hedwig and Iso were fortunate: they were young, had the resolve, and were sharp enough to extrapolate to the probable consequences in time still to be able to exercise a choice and leave Germany for England. Afterwards it was not necessary to speak much about that part of their lives. Nonetheless, Hedwig had an additional burden to bear. Most émigré stories evoke sympathy because they are about those who have themselves experienced persecution, or have strong indications that they are likely to do so. Hedwig and Iso clearly fall into this second group. But for Hedwig there was a concealed bitterness: the knowledge that her father had belonged to the Nazi party, and had not only cooperated in its furtherance, but gone out of his way to do so. Whatever the underlying reasons – and as we have seen, they remain unresolved – they were inescapable facts and must have caused her distress. Burning letters does not erase the memory of their existence, as the retelling of the act in her Diary shows so clearly.

Having taken the leap, Hedwig and Iso's entrée into British musical life was far from straightforward. Carving out a niche as a performing musician was no less taxing then than it is today: finding people willing to offer a performance platform; not being too proud to explore any option, even at the very bottom; and securing enough openings to be able to pay the rent, eat, and to purchase a suitable instrument. Here, too, fortune was with Hedwig and Iso. Coming onto the scene with a considerable reputation, as Iso did, and at a catastrophic time in history, led benefactors to them. And they also had the thin cushion provided by Luise Czerny's legacy and Hedwig's good friend from her Heidelberg days, Görli, who was able and willing to send their regular instalments.

What has emerged by way of Hedwig's story is rather front-loaded. It could hardly be otherwise. Most of the big events in Hedwig's life were in her early to middle years, though there was one or the other shocking event later. But these were not accompanied by the dramatic political turns that so shaped the 1930s and '40s; rather, they were personal shocks. These were shocks of the sort that go so deep they can hardly be allowed out into the outer self, let alone the external world, but are continually present internally, even if subdued, reordering memories and emotions and themselves being reordered and reshaped. For the rest, these later years saw the ongoing flowering of established friendships and the reaching of a steady state in Hedwig's musical career. Everything I have read and heard and remembered myself makes me think she felt largely in equilibrium with her world.

Equilibrium undoubtedly suggests a knowledge of oneself and, from early on, Hedwig showed resolutely that she was her own person, as she fixed on a joint life with Iso in the face of wholesale opposition from her parents; as she came to her own conclusions, early on, about Nazism; as she did no more than take note of Fritz's decisions about his and Gretel's path but stepped right back and rejected it for herself; about how she would pick up her life as a pianist as soon as the girls did not need her full time; and about her role in Iso's life. That was true of her approach to music also. Her pupil Nigel Simeone, now a musicologist, commented that Hedwig's playing showed no Russian influence whatsoever, despite her continuous seeking of advice from Iso. All this is not to say she did not have doubts about her own behaviour from time to time: witness her periodic self-examination and self-reproach in the Diary. A letter from Marga in 1957 talks about Hedwig allowing "the memory of past sacrifices and strains and stresses to dog her". Letters to Hedwig from others outside the family similarly respond to what must have been Hedwig's long-lasting churning about whether she could have done more to prevent Iso's early death or Tex's suicide. But she was steadfast in her cultural convictions. Her love and understanding of the classical European arts and traditions, coupled with a perpetual curiosity, a sharp eye, and thoughtfulness about how they relate to the unknown and the new, were the weft of the Hedwig fabric.

Researching and writing about someone, I have found, is quite unlike any other endeavour. In the quest to portray a character, a personality, you find yourself, over a prolonged period of time and more or less day in and day out, chewing endlessly over what they have chosen to reveal and how they describe the impacts of people and events, and what others have said about them. And the passing of each month, and the observations and reflections each contains, inevitably produces an adjustment to the picture. Virginia Woolf was spot on; my thoughts about Hedwig are no more than that: *my* thoughts, at this particular time.

At this particular time... I found myself now confronting yet another question: is the person I think of *today* as Hedwig the 'same' as the person I met back in 1973? The person with whom I became friendly for such a short but such a significant time – indeed, who I thought at the time, rather naively, I knew – was opened up to me far, far beyond the constraints of our evenings together, through her Diary and letters and reminiscences. I have become familiar, in some regards intimate, with facets of her entire life and know far more about her today than I, or she, could ever have conjectured in 1974. Surely though, the person, the character, who I found so intoxicating is unchanged. Yet surely too, my perspective must have changed in the intervening time. My own ideas and experiences have shaped me into the person I am today quite as much as my further reaches into Hedwig have shaped my impression of her. I ask different questions today and my uncertainties are other than they were 45 years ago, as indeed is my evaluation of the responses. Nonetheless, my feeling about Hedwig as I now 'know' her is fully congruent with that about Hedwig as I 'knew' her in 1974. It is the essence of a person that we as individuals respond to, and that is immutable over time. But the ways in which the essence is revealed do change, depending on all the external events and personalities that impact or impinge on a person. In Peter Handke's two-hour play *The Hour We Knew Nothing of Each Other*, no fewer than 450 characters do no more than traverse a square during the course of a day, observing others and what is going on around them, and in the odd case getting lightly caught up in various events, adapting their routes across the square to the movements of others. The entire play is without any dialogue, the only overt reactions being reflected through the characters' facial and physical reactions. It is a masterly expression of the nuance and consequence of human interactions. Each character is altered, in however small a way, and "...what went on before sculpts what is to come"[a] – and, I would add, without changing its essence.

Early on during the writing process, I went to Shakespeare's Globe Theatre in London to see a new play called *Emilia*, after Emilia Bassano, who was portrayed as Shakespeare's lover and the dark lady. It was one of the most engaging, compelling and energetic plays I have seen recently. Unsurprisingly, I was captivated hearing the playwright, Morgan Lloyd Malcolm, in a talk and Q and A session she gave with the director beforehand. Since there was no opening for me to ask my question, I wrote to her afterwards to ask: how had she decided which elements to use to portray Emilia and how had she remained true to her? Because of the paucity of information, Morgan said, she had had to interpolate and interpret in her own way. But she would keep pulling herself up and asking rigorously whether something really was in line with the few known facts and impressions of Emilia. I told her about my story of Hedwig and she advised me to do the same: keep going back to ask how Hedwig really would have felt or reacted to this or that. I tried. But oh, how difficult! Was I in any position to judge what Hedwig's attitude to, say, an issue related to politics or religion might have been? Could I do

---

a   Programme of the National Theatre production in 2008. Taken from an interview by Sigrid Löffler with Peter Handke in 1992.

any more than conjecture about her relationship with Tex or her feelings towards Hope Kilby, the other woman who played a role in Iso's life for a while? How much weight should I give to her expressions of irritation with Iso, and Anna, and Marga? And how could I possibly say to what extent the disintegration of their marriages had weighed on her? From all my probings, I might have a sense about the answers, but it could be no more than that. No, I felt and still feel able in the main only to pose questions. Some of those have remained in the background; others I have made explicit.

Nonetheless, there are powerful and unmistakeable elements about Hedwig that emerge from her writings. So too from the memories of her and Iso's students. Although each of them had led very different and separate lives, many threads were common to their stories: the profound effect Hedwig had had on each of their lives, how she had found springs in them they might not otherwise have discovered, and her sensitivity as she helped them to grow their talent while respecting their individual views. And each had been offered and had taken up inestimably more from Hedwig than just piano tuition and the invitation to her musical world. Like me, they had each been indelibly affected by Hedwig's sharing of her history, her loves in art, her pleasures of nature and cosmopolitanism, and her generosity of spirit. There are more well-known figures who, over and above their immediate musical legacies, show foresight and humanity by creating imaginative ways for others to follow their musical stars. Even without similar options, Hedwig kindled enormous inspiration through her involvement and empathy towards others, and the distinctive way in which she portrayed her experience and ideas. That awards her a similar qualitative standing.

What is a life? I find myself endlessly ruminating on the question at some length, not only in the context of Hedwig. We exist for a period of time, do certain things, think, converse, form relationships, and then – poof: we are gone. Except that almost without exception, something remains, however small, regardless of whether or not a person is well-known. That something might be a piece of creative art, a conversation, or simply the memory of a caring gesture. For ourselves, we can never know, can often hardly begin to imagine, what it might be, for whom. As I look at paintings by Monet and Holbein, try to fathom who the people really were who are captured in the portraits by Rembrandt or Freud, re-live the worlds of Tolstoy and Austen and Flaubert, Woolf and de Beauvoir, listen to performances of Bach and Beethoven and Brahms and hear old recordings by past maestri – Carlos Kleiber, Vladimir Horowitz, Maria Callas – I so frequently wish I could express to them the depths of what they give me. Instead, I have to be content simply with their legacies. But each individual history is both part of the legacy, and of my interaction with it. That history matters, therefore, and should be told. In trying to find out more about Hedwig's Wigmore Hall recitals, I went recently to meet the archivist Emily Woolf, who spends her days in a small cubby hole of an office at the back of the building, almost surrounded floor to ceiling by grey boxes with dates and names on them. These all contain programmes going back as long as there have been concerts at the Wigmore. Many of those names, like Hedwig and Iso, are no longer currency today. But Emily is starting to bring forgotten names back into life, to place them in the larger history, as I have tried to do with this portrait of Hedwig. They cannot but enhance our appreciation and understanding of the past, so becoming part of the present.

I was happy to hear that Hedwig had continued her musical life almost to the end, before spending the last weeks with Anna. She had been certain, when Gretel died, that it was a good thing because of her suffering. 'I wished for myself not to get so very old… The idea of death had no sting for me.' That wish came to be: Gretel had lived to be 88; Hedwig only 76. Whether or not linked to her on-and-off smoking habits, Hedwig developed lung cancer. But until the end, despite severe pain, she remained cheerful and jocular. Surely for Hedwig, whose entire life was in and around music, it could not have been more fitting that during her last hours Anna played a recording of Haydn's String Quartet Op. 76 No. 4 – poignant, since it is known as the 'Sunrise' quartet.

That brings me back to the question of essence. I commenced this venture hoping to convey the essence of Hedwig. I cannot know anything of her own internal conversations and since there is no more than the odd brief mention of an external conversation recorded in her Diary, I have not been able to expand on her deeper thoughts, attitudes and ethics. But she did open herself up by writing about her reactions to works of art, music and literature, to people and to landscapes. All these convey a great deal about her. They are contained within and behind this 'portrait' of Hedwig, and they add various hues to my painting. Mindful, however, of not wanting to give a particular wash to my portrait, I take comfort in knowing that readers are not wholly relying on me but have many of Hedwig's own words to allow her personality to emerge from the pages as well as any construct I might have fabricated. And if I have succeeded in my portrait, the two will harmonise, though necessarily not coincide. My fervent hope is that I have painted enough, and with a sufficiently broad spectrum of colours, to convey the sense of this unusual woman and artist against a backdrop of other remarkable personalities and earth-shattering events.

I have gleaned riches from Hedwig and writing about her that I simply could not conceive of when my canvas was bare. I emerge convinced of one thing: Hedwig's was a most meaningful, worthwhile and inspirational life. An exemplar as a musician, a teacher, an artist and – in the broadest sense – a friend. That is her legacy.

Dramatis Personae

Person	Associated place	Background
Adelmann, Ada and family	Germany, mainly Berlin	Close friends, especially Ada, who were also connected to Georg Döring (Görli). Ada was a painter. Hedwig lived with them as a paying guest when she was studying in Berlin.
Adler, Octavia	Sussex	Friend and neighbour of Hedwig and Iso's in West Chiltington, Sussex. Owned house named 'Kings and Princes'. Son Robin became photographer. Widow of Robert Nathaniel Eichholz, solicitor. May have had connection with John Sebag Montefiore.
Aggs, Sylvia and Jessica	Sussex	See Hanbury-Aggs.
Armstrong, Martin Donisthorpe	Sussex	Writer and poet. Visited Hedwig and family at Mill House for Sunday teas. Dedicated a book to Iso. May also have written books or poems for children.
Armstrong, Roy and Jean (and later Lyn)	Sussex	First approached Iso and Hedwig about lecture recitals for the Workers Educational Association branch. Lyn was Lyn Birtles when Hedwig and Iso first met her around 1940. She lived for many years in a ménage à trois with Roy Armstrong and Sheila, Roy's first wife. Daughter was Jean (now Macwhirter) and son David, who became county chess player.
Aronowitz, Cecil	Manchester	Viola player who Hedwig met. Teacher at RNCM.

Atterberg, Karl	Stockholm	Praised Hedwig's debut in Stockholm. He had won prize for finishing Schubert's Unfinished Symphony.
Auerbach, Arnold	London	Artist and acquaintance.
Barbirolli, Sir John and Evelyn	Manchester	Conductor and oboist. Iso played many concerts with Sir John. Hedwig was also friendly with him and his wife Evelyn.
Barkan, Adolf (Dr)	Kiel	Relative and close friend of Vincenz Czerny, from San Francisco. Heard Hedwig in concert and paid for her to study in Berlin.
Barlow, Lady Nora and Sir Alan	Sussex	Granddaughter of Charles Darwin and great friend of Beatrice Bateson. Lived in Wendover, near Aylesbury. She was also related to Josiah Wedgwood – possibly his granddaughter. The British Museum had a large collection of ancient Greek pottery and artefacts lent by her husband, Alan Barlow.
Bates, Martin	Manchester	Pupil of Hedwig's. She went to his wedding in 1974.
Bateson, Beatrice	Sussex	Took the family in from early on in the War because she had heard Iso on the radio and wanted lessons so as to play all the Bach 48 preludes and fugues before she died (she was already 72). Wife (widow by then) of William Bateson, naturalist and Mendelian scholar who knew Darwin well. Son Geoffrey married anthropologist Margaret Mead.
Bax, Sir Arnold	Sussex	Composer and friend who lived in Storrington, probably in an hotel. Hedwig and Iso often used to meet him on the station platform going up to London. Bax dedicated his piano solo, *Burlesque*, to Iso.
Bazley, Sir Thomas	London	Befriended Iso and was one of his pupils.
Bell, George	Chichester	Bishop of Chichester Cathedral (1929–1958). Strongly vocal in his opposition to Hitler and Nazism, and welcomed German refugees. In 1936 became chairman of International Christian Committee for German Refugees. Later condemned bombing of German cities. Many of the Elinson WEA lectures were in the Deanery at Chichester. Bell named much later in child abuse complaints; Sussex Police investigated and closed the case.

Benedik, Fritz	Heidelberg	Cousin of Hedwig's. Fritz attended Iso's funeral and produced a German Radio tape: 'In memoriam Fritz Stein'.
Birley, Sir Oswald and Lady	London	Portrait painter. Lived in Charleston Manor in Sussex where they hosted arts events. Iso played there.
Birtles, Lyn	Sussex	Dear and long friend. Lived in ménage à trois with the Armstrongs and subsequently became Roy's wife.
Blackshaw, Christian	Manchester	Pianist who was a student at RNCM when Hedwig was teaching there.
Boult, Sir Adrian	London	Conductor. Supportive in helping Iso to get teaching position. Iso gave a number of concerts with Boult, including in Albert Hall.
Brooke, Janet	London	Friend. Organised naturalisation and a good number of recitals for Iso in her London flat. Iso and Hedwig bought a very good Steinway from her when they lived in Hampstead.
Bülow-Jakobsen, Helle	Copenhagen	Staunch supporter of Iso and helped to arrange concerts in Scandinavia over many years. She and her husband often put on private concerts in their 'stylish' house. Visited the Elinsons in London pre-1940. Rowed to Sweden to escape Nazi invasion when the war started.
Buzengeiger, Lieselotte 'Lilo'	Germany	Long-standing and close childhood friend with whom Hedwig corresponded for many years. Lilo was an amateur pianist and professional book binder, also moving into textiles and tapestry. Granddaughter of landscape painter Professor Friedrich Kallmorgen (1856–1924). Karl Buzengeiger (1872–1948) was Oberlandesgerichtspräsident (President of Higher Regional Court).
Christie, John and George	Sussex	Founder of Glyndebourne Opera. Son George became friend of Hedwig's.
Clough, Joseph	Manchester	Student of Iso's. Very promising but died young.
Cooke, Muriel	Manchester	She and husband sponsored Iso's Festival Hall concert in 1955, conducted by Pope.
Cooper, John	London	Painter and acquaintance who taught Helen Page.
Cox, Frederic	Manchester	Principal at Royal Manchester College of Music. Greatly assisted Hedwig and Iso.

Crankshaw, Edward (Teddy) and Clare	Kent	Friends. Teddy was music critic and expert on Soviet politics. Tried to find Iso's parents/family in Russia. Invited Elinsons to live with them in Kent in early stages of the War.
Czerny, Vincenz and Luise	Germany	Hedwig's grandparents who she lived with throughout the First World War in Heidelberg. Vincenz was an eminent surgeon.
Dakyns, Frances	Sussex	Friend. Lived at Steyning, West Sussex. Instrumental in helping John Christie to get Glyndebourne off the ground and had many contacts in London musical world.
D'Aranyi, Jelly	Sussex	Joachim's grand-niece and violinist who played with Iso in early days and in Oxford concert at Margot Deneke's in about 1957.
Davies, Sir Peter Maxwell	Manchester	Eminent composer and conductor. Master of Queen's Music 2004–2014. Studied composition at Manchester University with Procter-Gregg and piano with Hedwig. Good and long-term friend of Iso and Hedwig.
Deneke, Marga	Oxford	Hosted concerts at her house in Oxford. Spent some of her earlier life in Africa with Albert Schweitzer.
Doggerts, John and Sara	Manchester	John (Irish) and Sara (Russian), very good friends for whom Iso would play at soirées when she hired special Bechstein (1961). Played supportive role for Hedwig after Iso's death. Hedwig gave Sara letter from Iso's parents' (in Russian) after Iso's death. Owned Friedland doorbells and started Sasha dolls and children.
Döring, Georg 'Görli'	Germany	Close friend. Trained as lawyer but aspiring painter. Spent much time with Hedwig when she was a teenager and stayed loyal. Sent regular instalments of money to Hedwig and Iso when they were in England and not allowed to earn.
Dorothy	Sussex	Beatrice Bateson's housekeeper at Mill House.
Du Cane sisters	Sussex	Lived at Fittleworth House and hosted many recitals by Iso and Hedwig, over many years. Kept in touch even when they lived in Manchester and formed a sort of 'Elinson Club'. The recitals were part of the WEA lectures organised by Roy Armstrong.

Epstein, Jacob	London	Famous sculptor. Iso and Hedwig went often to Epstein's Sunday receptions. Epstein wanted to sculpt Iso's head but they never managed to make the necessary arrangements.
Fergus-Thompson, Gordon	London	International concert pianist and Professor at Royal College of Music since 1996. Studied at Royal Northern College of Music and knew Hedwig well.
Forbes, Robert	Manchester	Principal of Royal Manchester College of Music in 1940s. Instrumental in getting both Iso and Hedwig teaching positions there.
Foucher, Hélène	Manchester	French, distant relation and frequent visitor of Tex Rickards. Lived in elegant house in France which Hedwig visited with Tex on occasion.
Furtwängler, Wilhelm	Germany	German conductor and composer, and Principal conductor of the Berlin Philharmonic Orchestra 1922–1945 and 1952–1954. Occasionally visited the Steins at home. Recommended Fritz Stein for the position of Director at the Musikhochschule in Berlin.
Glas, Richard	Kiel	Professor and Hedwig's first major teacher. Dismissed in early 1930s when the Nazis came to power, fled to UK and later interned on Isle of Man.
Groves, Sir Charles	Sussex	Conductor of Bournemouth Symphony Orchestra for some years and before that, of BBC Northern Orchestra. Hedwig played Chopin E min concerto at Bournemouth Pavilion with him.
Grünfeld, Ernst and Margarete	London	Family friends. Left Berlin for England in the 1930s. Probably after Ernst's death, Margarete became extremely friendly (Hedwig described 'ardent feelings') with Fritz Stein and did much for him; not liked by Gretel Stein. Great supporter of Iso's.
Hadjinikos, Georg	Manchester	Greek pianist and conductor. Colleague and friend at Royal Northern College of Music. Played 'fiery' duets with Hedwig.

Hanbury-Aggs	Sussex	Quaker family. Sylvia and her husband helped musicians who fled oppression by holding concerts at their house, Little Thakeham, in Sussex. Daughter Jessica became a good friend of the Elinsons. She was married to Daniel Aggs, the younger son of the Hanbury-Aggs, and they lived on the home farm of Little Thakeham, where about 50 land girls were quartered during the War to work on the estate. Jessica was a pupil and friend of Arnold Bax.
Harcourt, Cecil (Mrs)	London	Was the pianist Evelyn Suart; pupil of Leschetizsky and played under Hans Richter and Henry Wood. One of daughters by first marriage was Diana Gould, who became Menuhin's second wife; other daughter married Louis Kentner.
Hess, Myra	London	Pianist. Invited Iso to take part in one of the lunchtime recitals she organised in the National Gallery throughout the War.
Hitchens, Ivon	Sussex	Painter. Became good friend of Hedwig and Iso when he lived in Petworth. After the War he painted a 60-foot mural for the English Folk Dance Society at the Cecil Sharp House in Camden, London. The mural is still there.
Holt, Harold	London	Impresario who managed many of famous musicians from 1920s to 1950s. Concert agent for Iso.
Horsley, Colin	Manchester	Succeeded Iso at RNCM. Hedwig and he got on well and he was a regular guest of hers.
Ibbs and Tillett	London	Classical music artist and concert management agency, including for Iso.
Jeans, Lady Susi	Sussex	Organist (and collector of organs), musicologist and harpsichordist who also promoted Reger. Gave public concerts in her home (Clevedon Lodge) for over 40 years. The extension she had built to the house for concerts became the venue for an annual festival, which morphed into the Box Hill Festival. Hedwig first mistook Susi for a cleaner when she arrived! Married to Sir James Jeans, physicist.
Kilby, Avice, Hope and Ruth	Sussex	Friends and supporters from early days on. Avice became particularly close to Hedwig and the girls. Hedwig taught Hope's children and Hope was at Iso's final concert in London.

Kipnis, Ivor	USA	Harpsichordist. Son was a bass who recorded Iso in conversation/interview in New York.
Kussmaul, Adolf	Germany	Hedwig's great-grandfather, physician and leading clinician.
Kwast, James (Professor)	Berlin	Teacher of Hans Pfitzner, Percy Grainger, Otto Klemperer. Hedwig studied with him, mainly in communal lessons at the Kwasts' flat. Kwast had played duos with Clara Schumann and was a friend of Busoni.
Kwast-Hodapp, Frieda	Berlin	Wife of James Kwast. International concert pianist, regarded highly by Hedwig's parents. Later married Otto Krebs, entrepreneur and collector of Impressionist paintings, including 74 by van Gogh, Cezanne, Degas, Monet, and Toulouse-Lautrec, which were taken by Russians in 1945 and placed in the Hermitage in St Petersburg.
Lucas, Brenda	Manchester	Pianist and wife of John Ogdon. May have been pupil of Hedwig's.
Maufe, Edward	Sussex	Husband of Mervyn Stutchbury's sister Prudence. Architect who designed Guildford Cathedral. Prudence was a window dresser at Heals and later became a Director.
Mead, Margaret	Sussex	Anthropologist and Beatrice Bateson's daughter-in-law. She and husband Gregory lived in US, but she visited the Elinsons in Mill House in 1943. She commented on the lack of comfy chairs! 'Not at all handsome but with sparkling eyes and fine telling white hands,' said Hedwig.
Milling, Michael and Gladys, known as Gee

(actually Crowley-Milling) | Manchester | Michael was a physicist and engineer, including at CERN. Helped to invent first computer touchscreen. Millings were residents in same block of flats in Manchester as Hedwig and Tex. Very good friends. Hedwig went several times to their Wales cottage with Tex after Iso's death.. |
Milner, Martin	Manchester	Violinist and leader of Hallé Orchestra. Played concerts with Hedwig.
Montanana, Hans	Manchester	Pupil of Hedwig's but did much in addition with Hedwig and arranged concerts for her. Was music teacher at Rickstones School, Witham.
Moore, Sir Henry	London	Sculptor known for his monumental bronzes. Friend of Hedwig and Iso.

Ogdon, John	Manchester	Pianist and winner of Liszt and Tchkaikovsky (with Ashkenazy) Piano Competitions. As teenager, had lessons for several years with Iso, who thought he should have different teacher when he went to College. Also prolific composer.
Oster, Helene	Berlin	Sister of Luise Czerny (née Kussmaul), Hedwig's grandmother. Provided lodging for Hedwig while she studied in Berlin before she moved to the Adelmanns'.
Page, Helene	Kent	Wife of surgeon Dr Max Page. Iso and Hedwig spent much time with her in Selling, Kent, especially at the beginning of the War where they helped with hop picking on the Pages' land.
Pfitzner, Hans	Germany	Russian-born composer. Married James Kwast's daughter Mimi.
Priestley, JB	London	Novelist who Hedwig and Iso got to know in the 1930s.
Procter-Gregg, Humphrey	Manchester	Head of Music Department at University of Manchester and first Professor of Music, 1954–1962. Known as 'P-G'.
Raschèr, Sigurd		Saxophonist who put the classical saxophone on the map. Glazunov, Ibert, and Hindemith wrote works for him. Friend of Hedwig and Iso over number of years.
Rickards, Charles Edward Bernard (Tex)	Manchester	Senior consultant gynaecologist at St Mary's Hospitals in Manchester, and then Salford Royal Hospital and Hope Hospital, Salford, lecturer at the University of Manchester. Also amateur playwright, singer and pianist, and critic. One of Hedwig and Iso's closest friends for many years, until his death in 1970. Brothers Frank, Justin and Jim.
Sargent, Sir Malcolm	London	Conductor. Played several concerts with Iso as soloist. 'Perfect cooperation,' said Hedwig. 'Iso gets on well with these English musicians who come to know him.'
Schiffrin, Marie	Russia	Iso's mother. Studied with Anton Rubenstein.
Schweitzer, Albert	Germany	Theologian, organist, and philosopher. Nobel Peace Prize Winner in 1952 and founder of hospital in Lambaréné. Visited Steins at home where he conversed with Fritz about organs and Bach.

Sebag Montefiore, Violet and John	Sussex	Acquaintances. Became tenants of Ros's at Gayles. Banking family.
Simeone, Nigel	Manchester	Pupil of Hedwig's who became a very good friend. Writer, musicologist, teacher and conductor.
Stein, Max Martin 'Maertel'	Germany	Hedwig's brother, and pianist. Stayed in Germany throughout the War and afterwards. Married Ilsabe von Löw.
Stones, Barbara	Manchester	Pupil of Iso's. Frank Stones, her father, was instrumental in arranging the reunion between Fritz and Gretel Stein after the War. Iso and Hedwig visited them in Derbyshire several times. Christian Scientists. Frank was the head of the Arthur Lea Steelworks in Sheffield and involved with the European Iron and Steel Federation, pre-EU. Barbara died at a young age from anorexia.
Stutchbury, Ros(a-mond)	Sussex	Long-standing and close friend. Cellist and friend of many émigré musicians. Also advised John Christie on establishing Glyndebourne Opera. Descendant of Wycliffe, who translated the Bible.
Swaythling, Lady	Sussex	Gladys Helen Rachel (née Goldsmid), Lady Swaythling (1879–1965) (series of photo-portraits in National Portrait Gallery). Co-founded the anti-Zionist League of British Jews, and opposed Balfour Declaration. Helped with concert opportunities for Iso. Husband Louis Samuel Montagu, 2nd Baron Swaythling, who died in 1927.
Taylor, Muriel	Grange	Private pupil and friend. Ran Royal UK Beneficent Association (RUKBA), which aimed to provide people in poverty with a small income for life and which engaged Hedwig and Iso for many concerts.
Von Bülow, Marie	Berlin	Second wife of conductor Hans von Bülow who in turn was pupil of Liszt. Friend who supported Iso and Hedwig's marriage in face of opposition from Fritz Stein.
Walsh, Mary	Manchester	Long-term friend. Catholic. Owned a private nursing home where Tex sent his private patients. Took in unmarried pregnant girls and helped them to find jobs afterwards.
Wilde, David	Manchester	International concert pianist and composer. Studied with Solomon and then with Iso. Hedwig also taught him on occasion.

Wilson, Sally	Manchester	Child pupil of Hedwig's.
Wolfrum, Philipp	Heidelberg	Conductor, organist, composer, and musicologist. Chief Director of Music at University of Heidelberg from 1885. Friend of Max Reger and Richard Strauss. Teacher of both Hedwig's parents.
Wood, Sir Henry	London	Conductor and founder of the Proms. Helped Iso get the professorship at the Royal Manchester College of Music and played a number of concerts with him, including Proms, from which broadcasts followed. Iso attended his Jubilee concert and Savoy lunch.
Worthington, Alan	Manchester	Friend, particularly of Tex.
Zimbler, Dr	London	Elinson family GP during early years in London.

SOURCES, REFERENCES, AND PERMISSIONS ACKNOWLEDGEMENTS

1   Woolf, V. 1966–67. Collected Essays, edited by Leonard Woolf, Vol IV. *Chatto & Windus. London.* p54.

2   Schnabel, A. 1961. My Life and Music. *Longman, Green and Co. Ltd. London.* pxv.

3   Kussmaul, A. 1985. Jugenderinnerungen eines alten Arstes : Vom Heidelberger Medizinstudenten zum Kanderner Landarzt und Mitinitiator des 'Biedermeier'. *Waldkircher Verlagsgesellschaft, Badeischer Reihe 14.*

4   Czerny, V. 1967. Aus Meinem Leben. *Sonderdruck aus 'Ruperto Carola' Zeitschrift der Vereinigung der Freunde der Studentenschaft der Universität Heidelberg e.V., XIX Jahrgang, Band 41.*

5   Avins, S. 1997. Johannes Brahms: Life and Letters. *Oxford University Press. Oxford.*

6   Stein-Czerny, M. 1936. Gedichte und Tagebuchblätter. *Walter G. Mühlau. Kiel.*

7   Stein, M. 1969. Der heitere Reger. *Breitkopf & Härtel. Wiesbaden.* p12.

8   Popp, S (herausgeber). 1982. Max Reger: Briefe an Fritz Stein. Veröffentlichungen des Max-Reger-Instituts; Elsa-Reger-Stiftung Bonn. *Ferd. Dümmlers Verlag. Bonn.*

9   Plaskin, G. 1983. Horowitz, a biography. *Macdonald & Co. London & Sydney.* p 40. Reproduced with kind permission of Glenn Plaskin.

10   Plaskin, G. *op. cit.* p65.

11   Plaskin, G. *op. cit.* p64.

12   Popp, Susanne: *op. cit.*

13   Stein, M. *op. cit.*

14   Pfadt, M. 2004. 'Bande – Bande – Bande der Freundschaft umschließen
     uns' – Fritz Stein und Max Reger. In: Siegfried Schmalzriedt u. Jürgen
     Schaarwächter (Hrsg.): *Reger-Studien 7. Festschrift für Susanne Popp. Carus-
     Verlag. Stuttgart.* p512.
15   See Kater, M. 1997. The Twisted Muse. *Oxford University Press, Inc,* in
     which 'Kampfbund für deutsche Kultur' is translated as 'Combat League for
     German Culture'.
16   Kater, M. *op. cit.* pp158–162.
17   Kater, M. *op. cit.* p156.
18   Haffner, S. 1979. The Meaning of Hitler. *Weidenfeld and Nicolson.*
19   Sadie, S (editor). 1980. The New Grove Dictionary of Music and Musicians:
     Fritz Stein. *Macmillan Publishers. London.* p105.
20   Pfadt, M. *op. cit.* p217.
21   Das deutsche Führerlexikon 1934–35. *Verlagsanstalt Otto Stollberg, GmbH.
     Berlin.*
22   Haffner, S. 2002. Defying Hitler. *Weidenfeld & Nicolson. London.*
23   Kater, M. *op. cit.* p156.
24   Kater, M. *op. cit.* p12 and p157. Reproduced with kind permission of
     Michael Kater.
25   Snowman, D. 2002. The Hitler Émigrés. *Chatto & Windus. London.* p87.
26   Feigel, L. 2013. The Love-charm of Bombs. *Bloomsbury Publishing. London.*
     p 127.
27   Stutchbury, O. 1970. The Spirit of Gayles. Reproduced with kind permission
     of Gayles Archive.
28   Stutchbury, O. *op.cit.*
29   Stutchbury, O. *op. cit.*
30   Hare, David. 2015. The Moderate Soprano. *Faber and Faber Ltd. London.
     2015.* Reproduced with kind permission of David Hare.
31   Matar, H. 2016. The Return: Fathers, Sons and the Land in Between. *Viking-
     Penguin. London.*
32   Snowman, D. *op. cit.* pp107–109.
33   Litten, I. 1940. Die Hölle sieht dich an: Der Fall Litten. *Editions nouvelles
     internationals. Paris.* Also published in English as: A Mother Fights Hitler.
     George Allen & Unwin Ltd. London.
34   Hayhurst, Mark (Playwright, UK). 2015. Taken at Midnight. *Bloomsbury
     Publishing PLC. London, New Delhi, New York, and Sydney.*
35   Snowman, D. *op. cit.*
36   Feigel, L. 2016. The Bitter Taste of Victory. *Bloomsbury Publishing. London,
     New Delhi, New York, and Sydney.* p33.
37   https://www.rcm.ac.uk/singingasong/interviewees/janetbaker
38   Snowman, D. *op. cit.*

About the author and this book

Helen Marquard's life embraces both the arts and the sciences. She was a researcher in molecular biology and medicine in the UK and Germany, and worked as a UK government policy maker and the Executive Director of a UN-founded organisation supporting start-up social and environmental enterprises in developing countries. She is also a passionate music lover and an avid theatre-goer.

Part her own reflections, part Hedwig Stein's, The Musical Life is Helen's first publication outside the scientific arena. In writing about her friend and piano teacher Hedwig, she charts Hedwig's youth in the First World War, the start of her performing career, and later her decision to leave her family and flee from Berlin in 1933 with her Jewish Russian husband Iso, also a concert pianist. Although they knew no-one in the UK, from the very start they encountered extraordinary generosity. Drawing on Hedwig's diary and letters, Helen relates their experiences through the Second World War, the recognition she and Iso were awarded, and the challenges Hedwig faced in pursuing her own career alongside raising children and supporting Iso.

Helen speaks fluent German, is married, has two grown-up children and three grandchildren, and lives in the UK near Farnham, Surrey.

For exclusive discounts on Matador titles,
sign up to our occasional newsletter at
troubador.co.uk/bookshop

p. 230 — 'Marga... Julian...
         little Matthew...'

291 'Marga... Letchworth'

256 'Matthew, one of her grandson